THE MATERNAL TUG

Ambivalence, Identity, and Agency

Edited by Sarah LaChance Adams, Tanya Cassidy, and Susan Hogan

DEMETER

The Maternal Tug
Ambivalence, Identity, and Agency
Edited by Sarah LaChance Adams, Tanya Cassidy, and Susan Hogan

Copyright © 2020 Demeter Press

Individual copyright to their work is retained by the authors. All rights reserved. No part of this book may be reproduced or transmitted in any form by any means without permission in writing from the publisher.

Demeter Press
140 Holland Street West
P. O. Box 13022
Bradford, ON L3Z 2Y5
Tel: (905) 775-9089
Email: info@demeterpress.org
Website: www.demeterpress.org

Demeter Press logo based on the sculpture "Demeter" by Maria-Luise Bodirsky www.keramik-atelier.bodirsky.de

Printed and Bound in Canada

Front cover photography: Brooke Burton
Front cover artwork: Michelle Pirovich
Typesetting: Michelle Pirovich

Library and Archives Canada Cataloguing in Publication
Title: The maternal tug : ambivalence, identity, and agency / edited by Sarah LaChance Adams, Tanya Cassidy, and Susan Hogan.
Names: LaChance Adams, Sarah, editor. | Cassidy, Tanya, editor. | Hogan, Susan, 1961- editor.
Identifiers: Canadiana 20200153838 | ISBN 9781772582130 (softcover)
Subjects: LCSH: Motherhood. | LCSH: Mothers. | LCSH: Motherhood—Psychological aspects. | LCSH: Mothers—Psychology. | LCSH: Motherhood—Social aspects.
Classification: LCC HQ759.M38 2020 | DDC 306.874/3—dc23

This book is dedicated to my sisters, Diane and Kristan; to Audrey Devine Eller; and to my comrades in the Mental Labor Union.
—Sarah LaChance Adams

I wish to dedicate this book to my sister (Andrea), my mother (Laura) and her sister (Gloria), and their mother (Evelyn), and her mother (Gloria), whom I heard so many stories about, despite her having died shortly after giving birth to her only child, my grandmother.
—Tanya Cassidy

In memory of my grandmother Adah Clara Hogan, known as "Pips," who developed a life-long love of vegetable gardening during WWll scarcity, providing me with delightful early memories of sitting on her lap shelling peas and eating freshly picked strawberries in her beautiful garden.
—Susan Hogan

Acknowledgments

This book has been written in collaboration with the research project "Philosophy of Birth: Rethinking the Origin from Medical Humanities" (PHILBITH) (FFI2016-77755-R), Program for Research, Development and Innovation Oriented to Societal Challenges, Ministry of Economy in Spain, 2016-19, (AEI/FEDER/UE).

Jade Tucker and Isabella Restrepo Toro provided research assistance.

We express thanks to Rachel Teannalach for sharing the art of her painting and her life on our cover. Photo by Brooke Burton. Tugging by Mairead.

Contents

Chapter Eleven
Ambivalence and Identification:
Avenues for Reification or Change
Joan Garvan

Section III
Mothering in Context

Chapter Twelve
Unpacking Monomaternalism within a
Queer Motherhood Framework
Mel Freitag

Chapter Thirteen
Mothering Children with Disabilities:
Navigating Choice and Obligations
Sophia Brock

Chapter Fourteen
Unnatural Women: Reflections on Discourses on
Child Murder and Selective Mortal Neglect
Susan Hogan

Chapter Fifteen
"Mother, Is This Our Home?" Mothering in the Context of the
Lord's Resistance Army Captivity: Understanding the Perspectives of
Mothers and Children in Northern Uganda
Myriam Denov

Notes on Contributors

Introduction

Sarah LaChance Adams and Tanya Cassidy

In the novel *Circe*, by Madeline Miller, the goddess daughter of the Sun grapples with new motherhood in a conspicuously human fashion, despite having the powers of magic and prophecy:

I did not go easy to motherhood. I faced it as soldiers faced their enemies, girded and braced, sword up against the coming blows. Yet all my preparations were not enough.

Thank the gods I did not have to sleep. Every minute I must wash and boil and clean and scrub and put out to soak. Yet how could I do that, when every minute he also needed something, food and change and sleep. That last I had always thought the most natural thing for mortals, easy as breathing, yet he could not seem to do it. However I wrapped him, however I rocked and sang, he screamed, gasping and shaking until the lions fled, until I feared he would do himself harm. I made a sling to carry him, so he might lie against my heart. I gave him soothing herbs, I burned incense, I called birds to sing at our windows. The only thing that helped was if I walked.... This was the child I deserved.

We did find some moments of peace, when he finally slept, when he nursed at my breast, when he smiled at a flight of birds scattering from a tree. I would look at him and feel a love so sharp it seemed my flesh lay open. I made a list of all the things I would do for him. Scald off my skin. Tear out my eyes. Walk my feet to bones, if only he would be happy and well.

He was not happy. A moment, I thought, I only need one moment without his damp rage in my arms. But there was none. He hated sun. He hated wind. He hated baths. He hated to be clothed, to be naked, to lay on his belly and his back. He hated this great world and everything in it, and me, so it seemed, most of all.

I thought of all those hours I had spent working my spells, singing, weaving. I felt their loss like a limb torn away. I told myself I even missed turning men to pigs, for at least that I had been good at. I wanted to hurl him from me, but instead I marched on in that darkness with him, back and forth before the waves, and at every step I yearned for my old life. I spoke sourly to the night air as he wailed: "At least I do not worry he is dead."

I clapped a hand to my mouth for the god of the underworld comes at much less invitation. I held his fierce little face against me. The tears were standing in his eyes, his hair disordered, a small scratch on his cheek. How had he gotten it? What villain dared to hurt him? Everything that I had heard of mortal babies flooded back: how they died for no reason, for any reason, because they grew too cold, too hungry, because they lay one way, or another. I felt each breath in his thin chest, how improbable it was, how unlikely that this frail creature, who could not even lift his head could survive in the harsh world. But he would survive. He would, if I must wrestle the veiled god myself.

Circe lives in exile, banished by her father for giving water to Prometheus. She makes the potion that turns Glaucus into an immortal. She turns the nymph Scylla into a monster. She makes lovers of Hermes and Odysseus. She tames lions and turns brutal men into swine. Despite her courage, powers, and charms, this baby's slightest injury commands her; his needs enslave her; his fleeting moments of peace seem to flay her. She bears his hate and rage as a torment that she deserves, and she fights other gods to protect him. Motherhood takes away everything that gives her comfort, pleasure, and a sense of her own identity. What is it about motherhood that can possess even the sorceress Circe?

In Circe's account, we see how the tensions of motherhood are distilled in its early days. All of its piercing affects crowd and tumble over one another: fear, guilt, rage, and love. Indeed, to take responsibility for another person's fragile life is to invite physical labour, terror, feelings of failure, insane devotion, mournful regret, rage, claustrophobia, fierce protectiveness, amazement, and poetic inspiration.

Children's vulnerability is so rooted and tangible that it may feel like a metaphysical principle. Their mortality is certain. Moreover, we carry the unspeakable knowledge that the world was just as real before they existed and that they might never have been. The questions can linger. Who might we have been without them? Who would they be without us? What would happen to them if we abandoned them or died? How will they take it when we do die, if we do indeed die first? We find ourselves utterly responsible and ultimately powerless.

Children's needs are relentless and never ending. This can cause time to take on a peculiar character—disordered and anarchic. The days are long, and the years are short. On top of that, we are in suspense: Who will our children be? How can we make them ready for possibilities that cannot be foreseen or imagined? How can we prepare them for a future that we may never know ourselves? We may find ourselves hesitating and freezing time while trying to predict the future effects—good and bad—that our actions will have. Sometimes time rushes past, and we are unmoving while this other life flashes before us. The newborn's stare seems to hold ancient wisdom and judgment. The toddler's tantrums anticipate the teenager. When the future arrives, it echoes the past. It was only yesterday that they were starting school. A baby picture reveals the older child's recognizable expression. Past generations resonate in their faces, bodies, choices, and dispositions. Yet to them, their infancy and early childhood seem like an abyssal history; the years before their existence, mythological.

Being close to a child often makes one's own infancy and childhood appear more real. Memories and fantasies of mothers mingle. We may hold ourselves up to these images of benevolence and failure. We may find our own mother's caresses or strikes reincarnated in our hands. We may measure our breaking point against hers.

Motherhood brings the paradoxes of being human into blinding light. It can be both strenuous and empowering. It can give one's own life a new sense of legitimacy, yet it simultaneously certifies our finitude. It reconfigures our places in the familial and social nexus. It is no wonder that mothers, mothers-to-be, and those who even imagine themselves as mothers find themselves tugged in multiple directions.

Certainly many of these experiences and impressions will also be familiar to fathers and other caregivers. However, the authors herein assert the importance of understanding how individual experiences are socially and materially situated. Gender, as we know, powerfully affects other aspects of our lives, just as class, race, nationality, and other factors do. There are some important differences in how mothers and fathers are treated, what they expect of themselves, as well as the resources and limitations they tend to have. These will affect the institutions and the experiences of motherhood, fatherhood, and parenthood more broadly. A book such as this, with a focus specifically on maternal ambivalence, invites us to consider intersectional commonalities and differences within this role. In this way, we may better understand what it is, what it has been, and what it may become.

Adrienne Rich's highly influential book, *Of Woman Born*, provides a powerful example of how motherhood is contingent upon its material, social, and other conditions. She conveys her experience with poignant specificity, never generalizing or essentializing. Yet its individuality is firmly rooted in the gender roles and other systemic constraints of her time. This quote originates from her 1960 diary:

> My children cause me the most exquisite suffering of which I have any experience. It is the suffering of ambivalence: the murderous alternation between bitter resentment and raw-edged nerves, and blissful gratification and tenderness. Sometimes I seem to myself, in my feelings toward these tiny guiltless beings, a monster of selfishness and intolerance. Their voices wear away at my nerves, their constant needs, above all their need for simplicity and patience, fill me with despair at my own failures, despair too at my fate, which is to serve a function for which I was not fitted. And I am weak sometimes from held-in rage. There are times when I feel only death will free us from one another, when I envy the barren woman who has the luxury of her regrets but lives a life of privacy and freedom.
>
> And yet at other times I am melted with the sense of their helpless, charming and quite irresistible beauty—their ability to go on loving and trusting—their staunchness and decency and

unselfconsciousness. *I love them.* But it's in the enormity and inevitability of this love that the sufferings lie. (Rich 1)

This quote has provided inspiration for much of the motherhood scholarship that has followed it (Ruddick; Parker; O'Reilly; Brown). Rich might have been the first person to describe maternal ambivalence—a strong contradictory desire to both nurture and abandon or hurt one's children—in such vivid and honest terms. This topic has become increasingly important, given the necessity to debunk romantic ideals of an exclusively nurturing, maternal nature.

This wide-ranging, interdisciplinary, and international collection takes up the call to recognize the widespread existence of maternal ambivalence. The authors and editors in this book deny the assumption that mothers who experience ambivalence are bad, evil, unnatural, or insane. In fact, historical records, as well as cross-cultural narratives, indicate that maternal ambivalence appears in a wide range of circumstances. However, we also assert that it becomes unmanageable in circumstances of inequity, deprivation, and violence. As such, societies must understand their role in perpetuating ambivalence to intolerable levels, sometimes resulting in maternal abuse and neglect as well as filicide and suicide.

Ambivalence, a term that describes how one can be pulled in opposite directions, is a concept with a long theoretical and interdisciplinary history. Although it is often thought that Sigmund Freud coined the concept, it was actually the Swiss psychiatrist Eugen Bleuler (Falzeder 343-68; Troha 217-44).[1] Bleuler was later to reject psychoanalysis, which would lead to difficulties between him and Freud. However, it is significant that both Bleuler and Freud drew from their clinical considerations of women in understanding the phenomenon. Bleuler's clinical example is a mother who "poisoned her child; but afterwards she is in despair over her act; it is striking that even with the worst moaning and crying the mouth laughs quite clearly"[2] (see Bleuler's *Die Ambivalenz*). Bleuler's conception is not only emotional but also intellectual, as it could manifest as inabilities to choose between actions or behaviours.

The complicated relationship between the psychological, the social, and the cultural is captured by later theorists. They dispute whether the social and cultural considerations of ambivalence are more or less fundamental than psychological roots. Robert K. Merton and Elinor

Barber (Merton; Merton and Barber), for instance, developed the concept of "sociological ambivalence," emphasizing that ambivalence is built into the very structure of social relations. Later critics, in particular Robin Room, argue that Merton's understanding of ambivalence is primarily linked to those social problems that he sees as constitutive features of a complex industrial society. In other words, he thinks that ambivalence is the fault of modernity and that to change it requires changing society itself.

Exploration of the tension between sociological and psychological accounts of ambivalence persisted toward the end of the twentieth century. In his 1997 address to the American Sociological Association, Neil Smelser argues for a complex recognition of ambivalence, one that links the social and the individual levels. Following this call, some scholars have returned to the early works (1908) of the German philosopher Georg Simmel (Levine; Bauman). Simmel argues that society itself is built around the conception of the "stranger," who is at one and the same time both potential friend and foe (Cassidy). Bauman goes on to say we are living in "a time of reconciliation with ambivalence" and that the promise of modernity to make the world understandable and controllable is now no longer believed. Unfortunately, these interpretations of Simmel do not take into consideration his extensive discussion elsewhere of gender and culture. These are important to the discussions of Simmel and maternal ambivalence presented in Rozsika Parker's influential book *Torn in Two: The Experience of Maternal Ambivalence*. Parker draws on Simmel in recognizing that pregnancy and childbirth can be linked to thinking of the infant as a "little stranger" from within.

The notion that the child is "a stranger from within" is key to understanding the lived experience of maternal ambivalence. The living child, if not completely rejected or denied, comes from the mother's own body or was adopted into her home. Mothers, both adoptive and biological, have reported that they have a hard time drawing any firm line between their own interests and their children's interests. Indeed, this is the realization of the existential fact of human intertwining. The human person is not a separable monad. As such, maternal ambivalence is not merely directed from mother to child. One's child, though radically other, is also seamlessly one's own. Maternal ambivalence is simultaneously directed from oneself and towards oneself. Thus, it involves a self-estrangement that earlier theorists did not always recognize (LaChance Adams).

This anthology examines the diverse and complex experiences of maternal ambivalence from an interdisciplinary perspective. The authors draw on a rich legacy of cultural, social, and economic analyses; feminist traditions; philosophical insights; literary criticism; and more. They represent an array of writing styles and epistemic practices, and attend to a variety of circumstances and situations. This provides the collection with a multifaceted perspective that cannot be attained by a single author or from a single disciplinary perspective.

If we claim that mothers are ambivalent, does this mean that we think that they are fragmented? Or that they are incapable of coherent action, emotion, or thought? On the contrary, the editors and authors of this book believe that reflection on maternal ambivalence can provide more nuanced and variegated understandings of rationality, agency, and identity.

The first two essays introduce us to the phenomenon of ambivalence. In Chapter 1, "Ambivalent Intersections," Sagashus T. Levingston gives a raw, first-person account of her own maternal ambivalence in conditions of poverty, sexism, and racism. She reveals the struggle for bare survival, paired poignantly with the additional sacrifices demanded by academia. She performs, via her writing, the risks and the sense of vulnerability in revealing one's ambivalence. However, she does so unapologetically and reveals the fire in her that is also the source of her children's defiance, which is likely the key to all of their survival. The careful reader will see that Levingston's ambivalence does not reveal instability; rather it is her manifest existential awareness of too many demands and too few resources.

Levingston's essay poises us well to receive the message of Chapter 2—ambivalence may be virtuous. In "The Virtue of Ambivalence to Maternity," Joan Woolfrey explores how virtue ethics provides a lens through which maternal ambivalence can be understood as both "appropriate" and "morally admirable." Given the moral tone and prevalence of the maternal mandate, along with the general lack of support for childrearing, a rational creature would have to be rather insensible not to experience some ambivalence. Thus, she argues that given the circumstances, a unified self must also be a conflicted self.

Section I of the book, "Ambivalence in Pregnancy and Childbirth," begins with Amanda Roth's Chapter 3 "What Is Pregnancy Ambivalence? Is It Maternal Ambivalence?" Roth argues that pregnancy ambivalence is not just a subset of maternal ambivalence, since it is not primarily about inconsistent feelings towards the fetus; rather, it is about the fact that the pregnant body is both one's own and not one's own. Thus, to be ambivalent about being pregnant is not the same as being ambivalent about becoming a mother, and it may be completely unrelated to the question of whether or not to terminate a pregnancy. Roth affirms this distinction through a discussion of thick and thin relationships. She asserts that it is "neither rare nor worrisome for some periods of pregnancy to involve only the thin sort of gestational relationship," whereas for parents of a living child, it is highly problematic. As Roth indicates, this distinction is clearly important to abortion politics.

In Chapter 4, "The Unspeakables: Exploring Maternal Ambivalence through the Experience of Depression and Anxiety during Pregnancy," Aleksandra Staneva discusses the wide range of emotions, as well as their complexity, during pregnancy. She claims that even in women-centric online spaces, there is active censorship and surveillance, which minimize discussions of pregnancy distress. As part of this research, Staneva analyses the language of eighteen pregnant women as they discuss their distress and ambivalence. She uses the theoretical framework of Julia Kristeva's philosophy, which claims that the maternal is semiotic—the creative, emotive, and poetic aspect of language. Drawing on this concept, Staneva finds that pregnant women's internal conflicts were ultimately liberating if they were not stifled but rather expressed through language.

With Chapter 5, "On Ambivalence and Giving Birth: Reflecting on Labour through Beauvoir's Erotic," the attention turns from pregnancy to childbirth. Here, Sara Cohen Shabot considers labour as an existential project— a work through which one reveals her values and challenges her apparent limits. This is in contrast to the medicalization of childbirth, which often "abandons the experiential body," treating it merely as a medium or vessel. Overmedicalization focuses on the end product—the children—over the intrinsic value of the labouring process itself. In reclaiming the birthing experience, Shabot employs Simone de Beauvoir's notions of the erotic. She does so despite the fact that Beauvoir did not explicitly think of childbirth as empowering. Cohen Shabot finds the ambivalent erotic to be a useful conceptual tool because it shares several kinds of embodied ambiguity with pregnancy and child labour. These include the subject's simultaneous immanence and transcendence, the intertwining of self and world, the otherness within one's own body, and the dependence of one's freedom on the irreducible freedom of others.

In Chapter 6, the final chapter of this section, "A Healthy Baby Is Not All that Matters: Exploring My Ambivalence after a Caesarean Section" Bertha Alvarez Manninen discusses a similar theme: her sense of ambivalence towards her daughters' Caesarean-section births. Unable to take the active role she desired in bringing her children into the world, Manninen felt alienated from what she felt was a vital aspect of becoming a mother. Employing and extending Marx, Manninen describes the role of technology in alienating workers from their labour as parallel to the overmedicalization of childbirth. Similar to Marx, she argues that the product of one's labor is not all that matters; rather the *process* itself may cause disappointment and ambivalence. Focusing solely on the ideal product of child labor—healthy babies—minimizes the importance of the birth process.

Section II, "Seeking Perfection, Finding Despair," includes four chapters that explore different ways in which ambivalence is heightened due to attempts to be perfect parents. For women, this desire for flawlessness is decidedly gendered. These chapters show that cultural roles and habits need improvement, not the individuals themselves. The section begins with Chapter 7, suitably named "I'm So Tired: The Labour of Care, Infant Sleep Management, and Maternal Ambivalence," in which Patricia MacLaughlin and Gwen Scarbrough discuss sleep deprivation and infant care. The nightshift is an underresearched area in sociology. However, in the research that has been done, night time care has been found to prioritize men's sleep, leading women to experience chronic exhaustion, intensifying their rage and ambivalence toward both their children and male-partners.

In Chapter 8, "Maternal Guilt and the First-Time Mother," Claire Steele LeBeau's interviews with mothers reveal the maternal guilt regarding several features of new motherhood: the high stakes of personal responsibility, the mother's need for separation, her self-estrangement, miscommunication at the pre-verbal stage, feelings of inexperience, conflict between reality and one's expectations, and the intensity and variety of one's mixed emotions about this new role. As many of the other chapters indicate, ambivalence itself is a powerful source of maternal guilt. However, it is also an opportunity for insight and solidarity among mothers.

In Chapter 9, "Meta-Helicopter Parenting: Ambivalence in a Neoliberal World," Talia Welsh describes a type of situational ambivalence that comes from popular discourse on helicopter parenting. Helicopter parenting can be described as supervision so intrusive that all of a child's time is scheduled between school and activities, with very little time for spontaneous play and relaxation. This style of parenting is considered smothering by some and is blamed for young adults not being prepared for independence. Contrasted with helicoptering parenting is a style underlined with nostalgia for a time when children were more free range. This so-called natural parenting style is thought to resolve ambivalence for the excessively devoted parent. Against both of these perspectives, Welsh doubts that making a choice to parent differently can actually address ambivalence. She thinks that it has more to do with the larger issues that plague parents, such as economic exploitation, diminished funding for public education and healthcare, and environmental degradation. Meanwhile, the debate over free-range and helicopter parenting ignores the socioeconomic context; it offers a neoliberal and "personal-choice" resolution and treats children as their parents' personal project.

In Chapter 10, "Sustainable Ambivalence," Kate Parsons describes her growing ambivalence and resentment when taking her children on a Fulbright-Hays group trip to Brazil. Falling prey to the conflict between the "good mother" trope and her feminist consciousness, Parsons finds herself torn internally between two visions of who she wants to be. As she explores her ambivalence, she discovers a related divide between herself as an environmentalist and herself as a wealthy world-traveller. These divides share the same false dichotomy between self-care (enjoying comforts that are environmentally unsound) and taking care of others (fighting environmental degradation). Indeed, many of our lives are structured to oscillate between enjoying the comforts, employment, and culture of the city as it absorbs the resources of the rural, and then fleeing to the wilderness on the weekends or vacations. Parsons affirms that this incoherence is the result of colonially manufactured privileges and, thus, has political and ethical consequences. By bravely sinking into both her environmental and maternal ambivalences, Parsons finds inspiration for effecting cultural transformations that may alleviate them both.

In Chapter 11, "Ambivalence and Identification: Avenues for Reification or Change," Joan Garvan focuses on the identity crisis that many women experience upon becoming mothers. Despite some progress towards gender equity, the birth of a child often leads to more gendered roles in heterosexual couples. As a result, many women experience depression over their increasing estrangement from their male partners, anxiety in comparing themselves to their own mothers, and general distress in this ill-fitting new role. Garvan concludes that the insights into maternal subjectivity that have been achieved in motherhood research indicate that new narrative representations of mothering are needed.

Although all of the authors in this collection consider the circumstances in which maternal ambivalence occurs, those in Section III, "Mothering in Context," give attention to more specific socio-historical circumstances: contemporary queer mothering, mothering children with disabilities, England in the nineteenth and early twentieth century, and mothering in the aftermath of wartime rape in Uganda. In Chapter 12, "Unpacking Monomaternalism within a Queer Motherhood Framework," Mel Freitag explores the role of the nonbiological mother whose partner is the biological mother. She argues that such mothers need their own narrative that is distinct from the fathers,' from those who adopt, and from simply being defined in secondary terms as "the other mother." This lack of a socially identifiable role perpetuates maternal ambivalence; however, it also raises important challenges to heteronormative motherhood that can inspire us all.

In Chapter 13, "Mothering Children with Disabilities: Navigating Choice and Obligation," Sophia Brock draws on the experiences of mothers of children with disabilities. Their ambivalence can be amplified under these circumstances as the mother struggles to establish her identity while coping with the intensive and prolonged care that they are expected to provide without adequate social support.

In Chapter 14, "Unnatural Women: Reflections on Discourses on Child Murder and Selective Mortal Neglect," Susan Hogan takes the reader to England in the nineteenth and early twentieth century. She argues that this society had a great deal of social tolerance towards child murder—from severe neglect to purposeful filicide. She looks at a number of cases in which there was hesitance about prosecuting or punishing women who killed their newborns, especially when those children were illegitimate. Hogan references Nancy Scheper-Hughes's hypothesis that maternal expectations play a role in many children's deaths. She notes that the vague illnesses that were blamed for the deaths of many infants might have been caused, or assisted by, the neglect of children whose deaths seemed inevitable.

The book concludes with Chapter 15, "'Mother Is This Our Home?' Mothering in the Context of the Lord's Resistance Army Captivity: Understanding the Perspectives of Mothers and Children in Northern Uganda" by Myriam Denov. Denov describes the plight of girls who became pregnant while held captive by the Lord's Resistance Army in Northern Uganda between 1986 and 2007. Girls were selected for marriage against their will; they were forced to become pregnant, give birth, and raise the children. Many of them understandably felt ambivalent towards these children—for some it was a reason to carry on living, but a child also severely limited their ability to escape. Denov concludes that if children are to be well protected and cared for, then their mothers must also be supported.

This interdisciplinary and international collection adds to the growing recognition of the complexity of mothering. Maternal ambivalence—the simultaneous and contradictory emotional responses of mothers towards their children—is not merely an emotional reaction. Affects, intentions, and behaviour are socially and culturally responsive. They reveal social contexts and aspects of the human condition that are relevant to us all: the false dichotomies of good and bad in our ethical lives; the visceral impacts of gender normativity, violence, and racial discrimination; and the importance of first-person embodied experience. The authors in this collection reveal that maternal ambivalence may be wise, virtuous, and creative. Perhaps even more importantly, it presents opportunities to realized solidarity across difference.

Endnotes

1. Discussions of love-hate relations, what Wilhelm Stekel called "bipolarity," predate the use of the term "ambivalence."
2. Google translate provides translation for "Die Ambivalenz" to "The Ambivalence" and the above translation for the original quote in

German, which is *"hat ihr Kind vergiftet; aber nachträglich ist sie in Verzweiflung über ihre Tat; nur fällt auf, daß auch beim ärgsten Jammern und Weinen der Mund ganz deutlich lacht. Letzteres ist der Kranken unbewußt"* (see www.sgipt.org/medppp/gesch/ambiv-g.htm)

Works Cited

Bauman, Zygmunt. *Modernity and Ambivalence.* Polity Press, 1991.

Bleuler, Paul Eugene. "Über Ambivalenz [About Ambivalence], *Zentralblatt für Psychoanalyse,* 1, 266, (published 1911). www.sgipt. org/medppp/gesch/ambiv-g.htm. Accessed 1 Dec. 2019.

Brown, Ivana. "Ambivalence of the Motherhood Experience." *Twenty-First-Century Motherhood: Experience, Identity, Policy, Agency,* edited by Andrea O'Reilly, Columbia University Press, 2010, pp. 121-39.

Cassidy, Tanya M. "Irish Drinking Worlds: A Socio-Cultural Reinterpretation of Ambivalence." *International Journal of Sociology and Social Policy,* vol. 16, no. 5/6, 1996, pp. 5-25.

Castellini, Alassandro. *Translating Maternal Violence: The Discursive Construction of Maternal Filicide in 1970s Japan.* Palgrave Macmillan, 2017.

Kristeva, J., A. Jardine and H. Blake. "Women's Time." *Signs,* vol. 7, no. 1, 1981, pp. 13-35.

Falzeder, E. "The Story of an Ambivalent Relationship: Sigmund Freud and Eugen Bleuler." *J Anal Psychol,* vol. 52, no. 3, 2007, pp. 343-68.

LaChance Adams, Sarah. *Mad Mothers, Bad Mothers, and What a "Good" Mother Would Do: The Ethics of Ambivalence.* Columbia University Press, 2014.

Levine, D. N. *The Flight from Ambiguity.* University of Chicago Press, 1985.

Levine, Donald N., editor. *Georg Simmel on Individuality and Social Forms. Selected Writings.* University of Chicago Press, 1971.

Merton, Robert K., and Elinor Barber. "Sociological Ambivalence." *Sociological Theory, Values, and Sociocultural Change,* edited by E.A. Tiryakian, the Free Pres, 1963, pp. 91-120.

Merton, Robert K. *Sociological Ambivalence and Other Essays.* Free Press, 1976.

Miller, Madeline. *Circe*. Little, Brown and Company, 2018.

O'Reilly, Andrea. "Introduction." *Mother Outlaws: Theories and Practices of Empowered Mothering*, edited Andrea O'Reilly, Women's Press, 2004, pp. 1-28.

O'Reilly, Andrea. *Feminist Mothering*. State University of New York Press, 2008.

Parker, Rozsika. *Torn in Two: The Experience of Maternal Ambivalence*. Virago Press, 1995.

Rich, Adrienne. *Of Woman Born: Motherhood as Experience and Institution*. Norton, 1976.

Room, Robin (1976) "Ambivalence as a Sociological Explanation: The case of cultural explanations of alcohol problems." ASR.

Ruddick, Sara. *Maternal Thinking: Toward a Politics of Peace*. Ballantine Books, 1989.

Simmel, G. *Philosophische Kultur*. Alfred Kröner Verlag, 1919.

Smelser, Neil. "The Rational and the Ambivalent in Social Sciences." *American Sociological Review*, vol. 63, no. 1, 1997, pp. 1-16.

Troha, Tadej (2017) "On Ambivalence." *Problemi International*, vol. 1, no. 1, pp. 217-44.

Chapter One

Ambivalent Intersections

Sagashus T. Levingston

I s this a safe space? Can I speak openly and candidly here? As a
mother, I am supposed to tell you about all the ways in which I
adore all my children. I have six. And the assumption is that I have
no favourites. I think that I am expected to tell you about all the ways in
which I sacrifice for them; how I would die for them; that everything I
do—eat, breathe, and sleep—is for them. Maybe you want to hear
about how my life stopped the day my first one's began. But those
would all be lies. I do not adore all my children. I do have favourites. A
lot of our life is about survival. My favourite children are the ones who
are not currently threatening that survival with all of their rebellious
back talk and defiance. I live in a community that would rather us be
seen and not heard. My favourites, today, are the ones who help me get
out of this place we are passing through—the ones who help us do it
quickly and quietly without drawing more attention to ourselves. For us
to survive, I often put myself first. I am not a martyr. I want to live just
as much as I want my babies to live. So, no, I will not blindly and
valiantly die for them. I will fight for them, though, if I have to. If dying
is the result of that fight, then I would think that it must have been my
time. I say all of this with conviction now when, in reality, I am filled
with all kinds of ambivalence. There is always a conflict rising between
my needs and the needs of my children, tension between my survival
and theirs. Which do I choose? Those lines are always blurred.

I birthed my nemesis. I swear this kid will be my downfall, my ruin.
Every day, when she wakes up, it is like there is a poltergeist in my house.
As soon as her eyes opens, the atmosphere changes. It feels like the
cabinets are opening and slamming shut on their own. It feels like the

window shades are rolling up and down on their own. The faucet, the lights, the electricity all seem to take on lives of their own. And then her feet hit the floor, and her mouth opens. "Who took my hair pick?" "Somebody ate my this..." "I hate this house for that..." She goes on like this for minutes as she scrambles to get out the door. All the while I am in my bed, shrinking, dying on the inside. Her voice is like nails on the chalkboard or grinding teeth. It pierces my soul, and then it stops. The poltergeist, the cabinets, the shades, the hurricane all stop as she storms out the door. Then the atmosphere goes back to normal.

I regret not touching her or getting up to ask her if she needs me to do something to ease her anxieties. I want to hug her and tell her I love her and that things are going to be ok. I cannot. Something in her triggers something in me, and for my own safety, I don't reach out. In fact, she is a version of me when I was her age—awkward, insecure, and depressed, full figured, emotional. Like me, she cries almost instantly about almost everything. She is a fighter who stands up for what she believes in and for those she believes in. She hates bullies. Even when she's up against a fight she knows she is going to lose, she challenges people that intimidate and mistreat the powerless and vulnerable. She is loud and rebellious and funny and beautiful and verbally aggressive— all the things I was her age, all the things I believe and promote in a girl (a woman).

Yet I cannot touch my own child and embrace all of her because she reminds me too much of the girl I was her age—the girl who remained untouched for all those same reasons. I am torn between giving her the comfort she needs and reassuring myself against my own unresolved hurts. For my own protection, I do not touch her. I do not jump out of my bed to comfort her because I cannot face the image of me that I see in her. I leave her to storm through our home, as I lay in my own bed terrified about what will happen to me if I reach out for her. My terror appears to her as resentment—a much safer, more socially acceptable emotion from a mother to a daughter.

May I write openly and candidly? May I tell you about all the ways in which I experience maternal ambivalence? Will there be a social cost? I am always torn and pulled between multiple minds. The projections show that in less than six months, my business is going to skyrocket, bringing in an amount of money that can change the course of our family forever. The problem is this: we're falling apart today. My son is starving for my attention. My seven-year-old is playing with fire—literally. My entire house is in survival mode. Do I put it all on hold and nurture them and be the mother they want and need me to be? Or do I plough through so that I can create pathways that remove some of our barriers? Rent is already four months behind. The engine just went out on the car. Food is sometimes scarce.

As a woman who is poor, Black, single, the mother of six children by four different men ... as a PhD candidate, an entrepreneur, a woman, I find myself always stuck in the balances, trapped in these kinds of dilemmas. The trade-offs are never simple. It is always something like this—choose between getting on the plane to present my innovative work to an international audience at a conference in Montreal, Canada (a place I have always wanted to visit), or rush home because my daughter needs to have emergency surgery so that her arm does not get amputated. This happened to me for real, by the way. As much as I would like to say I would make the obvious choice, I never take that for granted. In fact, each time I choose my children, I am always both surprised and relieved.

Poverty is a cruel master. For its own entertainment, it forces you to make impossible choices. Pay for parking so that you can drop off and pick up your children from school on time or use that money to buy toilet paper. It's sadistic. Spend time with your children so that they can be nurtured while living in a war zone, or move them into a safe community, work three jobs, and make them latchkey kids.

Sexism is even crueller. Here are the options for many impoverished, Black, single mothers. Option one is to stay in an abusive relationship with a jealous man because his being there makes the neighbours feel safe. You know? He makes her look respectable and her family less of an eye sore. His being there decreases their anxiety about illegitimate families and non-normative heterosexual sex. He rights her wrongs, easing the public's mind. Meanwhile, in fact, he makes her home highly dysfunctional and broken. While she is privately beaten, the neighbours stroll by their home, pushing their carriages, happy that he has legitimized her and eased their discomfort. There is always option two. She can raise her children alone, as a single mother in a highly functional and loving family and have Child Protective Services always showing up because the neighbours suspect the children are hungry. Sometimes, it is not even that. They call "just in case"—just in case she has too many children to handle, just in case someone is being abused, just in case she is too Black to mother, just in case she is a stereotype. I have been in different versions of these scenarios on both sides. I cannot help but wonder: do I teach my girls to have ambition and to accept the world hating them, including their lovers, for accomplishing too much? Or do I teach them to play themselves small to be more likeable, marriageable? If I am to lead by example, which do I choose?

Racism is a monster. It taunts and divides. For years, I taught at a top-tier research institution. I was good. Each day, I would show up to give my students—often very white and sometimes very wealthy—the best parts of me. I loved it. At some point, while I was there, my son was in elementary school, struggling. In fact, he always struggled. But at the time, it was important for me to not see it. I needed to believe that the teachers would resolve his problem because I had another fire to put out. I had to move us from one social class to another. I had to follow my dreams of becoming a college professor. I did. Meanwhile, he grew taller, and his reading stayed the same. The teachers promoted him from second to third grade and then from fourth to fifth grade, all the while he kept reading at a first-grade level. I stood at that chalkboard and then the whiteboard, year after year, teaching, because it fulfilled me. The discussions, the assignments, the grooming, the influence, it all gave me a rush. So I kept lecturing and kept teaching and kept inspiring, while my baby was falling deeper and deeper into an academic hole. He was so uncomfortable with reading that he grew anxious about it, so much so that when he knew he would be called upon to read out loud, he would misbehave or walk out of the classroom to avoid the embarrassment. And I kept teaching. While he was being placed in cinder block rooms that look like solitary confinement in the name of protection—protection for him and the population—I kept teaching. When he was nodding off in school and losing weight because of the "focus medicine," the Adderall or the Vyvanse, still not making progress, I kept teaching. I kept teaching until, finally, one day, I picked my son up from school. He was drugged from the medicine. On either side were two staff members, ushering him to my van. He looked so lost. In that moment, I saw him being pushed right through the school-to-prison pipeline. I had read the Moynihan Report. I knew that we lived in a society that was quicker to elevate Black women while leaving behind Black men and boys—even if the women was a mother and the boy her son. I was loving the high, the power, the rush. But what would it cost me in the long run?

I imagined my son screaming at my graduation, "Yeah, my mom has a PhD in literature. But I can't read." I can see it now. The crowd is cheering, excited about my accomplishment. And there he is, working his way to the stage or standing in his seat screaming, "Shame! I can't even read, and she's taught all of these people. Shame. Stoooooone her!" I imagine what would happen to my boy once he made it to middle and then high school. How would he try to cover up for his inability then? Ditching? Fighting? Guns? I needed to teach and research and inspire. I needed to be in a space that valued me without arguments and fights. For my own mental health, I needed to matter outside of my home. I needed a life of my own. I needed to create. I needed instant gratification because mothering is such a thankless job. The rewards are always uncertain, often delayed. Yet what was more uncertain was my boy's future. He could not read, and I could. How unfair was that? So I began imagining my exit.

To be honest, although my son was a crucial factor in my decision to exit academia, he was not the only one. My research focuses on Black mothers. That meant I was going to buy my first house on their backs. My first brand new car was going to be purchased using money from research about them. My younger children would go to private school because of the life I built telling a very small group of people stories about these women, and probably not one Black mother would ever hear, let alone benefit from, my work. That became an ethical problem for me. I had to bring my research to these women in a way that made an impact. I was so close to graduating, completing my PhD, and going on the job market. I was so close to entering into another financial class. I was so close to finally being able to provide for my children in a significant financial way, and there I was deciding to go down a new and unknown path because it was ethical. Well, wasn't this another ethical problem— choosing to take my children down such an uncertain path, prolonging their struggles when we were right at the threshold of a new era? I was torn.

To many others, the choice was obvious. Be safe. Take care of my family. But for me, it was obvious that playing it safe was not going to protect me or my babies from poverty or Blackness. It was not going to protect my girls from sexism and my boys from becoming perpetrators. It was not going to protect any of us from being complicit in our own oppression. I am a feminist. So for me, the personal is always political.

I made the personal choice to bring my research to mothers. It was more than an act of rebellion; it was an act of survival, not just for me and my babies, but for other mothers and their children as well.

When I think of all the things I am up against in this society, sometimes I just want to sell out. I want to make love to the man who disrespects me—because he is beautiful and muscular and his just being there validates all my insecurities. I want to be the shrinking violet because it is easier than the daily fight. Make me a damsel in distress. I am more palatable that way. Everyone wants to be a hero. Let me spread my body across the train tracks and give them a reason. I want to drive my car into the lake or jump from the highest building. I want to play nice, think small, and spend big. I want to be pocket sized and manageable and give up all sense of personal responsibility and agency. I want to just be. But I have these babies, three of them are almost adults now and three are growing rapidly. They're watching me. So I stand tall, defy odds, break barriers, shatter moulds, overcome obstacles, set trends, reframe narratives, and explore new possibilities. I do all of this while struggling with my own maternal ambivalence. I fight all of these fronts while standing at the centre where my ambivalence intersects.

Chapter Two

The Virtue of Ambivalence to Maternity

Joan Woolfrey

Maternal ambivalence has most often been described in terms of already existing mother-child relationships (e.g., Almond; LaChance Adams). In this essay, I consider contradictory feelings towards becoming a mother in the first place. At its best, motherhood can be deeply rewarding, and having a desire for that experience is perfectly common and appropriate. At the same time, understanding the challenges and burdens that motherhood presents, wanting to resist social and familial pressure to become a mother, and valuing the rewards of childlessness are also justifiable. Thus, one may simultaneously appreciate the advantages of not having children while also understanding the merits of becoming a mother. In this essay I claim that such ambivalence is morally appropriate and that there are morally better and worse ways of engaging with this ambivalence. Moreover, the attitude taken towards maternal ambivalence may be considered a virtue or not depending upon the level of understanding about ambivalence and the circumstances in which it develops.

The very phrase "maternal ambivalence" seems loaded with immediate concerns. Why maternal ambivalence? How does it differ from paternal ambivalence, if there is such a thing? There are numerous historical and cultural reasons for discussing parenting within its gendered contexts. Men experience neither the same social sanctions as women for childlessness nor the same pressures to make parenting into a fulltime occupation.[1] Traditionally, the role of the father has been limited, as Nancy Dowd writes, to the "biological or economic" (4) and has thus been peripheral to hands-on childrearing. Men have not, until recently, been likely to spend the majority of their days, energies, and mental and emotional resources in active childrearing. The job has been left to women for millennia. A female's ambivalence to motherhood stems, in large part, from the historic gendered division of labour and from the generally oppressive social context within which females find themselves under patriarchal structures.[2] Thus, although the experience of ambivalence will be relevant, predictable, and appropriate for anyone becoming a parent, some aspects are unique to people who identify as women or who are identified and, thus, categorized as such by society.[3]

Throughout recorded history, females have been expected to be the nurturers. Unmarried and childless women have been pitied, scorned, and labeled pejoratively as "spinsters" and "old maids." In contemporary times, women still feel pressure to become wives and mothers, and to perform these roles according to elevated and rigid expectations. In "The Modern Mystique," Harmon Newman and Angela Henderson document a set of persistent presumptions about "ideal mothering" identifiable throughout (at least) the Global North: "(1) the mother must be the primary caregiver of children because men cannot be relied upon for the duty; (2) child rearing logically requires extensive time, energy, and material resources; and (3) the children are priceless and incompatible with paid labor" (474). Many women choose to become mothers while resisting these ideals. These shared assumptions affect women's experiences and may contribute to ambivalence both before and after motherhood. As I argue below, under such social pressures, ambivalence towards becoming a mother is not only comprehensible but even morally appropriate.

Virtuousness

Aristotle, who understood a great deal about the human psyche, believed that we have some control over the development of our personalities. He argued that we ought, with the engagement and oversight of already virtuous members of our community, to develop those character traits—those virtues—that increase our chances for *eudemonia*, or human flourishing. Such virtues generate automatic responses or actions inhabiting the middle ground between extremes, relative to the context and the individual. To be generous, for instance, is virtuous when it shows the right amount of generosity, in the right manner, and in the right circumstances. Being too generous would mean that we give more than we can afford, we give an amount too large for the need, or we give to the wrong person or project. Not being generous enough may be giving too small of an amount to make a difference. According to virtue ethics, over the course of a lifetime, we should be moulding our character to comprise a variety of virtues, such as generosity, which allow us to respond automatically in the best possible way—moderately—whether in common or novel situations. As Aristotle says, being virtuous entails acting "to[wards] the right person, to the right extent, and at the right time, for the right reason, and in the right way" (*NE*, II.vi.1106b20) and doing all that without having to think about it in the moment.

What is most rich about Aristotle's account of virtue is that one's emotional responses are just as important as one's rational responses— that is, the goal in developing virtue is to mould one's emotions to be in sync with and, indeed, in service to our rationality so that our actions emerge automatically from our desires (*NE*, 1102b26-1103a3). The goal is to mould oneself into someone who wants to do what one also knows is the right thing to do and who does that thing automatically because it is emanating from an engrained character trait. Aristotle posits the need for a harmonious collection of these virtues in each of us, which suggests, among other things, that we should not spend so much time on the development of one virtue that we neglect the others. The aim is a unified, virtuous self (e.g., *NE* 1145a1-2). Acquisition of the moral virtues takes patience and repetition over a lifetime.[4] In this essay, I examine what ambivalence to motherhood looks like and why given present societal norms and pressures it seems morally appropriate to have a certain amount of ambivalence about taking on the maternal role. And I also want to suggest, one can be virtuous—or not—towards one's maternal ambivalence.[5] To that end, a look at moral ambivalence, more generally, will lead us back into a discussion of maternal ambivalence specifically.

Ambivalence

For Harry Frankfurt, ambivalence is an inability to make up one's mind that suggests a threat to a cohesive, authentic self ("Identification" 172). Frankfurt argues that one cannot wholeheartedly embrace competing desires at the same time because to value A and not A at the same time is like approving and not approving of a thing you approve of, and this is incongruous. One can see how ambivalence would pose a danger to Frankfurt's view. One could be so torn between one's contradictory desires that one would be too paralyzed to act, and thus be significantly less capable of moral agency than someone without such ambivalence. The irrationality of holding both values simultaneously suggests a defect of character for Frankfurt, a lack of a unified self ("The Faintest Passion" 100).

Moral ambivalence, as described by Patricia Marino in "Ambivalence, Valuational Inconsistency and the Divided Self," involves desiring and valuing two things that are mutually exclusive simultaneously. Marino argues, in contrast to Frankfurt, that ambivalence of some kinds can be moral goods and come from morally whole selves. She challenges Frankfurt's assessment by describing two purportedly different kinds of ambivalence and the values they imply: the kind containing values that have an "essential conflict" and those which have a "contingent conflict" (44-45). For example, if I desire to smoke a cigarette and to not smoke this cigarette simultaneously, then I have an "essential conflict." It is impossible to fulfill both desires under any circumstances. However, in "contingent conflicts," there are two desires that in current circumstances conflict but under different circumstances would not. If I want to be at a meeting, while I also want to be at my child's school play (Marino 55) this is a contingent conflict. If the play or the meeting were on a different day, I could fulfill both desires. Thus, this is not a threat to a unified moral self, since one could wholeheartedly do both things if the timing were right.

The pivotal issue for contingent conflicts is that given a different context, the conflict would be averted, and the conflicting desires could both be fulfilled without contradiction. For a variety of social, economic, and political reasons, contemporary motherhood provides innumerable examples of contingent conflict. In a world where the burden of childcare were more evenly shared, women could be mothers without having to forego other equally desirable opportunities, experiencing a loss of social status[6] or income,[7] or minimizing the professional respect they receive.[8] To imagine that world, consider one of the first systematic proposals for a just society in the Western world—Plato's *Republic*. While there are significant feminist concerns with Plato's vision, he at least attempts to eliminate some of the contingent conflicts between childcare and the flourishing of (some) individuals. Or consider Charlotte Perkins Gilman's advocacy for socialized childcare (and all other domestic labour, albeit with an unacceptable racist component) in *Women and Economics*.[9] If we were living in either of those theoretical worlds, particular versions of maternal ambivalence (to motherhood) that contain contingent conflict would not arise because the relevant conflicting desires and values would not exist.

Utopian visions aside, we can also imagine a woman who has an essential conflict between motherhood and remaining childfree. Marino uses the example of a mother who equally values her fulltime career and being a stay-at-home mother (55). For Marino, this presents an "essential conflict" but not an irrational one. Both desires are reasonable, even though they are mutually exclusive, and a unified self or a virtuous person could be imagined to possess both. Marino takes this argument further when she claims that even when one's desires are contradictory and unresolvable, this is not necessarily a moral defect or, in Frankfurt's phrase, "volitionally inchoate" ("The Faintest Passion" 100). Following Marino's logic, valuing the freedom that comes with being childfree as well as the rewards that may come with mothering may be an essential conflict but still leaves open the possibility of a morally consistent self.

Following Marino's thinking, whatever choice this woman (the one with this ambivalence) makes, "she will be dissatisfied, feeling under any arrangement that something has been lost" (46). A woman with maternal ambivalence perhaps yearns to pursue motherhood but sees the enormous sacrifices required and equally values the freedom that comes with not pursuing motherhood. Marino differs from Frankfurt here in that she can imagine that such a person could still be "a fully rational and good self" (46). Such a person is deeply uncertain about which value should take precedence in this case. As Amelie Rorty argues in "The Ethics of Collaborative Ambivalence," if one values two mutually exclusive options and has good solid reasons for both of those options, then one's ambivalence is "internally appropriate" (395). How one responds to one's own ambivalence as it relates to the prospect of motherhood can be elucidated through the lens of virtue ethics, as I discuss below.

Virtue Ethics

Martha Nussbaum—a philosopher occasionally accused of being a full-blown Aristotelian but who has spent time uncovering Aristotle's faults as well as his own virtues—offers a nonrelativist account of Aristotle's approach to virtue ethics in "Non-Relative Virtues: An Aristotelian Approach." She claims that to have virtuous traits means "to be stably disposed to act appropriately" in a given context (441). This means that a virtuous person is likely to consistently behave in a particular way in similar types of situations. For example, if I am possessed of the virtue of honesty, I will automatically (almost) always tell the right amount of truth based on a valid assessment of the situation. I won't bore you with unnecessary details. I won't leave things out that are relevant to your decision making. It won't cross my mind to lie for convenience's sake. As the sort of person who has developed the habit (and who has trained herself) to tell the truth, I am "stably disposed" towards honesty.

What it is "to act appropriately" in a given situation will come partially out of the cultural context of the action. Societies develop norms which their members will be conditioned to accept. Being a rational moral agent also requires one's active participation in deciding how to act in evaluating those norms. True moral virtue (moral virtue in the "strict sense"[10]) requires that we have an understanding of the appropriateness of the habits we acquire. That deliberation may produce actions that develop into character traits outside our society's dictates. Individuals deliberating can also have an effect on their society's norms. Virtuous individuals acting collectively can influence their society. For example, support for legal slavery in the United States predominated from early colonial times. Early abolitionists publically evaluated and deliberated about this view. Speeches were made, tracts were written, and arguments were repeated over and over about the moral abhorrence of the practice. Slavery was eventually banned in the U.S. and attitudes about slavery slowly changed because of the efforts of single-minded, principled, and virtuous people acting independently of the dominant cultural beliefs. My point here is that both individuals and—holding with Aristotle—communities can acquire moral virtue in the strict sense through public discourse and deliberation.[11]

All of this is to suggest that individuals who have ambivalence to motherhood can acquire a virtuous attitude about that ambivalence. If one deliberates about the ambivalence—bringing its tensions to light and examining the social context in which it emerges—and sees good solid reasons for both options, one is in a position to acknowledge one's ambivalence as internally appropriate. A critique of societal norms will be a part of that deliberation. Developing that deliberative practice into a virtue will occur over time with repetition. And if one does this deliberation publically, one may play a role in shifting dominant beliefs about motherhood. Morally appropriate maternal ambivalence to motherhood could be valuable in drawing attention to societal injustice.

Attitude towards Maternal Ambivalence as Virtue

Although opportunities for women have been increasing in many nontraditional directions, women still experience the maternal imperative across race, class, ethnicity, and religion. Some level of ambivalence towards motherhood is, I have been arguing, morally appropriate as a response to those messages. If the social context were different, it might be easier to resolve one's ambivalence, but this is—though contingent—merely hypothetical. In the current social context, I claim that it is morally appropriate to be ambivalent about becoming a mother and particular versions of the attitude one holds towards that ambivalence could be seen as virtuous.

Reasons for having children are multiple: mothering can yield many joys and much enrichment. Many confirm that it is deeply rewarding to contribute to a child's increasing mastery of their surroundings, that the bonds of love for a child are like no other, and that caring for a child can develop positive aspects of oneself that would not be realized through other means. There are also numerous factors that weigh against the impetus to have children, especially for women. For one, an individual's capacity to flourish is dependent upon having the room to develop one's talents and abilities. The pressures to become a mother, and the pressures of living up to the ideals of motherhood for those who become mothers, often leave one with too little time for the development of one's unrelated capabilities and interests. Thus, to choose motherhood could limit one's own flourishing. One may also see it as morally problematic to bring a child into a world where environmental, resource, terrorist, and social justice crises are compounding daily. These concerns have profound ramifications that are differently textured depending on one's class, race, gender identity, religion, and so on.

Overall, many of the desires and values embedded in both wanting children and wanting to be childfree are reasonable and valid and can be held simultaneously by morally mature individuals. One's attitude towards this ambivalence can be more or less virtuous. This means that maternal ambivalence to motherhood is appropriate even if such ambivalence is not a norm for this society. What it means to act appropriately, per Nussbaum's definition, regarding motherhood is in flux in this society, but one can still be more or less virtuous towards the experience of that ambivalence.

I want to suggest (but will not argue here) that someone who unreflectively abides by her society's expectation that her role as a mother is an inevitability and a necessity in order to complete herself, while feeling no ambivalence, will not be fully engaging their moral agency and will not have the virtue under discussion. Those who experience ambivalence to motherhood, however, may have an attitude towards their ambivalence emanating from a character trait that could fit the definition of a virtue. If one's ambivalence motivates one to deliberate about their circumstances, critique the social norms that create the ambivalence, and publically engage others in conversations on that topic all from a character trait that makes those conversations and thoughts seem natural and more or less automatic, one can be said to have the virtue of which I speak. If, alternatively, one is overwhelmed by one's ambivalence—deeply conflicted about introducing a new life (that she really does desire) into a world fraught with overconsumption, environmental disasters, institutional injustice, and the risk of terrorism—one might become paralyzed by the thought of making this decision. One's deliberative capacity might shut down on this front, exposing, as Frankfurt suggests, a moral defect in one's character. Unable to justify her right to bring a new life into the world, she remains childless, and regretful, and that regret infects many other areas of her life.

Greater deliberation about the meaning of one's ambivalence is beneficial to individuals and society as a whole. To develop a virtue about ambivalence to motherhood, one would have to explore how the forces in society shape and mould us differently depending upon our perceived gender; one would need to examine one's own conditioned responses to those influences. To the extent that we can be aware of the power exercised over us, we may develop more flexibility in how we manoeuvre through the pressures of our communities and society generally. Ambivalence presents the opportunity to deliberate about how to make more active and nuanced choices about what traits we value and what messages we get from our society. To value both motherhood and childlessness is to be conflicted about two potentially rewarding, but contradictory, ways of living. The conflict one experiences has a great deal to do with the context in which one finds oneself. Whether one does or does not become a mother, the ambivalence will likely remain. Understanding why and being at peace with that may actually be virtuous in itself.

Endnotes

1. "Childlessness seems to be inconsequential for men's cognitive well-being" conclude Thomas Hansen et al. (354), suggesting that the social pressures to reproduce do not affect men's understanding of the best lived life. The opposite appears to be true for women generally: "the mere presence of offspring ... enhances women's life satisfaction and self-esteem, independently of age, marital status, education, or whether the children had left home" (354), suggesting that there are significant social pressures shaping the values and desires of women that do not affect men.

2. Although maternal ambivalence happens globally, I will be restricting my comments to the Global North. I will also note that there are certainly other morally relevant and appropriate reasons for maternal ambivalence to motherhood (e.g., financial, physical, emotional, etc.), but I will be focused on the sort just mentioned.

3. My use of "women" and "female" from here on is meant to be inclusive of both of these categories.

4. Aristotle distinguishes between moral and intellectual virtue (NE, Bk. VI), but my focus will remain on the moral virtues.

5. My thanks to Sarah LaChance Adams for pushing me to clarify this point.

6. Amany Gouda-Vossos et al. conclude that women's social status is perceived as lowest when paired with a man, and the reverse is true for men; Cecilia Ridgeway discusses, inter alia, how cultural beliefs differentiating men and women stereotype men as more competent and effective.

7. Tiantian Yang and Howard Aldrich cite several studies that document that motherhood has a negative effect on women's earnings while the reverse is true for fatherhood.

8. Physician X "notice[s] how far her social status plunged when she began walking around with a baby instead of a stethoscope" (Efron); "when motherhood becomes a salient descriptor of a worker it, like other devalued social distinctions including gender, downwardly biases the evaluations of the worker's job competence and suitability for positions of authority" (Ridgeway and Correll, 683).

9. For a careful discussion of those feminist concerns for Plato, see Annas, and Tuana. For resources on Gilman's racism, see, Rudd and Gough (especially Catherine Golden's chapter titled "'Written to Drive Nails With': Recalling the Early Poetry of Charlotte Perkins Gilman" and Lisa Ganobcsik-Williams's "The Intellectualism of Charlotte Perkins Gilman: Evolutionary Perspectives on Race, Ethnicity, and Class").

10. Aristotle distinguishes between natural virtue—the kind that develops unreflectively due to moulding by society—and moral virtue in "the strict sense" (NE VI.xiii.1144b). It is the latter than I am discussing.

11. Regarding how groups acquire virtue, see Beggs; Woolfrey.

Works Cited

Almond, Barbara. *The Monster Within: The Hidden Side of Motherhood.* University of California Press, 2010.

Annas, Julia. "Plato's *Republic* and Feminism." *Philosophy*, vol. 51, no. 197, 1976, pp. 307-21.

Aristotle. *The Nichomachean Ethics [NE].* Translated by W.D. Ross. *The Internet Classics Archive.* MIT, classics.mit.edu/Aristotle/nicomac haen.html. Accessed 2 Dec. 2019.

Beauvoir, Simone de. *The Second Sex*. Translated by Constance Borde and Sheila Malovany-Chevallier. Alfred A. Knopf, 2010.

Beggs, Donald. "The Idea of Group Moral Virtue." *Journal of Social Philosophy*, vol. 34, no. 3, 2003, pp. 457-74.

Carr, David. "Virtue, Mixed Emotions and Moral Ambivalence." *Philosophy*, vol. 84, no. 327, 2010, pp. 31-46.

Dowd, Nancy. *Redefining Fatherhood*. New York University Press, 2000.

Efron, Sonni. "The World; Sunday Report: Japan's Demographic Shock; A Young Physician Decides One Child Is Enough; Motherhood Means a Drop in Social Status, Mio Masuda Has Found. A Second Baby Would Thwart Her Career." (Part A). *Los Angeles Times*, 24 June 2001, www.newspapers.com/newspage/188360901/. Accessed 2 Dec. 2019.

Frankfurt, Harry. "Identification and Wholeheartedness." *The Importance of What We Care About*. Cambridge University Press, 1988, pp. 159-76.

Frankfurt, Harry. "The Faintest Passion." *Necessity, Volition, and Love*. Cambridge University Press, 1999, pp. 95-107.

Gilman, Charlotte Perkins. *Women and Economics: A Study of the Economic Relation between Men and Women as a Factor in Social Evolution*. Boston: Small, Maynard & Co., 1898. *UPenn Digital Library*, digital. library.upenn.edu/women/gilman/economics/economics.html. Accessed 2 Dec. 2019.

Gouda-Vossos, Amany, et al. "Sexual Conflict and Gender Gap Effects: Associations between Social Context and Sex on Rated Attractiveness and Economic Status." *PlusOne*, vol. 11, no. 1, 2016, pp. 1-14.

Hansen, Thomas, et al. "Childlessness and Psychological Well-being in Midlife and Old Age: An Examination of Parental Status Effects across a Range of Outcomes." *Social Indicators Research*, vol. 94, no. 2, 2009, pp. 343-62.

Lachance Adams, Sarah. *Mad Mothers, Bad Mothers, and What a Good Mother Would Do: The Ethics of Ambivalence*. Columbia University Press, 2014.

Marino, Patricia. "Ambivalence, Valuational Inconsistency, and the Divided Self." *Philosophy and Phenomoenological Research* 83.1 (2011): 41-71.

Newman, Harmon D., and Angela C. Henderson. "The Modern Mystique: Institutional Mediation of Hegemonic Motherhood." *Sociological Inquiry*, vol. 84, no. 3, 2014, pp. 472-91.

Nussbaum, Martha. "Non-Relative Virtues: An Aristotelian Approach." *Ethics: Classical Western Texts in Feminist and Multicultural Perspectives*, edited by James Sterba, Oxford University Press, 2000, pp. 439-57.

Plato. *The Republic*. Translated by Benjamin Jowett. *The Internet Classics Archive. MIT*, classics.mit.edu/Plato/republic.html. Accessed 2 Dec. 2019.

Ridgeway, C. L., and S. J. Correll. "Motherhood as a Status Characteristic." *Journal of Social Issues*, vol. 60, no. 4, 2004, pp. 683-700.

Ridgeway, C. L. *Framed by Gender: How Gender Inequality Persists in the Modern World*. Oxford University Press, 2011.

Rorty, Amelie. "The Ethics of Collaborative Ambivalence." *Journal of Ethics*, vol. 18, no. 4, 2014, pp. 391-402.

Rudd, Jill, and Val Gough. *Charlotte Perkins Gilman: Optimist Reformer*. University of Iowa Press, 1999.

Tuana, Nancy. *Feminist Interpretations of Plato (Re-Reading the Canon)*. Pennsylvania State University Press, 1994.

Woolfrey, Joan. "Group Moral Agency as Environmental Accountability." *Social Philosophy Today*, vol. 24, 2008, pp. 69-88.

Yang, T, and H.E. Aldrich. "Who's the Boss? Explaining Gender Inequality in Entrepreneurial Teams." *American Sociological Review*, vol. 79, no. 2, 2014, pp. 303-29.

Section I

Ambivalence in Pregnancy and Childbirth

Chapter Three

What Is Pregnancy Ambivalence? Is It Maternal Ambivalence?

Amanda Roth

mbivalence refers to two-mindedness—the state of being torn or having conflicting emotions or attitudes. In speaking of maternal ambivalence, the notion is often expressed in terms of mothers experiencing both love and hate simultaneously for their children. As one parenting blogger puts it: "**I love this**. *I hate this. I want to eat you up I love you so much!* Oh my God, please leave me alone!" (Sprenger, emphasis and bold in original,). Similarly, Adrienne Rich reflects that "My children cause me the most exquisite suffering of which I have any experience. It is the suffering of ambivalence, the murderous alternation between bitter resentment and raw-edged nerves and blissful gratification. Sometimes I seem to myself, in my feelings toward these tiny guiltless beings, a monster of selfishness and intolerance" (1). Although such feelings are common, there is little room for them in a cultural context in which motherhood is an identity altering experience. That women may experience hate for their children—even fleeting hate, even hate joined with overflowing love— seems antithetical to motherhood as it is commonly imagined.

Yet if maternal ambivalence has not received enough recognition, the subject I have in mind has received still less. I focus here not on ambivalence about motherhood and the mother-child relationship but ambivalence about pregnancy and the gestator-fetus relationship. In this chapter, I describe pregnancy ambivalence and situate this phenomenon in terms of its relation to maternal ambivalence.

Doing so requires first getting clear about what maternal ambivalence consists in—what exactly is "maternal" about this experience? Next, I ask how pregnancy ambivalence is related to maternal ambivalence, and I consider two intuitively attractive conceptions of pregnancy ambivalence—one that takes pregnancy ambivalence to be a species of maternal ambivalence and one that takes these two phenomena to be wholly unrelated. I show that neither account is satisfactory, and suggest that instead of attempting to define pregnancy ambivalence in relation to maternal ambivalence, we approach the question of how the two are related by examining paradigm cases. Doing so highlights the ways in which pregnancy and motherhood are conceptually and morally distinct. I suggest then that a close analogy between motherhood and pregnancy is not suitable, even as some experiences of pregnancy ambivalence have much in common with experiences of maternal ambivalence.

What Is "Maternal" about Maternal Ambivalence?

One major challenge in theorizing about the experiences of pregnancy, motherhood, and ambivalence in pregnancy and motherhood—and especially of attempting to analyze the categories to determine their relation to one another—is avoiding "totalizing conceptions" of such experiences that ignore or erase some women's experiences of these phenomena (Lundquist 138). Given this, instead of offering an analysis or definition of maternal ambivalence here, I instead point to a number of apparent themes characterizing maternal ambivalence in the feminist literature—themes that may or may not be exhaustive. First, while characterizations of maternal ambivalence vary, the literature routinely points to the simultaneous or "side by side" emotions of love and hate towards one's child as distinctive of maternal ambivalence (Parker 17). Maternal ambivalence then presumably is not intended to capture just any conflicted emotions or two-mindedness related to motherhood. After all, there are many ways to be ambivalent about motherhood. A woman without children may be of two minds about wanting to become a mother. Or an assigned female at birth individual who is gender nonconforming and who carries and births a baby may be ambivalent about identifying as a mother given the gendering of the term and role. Neither of these situations seems to be what the term "maternal ambivalence" typically aims to include, which makes sense if maternal ambivalence is fundamentally a matter of having loving and hateful emotions about or towards one's child.[1]

A second theme is that maternal ambivalence is noted to be a state of mind "shared variously by all mothers" (Parker 17) as well as "a normal phenomenon ... ubiquitous ... [and] not a crime or a failing" (Almond 1). In fact, Rozsika Parker takes a generally positive outlook on the phenomenon and argues that manageable maternal ambivalence can be an important resource for mothers; after all, ambivalence, but not pure love or pure hate, encourages a parent to productively reflect on their child and parental relationship (6-7). From this perspective, the existence of maternal ambivalence is not a problem; rather, the problem is with the lack of acknowledgment of any negative sentiments towards motherhood.

Third, scholarly work on maternal ambivalence has looked to the specific social and historical construction of motherhood in the contemporary U.S. and Canadian context to understand the phenomenon. Sarah LaChance Adams, for instance, locates the experience as resulting from legitimate conflicts between the needs of mothers and their children (4-5). Presumably, any kind of parental relationship is likely to involve such conflicts, but the particular context of parenting—and especially mothering—here and now seems especially ripe for producing conflict. For instance, Barbara Almond points to historical events such as the rise of childhood as an institution and the idealization of the mother-child bond since the Enlightenment, along with the increasing primacy of the nuclear family and the rise in single-parent/mother family forms as important contributors to maternal ambivalence (4-5). All of these historical changes, after all, have greatly increased demands on mothers. The cultural dominance of intensive motherhood as the way to be a good mother as well as the increasing turn to methods of parenting that demand large amounts of time and energy—for example, attachment parenting, co-sleeping, "breast is best" ideology, and extended breastfeeding—arguably further this trend (Hays; Ennis.).

A final theme is the recognition that although maternal ambivalence is a common experience, it can have devastating results in some cases. Consider mothers who kill their children. LaChance Adams suggests that such "maternal aggression ... is often a sign that the mother is in need of physical and psychological distance" (183). Thus, although conflicts between mother's and children's needs may be a normal and an inevitable aspect of parent-child relationships, the lack of not only societal support for mothers but also acknowledgment of maternal ambivalence can lead to tragic outcomes.

Implicit in all of the themes described above, of course, is gender. In particular, notice that the very notion of maternal ambivalence is tied to the parenting role typically inhabited by women. No doubt parents of any gender experience significant conflict between their own needs and wants and those of their children at times. Parenthood done well in almost any imaginable social context must involve significant burden, sacrifice, and emotional turmoil—and this is clearly the case in the contemporary U.S. and Canada. However, the phenomenon of "paternal ambivalence" does not fill the pages of a well-developed scholarly literature, nor does it garner much discussion even in popular news or on blogs. Perhaps this reflects a simple neglect of men's experience of parenthood, but I suspect the abundance of discussion of maternal ambivalence is a reflection of both the biological reality of the bodily role women primarily, but not exclusively, play in bearing children as well as the gendered division of parenting labour that assigns women the primary care of children.[2]

Is Pregnancy Ambivalence Maternal Ambivalence?

Having laid out how the existing literature understands maternal ambivalence, what can we say of the nature of ambivalence in pregnancy and how it is related to maternal ambivalence? First, I must be clear by what I mean by pregnancy ambivalence, since this is not a commonly named and discussed experience. Two opposing conceptions of pregnancy ambivalence become apparent at first glance.

One seemingly attractive possibility is to make sense of pregnancy ambivalence in terms of ambivalence about continuing a pregnancy, most obviously in cases of unintended and unwanted pregnancies. Consider the dominant cultural representation of abortion-related decision making: a young woman or teenager in an uncommitted relationship finds herself pregnant. She is not ready to be a parent for a multitude of reasons—personal, educational, economic, etc. But she is torn, of two minds, about whether to abort or to continue the pregnancy (whether in order to become a parent to the resulting child or to relinquish the child for adoption at birth). There are reasons on both sides, and, thus, the young woman is ambivalent about the pregnancy. This makes for dramatic television or film watching, although it is not obvious whether such depictions capture much about the experience of real women and girls when it comes to terminating pregnancy. For instance, in contrast to media representations, in 2014, over half of women obtaining abortions were age twenty-five and over; 45 per cent were married or cohabitating with a male partner, and 59 per cent had already given birth (Guttmacher).

Moreover, popular culture representations of abortion also emphasize cases of ambivalence—about what to do about an unintended pregnancy—in ways that obscure experiences of women who do not agonize about what to do or do not find reasons on both sides in the first place.[3] Some empirical evidence suggests that only a minority of pregnant women face feelings of "decisional uncertainty" about whether to continue a pregnancy, as evidenced by their reporting doubt when approaching an abortion provider or withdrawing the request for an abortion prior to it being performed (Kjelsvik et al. 2). However, Maggie Kirkman et al. point out in a review of the literature on reasons women give for pursuing abortion that "ambivalence will be found only if researchers provide an opportunity to express it", which many authors of the papers included in the review did not explicitly provide.

In those studies in which ambivalence was recognized, it took a number of forms: women providing any reasons in favour of continuing the pregnancy (e.g., possible future regret of if one terminated the pregnancy); women viewing abortion as "not unequivocally desirable even if it was the best current option for them"; and women expressing "anti-choice attitudes" or acknowledging both "the desire for a child (on the one hand) and the conclusion that the timing was wrong (on the other)" (Kirkman et al. 376). At least for some women, then, deciding what to do about a not clearly wanted pregnancy does involve a sense of being torn. Should we focus on this particular kind of experience of having two minds about pregnancy and take it to be the meaning of pregnancy ambivalence?

Before evaluating this approach to pregnancy ambivalence, it is worth considering what the relation between maternal ambivalence and pregnancy ambivalence looks like in this approach. If pregnancy ambivalence is specifically about whether to abort or continue a pregnancy—a question that is perhaps most likely to arise in unintended pregnancies—then there is quite a large disanalogy between the two phenomena in three ways: 1) the lack of universality of pregnancy ambivalence; 2) the decisional rather than emotional and/or phenomenological emphasis of pregnancy ambivalence; and 3) the focus on ending the pregnancy relationship (by ending the life of the fetus) in pregnancy ambivalence.

Regarding the first aspect of the disanalogy—the lack of universality of pregnancy ambivalence—recall that maternal ambivalence is described not as something that some mothers experience but as universal. But as indicated above, ambivalence about whether to continue or end a pregnancy, though common, is certainly nowhere near universal. Some women have no doubt that termination is the right choice for them as soon as the stick turns blue. Others spend almost the entire length of a desperately wanted pregnancy threatened by a risk of loss hoping against hope that the pregnancy will endure and the baby will live, with deliberate termination of the pregnancy the farthest thing from their minds. So pregnancy ambivalence understood as being torn about whether to terminate or continue a pregnancy is something only some pregnant individuals ever experience. It is not something essential to pregnancy itself or even to pregnancy in this culture.

The previous point leads naturally to the second aspect of the disanalogy: the decisional, not emotional, emphasis of pregnancy ambivalence. Maternal ambivalence is generally characterized in the literature in terms of the emotional experience of being torn or experiencing conflicting emotions regarding one's child and oneself simultaneously. It is true that in some cases this may take the form of overtly considering options about what to do with that relationship or the child in question—e.g. whether to kill the child, whether to call a loved one for help so that one does not harm the colicky baby, whether to put one's own needs and desires aside to fulfill those of the child once again, etc. But more generally, maternal ambivalence is understood in terms of an emotional and a phenomenological experience. As LaChance Adams (35) puts it: "The ambivalent mother finds herself in two opposite orientations toward her child(ren). They share both a relationship of conflict and a relationship of happy mutuality" (35). Even more than this, "mothers often feel as though their own desires are directed against themselves when they are in opposition to their children's needs and wishes," which can leave a woman feeling "displaced by motherhood, as she simultaneously loses and finds herself in relation to her child" (LaChance Adams 36). But this sort of experience of displacement, of losing and finding oneself at the same time, need not play out in terms of ambivalence about what to do in some concrete choice situation. Yet taking pregnancy ambivalence as a matter of torn-ness about whether to continue a pregnancy does seem to commit us to a rather narrow "what to do" framing of the phenomenon.

Deeply related to that "what to do" framing is the third dissimilarity between maternal ambivalence and pregnancy ambivalence on this first approach to interpreting pregnancy ambivalence. Pregnancy ambivalence is here understood solely about whether or not to terminate a pregnancy—that is, for the pregnant woman to end her developing relationship to the fetus, to remove herself from pregnancy, and to do so more specifically by ending the life of the fetus. One may think this is not all that dissimilar from maternal ambivalence, which, after all, does sometimes tragically involve filicide, as LaChance Adams discusses. But even recognizing the connection between maternal ambivalence and filicide, there is more disanalogy than parallel here. Maternal ambivalence is not merely about ending a mothering relationship to a child, and is certainly not specifically about ending the child's life. After all, filicide is quite rare, although maternal ambivalence is taken to be universal.[4] On the view we are considering, however, pregnancy ambivalence involves nothing but consideration of terminating the pregnancy and thereby ending the fetus' life.

Given the three dissimilarities between pregnancy ambivalence and maternal ambivalence explained above, it seems that in this approach, pregnancy ambivalence and maternal ambivalence are just fundamentally different and, in fact, bear little relation to one another. This outcome, in itself, is not theoretically worrisome to me, as I see no reasons to assume the two phenomena must strongly parallel one another. Yet each of the above points of disanalogy does seem to raise some independent reasons to reject this way of interpreting pregnancy ambivalence. More fundamentally, the largest problem I see with taking the cultural representation of being torn about continuing an unintended pregnancy as a starting point is that this approach simply ignores all other ways to experience two-mindedness—the simultaneous pull of love and hate or the sense of loss of oneself in the pregnancy relation. Should not an understanding of pregnancy ambivalence try to accommodate all (or at least most of) the ways of being ambivalent in and about pregnancy? What, after all, is so special about the ambivalence of abortion decision making?

What if instead of the above framing—which emphasizes a particular kind of experience of pregnancy that is often associated with lack of clarity about what to do—we begin with the assumption that pregnancy ambivalence will likely parallel maternal ambivalence regarding the three dissimilarities laid out above? Let us think about ways in which all pregnant individuals may experience the conflict of love and hate or the sense of losing oneself regardless of whether they are considering ending the pregnancy. After all, if mothering can so often involve being of two minds, feeling a mix of love and hate, and seeming to lose oneself as a result of the intensive nature of the mothering relationship and the related social and emotional burdens, could not pregnancy also plausibly involve the same?

Indeed, pregnancy often does involve significant burdens that are influenced by cultural context and social forces. For instance, some of the cultural expectations and norms that have produced intensive mothering (Hayes; Ennis) are also applied to pregnant women leading to what we may call "intensive gestation." It may seem counterintuitive that gestation—at root, a bodily process, many aspects of which occur outside of one's control—could be intensive in the way mothering has come to be. Yet consider Rebecca Kukla's argument that pregnancy is a new symbolic site in which women's mothering is measured. For example, Kukla points to "birth as a maternal achievement test" (74-78), in which good pregnant women are expected to walk a narrow line of choices: "yes" to an unmedicated vaginal delivery following birthing classes and the writing of an extensive birth plan, but "no" to home birth, elective Caesarean section, epidural, or vaginal delivery after a Caesarean section, lest they (supposedly) risk the safety of their baby or the ability to immediately bond with the newborn. Similarly, pregnant women are told to make "every bite count" by popular guides to pregnancy (Kukla 81), are sometimes blamed for miscarrying by friends, family members, or acquaintances (Bardos et al), and are instructed—along with women who are not currently pregnant, but might accidentally become pregnant—to completely abstain from alcohol by the Centers for Disease Control and Prevention.

Moreover, similar to motherhood, there is little cultural acknowledgment of negative emotions in pregnancy. One is supposed to feel an almost immediate connection to the fetus, as indicated by media representations of pregnancy. In "the ultrasound moment" in television storylines, women are expected to swoon immediately at the image, and failure to react in this way appears to be reserved only for unplanned pregnancies as well as for cases in which doubts about the pregnant woman's maternal nature or abilities are raised as a comedic element (Kukla; Tropp).[5]

Finally the biological reality of pregnancy is perhaps even riper for the experience of ambivalence than mothering after birth. LaChance Adams points out that maternal ambivalence involves a double sort of being torn—"a fissure between the mother and her child ... [and] a fissure within the woman herself" (53). Nowhere is such a fissure in the self more obvious than in the case of pregnancy in which the boundaries of one's own body and self are disrupted; as Iris Young puts it, "the pregnant subject ... is decentered, split, doubled.... She experiences her body as both herself and not herself" (Young qtd. in LaChance Adams, 16).

These considerations make clear a number of likely similarities between pregnancy ambivalence and maternal ambivalence, such that pregnancy ambivalence could plausibly be interpreted as an earlier version or stage of maternal ambivalence. This second conception of pregnancy ambivalence avoids the problems associated with thinking about it only in terms of whether or not to terminate a pregnancy, leaving room for many different kinds of experiences of two-mindedness in pregnancy to count as pregnancy ambivalence. Ambivalence about terminating or ending a pregnancy may count as well, but so may the sense that one is no longer a whole person, a subject of one's own, since the physical and emotional demands of the fetus reshape one's body and mind. Moreover, there is no doubt that many women do understand their pregnancies as early forms of motherhood. Thus, the approach seems to have prima facie appeal. Yet I will argue that this second conception of pregnancy ambivalence is also ultimately unsatisfactory.

One reasonable objection is that analogizing motherhood and pregnancy threatens to obscure important moral and legal differences. A common tact in defending the morality and legality of abortion is to insist that fetuses are not (yet) babies and pregnant women are not (yet) mothers. But if we subsume pregnancy under motherhood in order to make sense of pregnancy ambivalence, do we not undermine this common defense of abortion rights? Accusations that women (or girls) who terminate a pregnancy are mothers killing their own babies, after all, appear to underlie much popular political and social antiabortion sentiment. And the analogizing of filicide to abortion has been put forth in academic discussion of abortion as well, such as in the parenthood argument:

> All mothers are parents. All parents (unless exceptional cir-cumstances obtain) have serious, special duties of care to their children. (Think here of your reaction to deadbeat dads.) There-fore, all pregnant women have serious, special duties of care to their children. Fetuses are children. Therefore, all pregnant women have serious, special duties of care to their fetuses. (Marquis 56)

The ultimate conclusion of the argument is that abortion violates the special duties parents have to their children. Thus, embracing the idea that pregnancy is just an early form of motherhood appears to run the high risk of undermining abortion politics.

Of course, some dispute the idea that embracing the pregnancy-motherhood connection undermines feminist abortion politics. For example, Judith Arcana's "Abortion as a Motherhood Issue" implicitly responds to the parenthood argument by denying that killing a fetus means failing to meet one's parental care-giving duties while still insisting that "conception is the beginning of maternity," which "women have always known" (160-61). In rebutting the idea that terminating a pregnancy violates parental duties, Arcana likens the decision to abort to other monumental parental decisions, such as choices about children's schooling, sleep habits, and religious training—mothering decisions that women take seriously (160-62). Far from being a failure to meet one's parental duties, then, Arcana frames abortion as a way of taking parental responsibility: aborting women make the choice they do because it is best for themselves *and* their babies; babies deserve to be well-mothered if they are brought into the world, and many women choose abortion because they cannot be a good mother at the point in their lives at which they find themselves pregnant (161-3).

Arcana's perspective is in some ways a welcome contrast to the tendency in prochoice circles to hang abortion rights on the claim that fetuses lack value or to deemphasize feelings of confusion, grief, loss, or regret on the part of women who abort (or experience pregnancy loss).[6] However, to my mind, Arcana's essay does little to alleviate the worry about abortion politics. Of note is that filicide is also a monumental parenting decision and the decision most obviously analogous to abortion if we take pregnancy to be just an early form of motherhood, yet Arcana does not discuss mothers killing infants or children as a form of parental responsibility. Why not? Presumably because Aracana—like most Western feminists—does not see abortion as in the same moral universe as killing infants or children, and the notion that filicide is simply women responsibly making the best choice for themselves and their children would strike most readers as absurd.[7] (See Hogan's chapter for further discussion of this topic.) Yet nothing in Arcana's discussion seems to explain why abortion is so different than a mother killing her child, and she, in fact, rules out many of the differences defenders of abortion typically emphasize.[8]

Moreover, Arcana's view highlights a deeper worry about drawing too close an analogy between pregnancy ambivalence and maternal ambivalence: subsuming pregnancy under the umbrella of motherhood risks failing to acknowledge the great variance in experiences of pregnancy. Consider Arcana's apparent dismissal of talk of embryos, fetuses, or "mass[es] of cells" as mere strategy women are forced into accepting by external forces; she insists instead that "we never didn't know that being pregnant meant having a baby growing inside of our bodies" (161). Who is the "we" that Arcana speaks for here and in the earlier quoted passages? It is not the woman who could be a perfectly fine mother and could give her fetus a wonderful life but simply does not want to and makes no apologies for it. Nor is it the woman who insists that her very much wanted but now deceased embryo was merely an embryo, not a baby.[9] This "we" is much too narrow, just as mainstream prochoice denial of fetal status and any connection between pregnancy and motherhood is too narrow.

More generally, Arcana's conception of pregnancy is here revealed to be a totalizing conception; it offers a response to the parenthood argument that can succeed only at the cost of failing to make room for the great diversity of women's experiences and self-understandings, and it should be rejected for that reason.

Building on these points in response to Arcana, my larger worry is that any approach that attempts to subsume pregnancy under the paradigm of motherhood will face a similar problem. Consider, after all, the variety of pregnancy-related experiences: intended pregnancies in which one counts the days after ovulation and wills the stick to turn blue; surprise pregnancies continued hesitantly and with uncertainty; surrogate pregnancies in which one does not view oneself as the child's parent at all; unplanned pregnancies continued with the intent to relinquish the child for adoption; pregnancies not consciously recognized until delivery; rejected pregnancies, etc.[10] It seems to me simply false and dismissive of so many women's experiences of pregnancy to hold that every pregnancy involves or is just an earlier form of motherhood. By parallel reasoning, then, it also seems a potential mistake to understand pregnancy ambivalence as merely an earlier form of maternal ambivalence.

Both of the conceptions of pregnancy ambivalence considered so far have offered valuable insights as to the promise and peril of conceptualizing pregnancy ambivalence as either wholly distinct from maternal ambivalence or as subsumed within it. Yet neither is satisfactory. Where does this leave us?

Motherhood and Pregnancy: Thick and Thin

I take the major lesson of the above section to be this—theorizing about pregnancy ambivalence must acknowledge the variety of different experiences of pregnancy. I would go so far as to suggest that there is perhaps more diversity among experiences of pregnancy than among experiences of motherhood. Perhaps an uncontroversial way to make this point is to direct attention to the fact that one can gestate without being consciously aware of doing so, most obviously in the case of rejected pregnancy or late discovered pregnancies, but more subtly in fact in the case of virtually every pregnancy—for at least a few days or weeks. In contrast, barring amnesia, there are few if any ways to be a mother without realizing that one is a mother.

I do not think the above is a mere obvious truth about the nature of gestation. I think it points, in fact, to fundamental differences between motherhood and pregnancy that are vital to recognize if we are to put forth a satisfying understanding of pregnancy ambivalence. Consider a distinction put forth by Margaret Little between parenthood thickly and thinly construed. In the paradigm case, according to Little "parenthood is a lived, personal relationship, not just a legal status, one that, in the ideal, involves a restructuring of psyches, a lived emotional inter-connection, and a history of shared experiences" (306); this is parenthood in the thick sense. But other cases of parenthood do not live up to this paradigm inasmuch as they do not involve a deep emotional connection, or a well-developed personal history, or a "lived intertwinement" (306). Anonymous ovum or sperm donors, for instance, are at most parents only in a thin genetic sense (although I would refrain from using the term "parent" in such a case at all.) Similarly, another thin sense of parenthood may be a mere legal relation in the absence of any personal history or deep emotional connection—perhaps in a temporary guardianship situation.

Little draws this distinction as part of a discussion of the ethics of abortion in order to make the point that the ethics of what a parent owes to their child depends greatly on the thickness or thinness of the parental relationship. What a merely genetic or legal parent owes a child is paltry compared to what a parent in the thick sense owes to their child, even when significant burdens are involved. Little employs the example of a child in need of a kidney transplant to illuminate this point. We would expect much more willingness to provide the kidney on the part of a parent with a personal history and lived intertwinement with the child versus an anonymous sperm donor or a temporary legal guardian (306). Moreover, it is not only that the parent thickly construed owes more than the parent thinly construed but also that we often expect the former not even to hesitate in making the relevant sacrifice. According to Little, to be unwilling to sacrifice or to require some time to "think over" the medical burdens when one's child's life is at stake would be "a betrayal of the [thick parent-child] relationship" (306).

How does this thick and thin distinction relate back to the question of how to understand pregnancy ambivalence and its relation to maternal ambivalence? It is striking that the scholarly literature on maternal ambivalence overwhelmingly depicts motherhood thickly construed. For instance, LaChance Adams, in illuminating the sense of splitting or losing oneself to one's children common in maternal ambivalence, quotes a woman who describes her child's need to hold her hand while sleeping, and another who fears she will harm her colicky baby in the middle of the night, and others who find that time away from the baby in the world of work or education is the only thing that convinces them of their continued existence (47-53). Common throughout these narratives is that motherhood for these women involves a personal history, an ongoing physical and emotional intertwinement, a deep emotional connection, and a daily caregiving responsibility.

On reflection, this should not be surprising. After all, maternal ambivalence is often understood in terms of simultaneous love and hate for one's child. Indeed, it seems only because we are so devoted to our children that feeling ambivalent towards them seems monstrous, in the way Rich (1) describes. The very devotion at issue in so many cases of maternal ambivalence is part of the emotional connection and intertwinement that characterizes the thick sort of parenthood.

This is not to claim, of course, that maternal ambivalence cannot also be present in thin mothering relationships as well, cases such as surrogacy, temporary guardianship, or, more controversially, egg donation.[11] And moreover, some cases may involve some mixture of thin and thick parenthood—perhaps in cases of birth mothers who have relinquished children for adoption yet have retained some form of a relationship with the adoptive family and the child. Contemplating such cases also raises questions about whether the phenomenon of ambivalence is most directly tied to the social relationship between mother and child (or pregnant person and fetus) or the intensity of the emotional tie, even if there is little or no social relationship. More investigation of these types of cases of thin or thick-thin parenting and experiences of ambivalence would be of great interest. Yet it remains the case, and not an accident in my view, that the paradigm case of maternal ambivalence— judging from the existing literature on the topic—involves thick parental relationships.

If the paradigm cases of maternal ambivalence are about thick parental relationships, then what about pregnancy ambivalence? Notice that we can also distinguish a thick and thin sense of the gestational relationship as Little points out. The thin sense is the underlying biological relation of gestation (Little 305-8), whereas the thick sense would be something more akin to the expectant mother and baby-to-be relationship, in which the pregnant woman has bonded with the fetus in some sense and views it as more than mere developing tissue. And presumably there might be many gradations of thickness in between, making room for the various experiences of different women in different pregnancies.

Like the mothering relationships described in the maternal ambivalence literature, the thick sort of gestational relationship is one that can involve deep emotional ties and strong duties of caregiving. Many a gestating parent has borne without hesitation the burdens of bedrest, hyperemesis (severe nausea), or life-threatening complications to her own health during pregnancy out of love for the fetus they carry.[12] For some, this relationship may begin immediately upon discovery of the pregnancy, but for others, it develops only over time (Little 310).

Yet at the same time, other pregnancies involve only a thin type of gestational relationship. A pregnancy that is desperately unwanted and reacted to with only resentment or animosity may be the most obvious example of gestation in the thin sense, with no emotional overlay of attachment or on the woman's part. Many such pregnancies end in termination, but others continue to full term. Sometimes what began as an unwanted pregnancy can generate a thick gestational relationship, but in other cases—what Lundquist calls "rejected" pregnancy (140-43)—the fetus may reach term with no embrace or acceptance of the pregnancy or fetus by the pregnant woman. Unrecognized pregnancies are another such case in which gestation occurs, but there is no more but the thinnest relationship at work between the pregnant woman and the fetus, as in the case of "denied" pregnancy—again using Lundquist's terminology (146-50)—in which one is not consciously aware of the existence of the fetus until labour and delivery commence. Finally, cases of mixed thin and thickness are presumably possible as well, such as in the case of gestating with the intent to relinquish the child for adoption or surrogate pregnancy.

If, as I suggest above, paradigm cases of maternal ambivalence involve thick parental relationships, should we assume the same about pregnancy ambivalence? I want again to emphasize the need for further empirical or narrative work involving women's actual experiences of pregnancies of different sorts to play a role in theorizing. But in the absence of such empirical or narrative accounts at the moment, there is a strong case to be made that we should expect pregnancy ambivalence to be associated with thick gestational relations; after all, the ambivalence in question is characterized by a simultaneous love and hate for the fetus, which implies an emotionally deep relationship.

This conclusion about what kind of torn-ness is required to count as pregnancy ambivalence reflects an important dissimilarity in maternal ambivalence and pregnancy ambivalence familiar from discussion in the previous section. Again, it looks as if pregnancy ambivalence will not end up being a universal phenomenon—far from it in fact, since plenty of pregnancies exist without an emotionally deep relationship between the pregnant individual and developing fetus. But in direct contrast to the first approach to pregnancy ambivalence discussed above, there is nothing in particular about the decision to terminate or continue a pregnancy that marks pregnancy ambivalence. In fact, many cases in which a woman is ambivalent about what to do in the case of an unintended pregnancy may not end up counting as pregnancy ambivalence at all, given a lack of deep emotional connection to the fetus.

Still, the understanding of pregnancy ambivalence as arising only in thickly construed gestational relationships also contrasts with the second approach discussed above, in which all pregnancies are understood as forms of motherhood. By distinguishing thin and thick forms of gestational relationships, we can allow that for those who relate to the fetus as a baby-to-be and become deeply attached a kind of ambivalence that is quite similar to maternal ambivalence is possible. Yet pregnancy ambivalence will still diverge sharply from maternal ambivalence with regard to its universality.

This would mean reaching as a provisional conclusion a conception that allows for pregnancy ambivalence in some cases to have similar origins and nature as maternal ambivalence, yet which resists any tight analogy between the two phenomena and rejects theorizing pregnancy as an early form of motherhood.

The Moral Consequences of Maternal Ambivalence vs. Pregnancy Ambivalence

An additional dissimilarity between maternal ambivalence and pregnancy ambivalence which supports the middle-of-the-road conception I offer (in which pregnancy ambivalence is neither wholly distinct from maternal ambivalence nor merely a species of it) has to do with the moral consequences of each sort of ambivalence. I want to call attention here to three differences between pregnancy and motherhood generally and pregnancy ambivalence and maternal ambivalence specifically:

1. the way in which the emotional and/or social nature of the relationship affects the fetus/child

2. the moral permissibility of ending the life of the fetus/child

3. the moral standing of the fetus/child and the way in which parental or gestational relationships do or do not play a role in determining this

Reflecting on thin and thick parental and gestational relations makes clear an important difference in what children vs. fetuses need—a difference that supports rejecting any tight analogy between maternal and pregnancy ambivalence. When it comes to social parenting—that is, having daily and ongoing caregiving responsibility for a child—the paradigm case is motherhood in the thick sense. Not only is it rare for women who have ongoing social parental responsibility for children to fail to be parents in the thick sense, but such situations rightly strike us as worrisome. Children, after all, need and deserve the kind of love and nurturance particular to the thick parental relation. Moreover, presumably the goods of the emotional connection and intertwinement of the thick parental relationship benefit primary caretakers as well. For both reasons, then, a social parenting situation in which only a thin parental relationship exists raises significant moral worry out of concern for both the caregiving parent and the child.

But these worries do not hold in the same way in the case of gestation. It is neither rare nor worrisome for some periods of pregnancy to involve only the thin sort of gestational relationship. Even with easily available over-the-counter tests that can detect a pregnancy on or before the day of a missed menstrual cycle, those who are not intending to become pregnant routinely gestate for weeks (and sometimes months) without discovering the pregnancy. Thus, the thick parental relationship is not even possible in most cases for the first few weeks of pregnancy, since most such pregnancies are not recognized. Furthermore, those who do discover pregnancy early on may or may not immediately bond with the fetus. Even in an intended pregnancy, for many women bonding in pregnancy is a gradual occurrence, and in the early period, the lack of possibility of interacting with the fetus—or even ensuring that it is still alive inside oneself—can constrain the development of an expectant mother and baby-to-be relationship. Moreover, it is no surprise that quickening—the point at which fetal movement can be felt by the pregnant individual—has often been pointed to as a turning point in pregnancy, a moment in which the baby becomes real and after which bonding is greatly enhanced (Lundquist 141). This is all to say that gestating in the midst of a merely thin gestational relationship is common and not inherently worrisome; fetuses simply do not seem to need a thick gestational relationship to thrive in the way that children do. And similarly, at least in the early stages of pregnancy, women's wellbeing does not seem any the worse for viewing the fetus as a mere biological entity or experiencing pregnancy as mostly an inconvenience rather than an emotional entanglement.

Whether this point can generalize to apply to the entire gestational length of pregnancy, however, is less clear. Is it true that fetuses thrive just as well even in the late stages of pregnancy even if the pregnant woman is completely emotionally unengaged or even rejects or denies the pregnancy? Lundquist's discussion suggests that denied and rejected pregnancies do involve various negative consequences for the fetus, either during gestation as in the case of denied pregnancies being associated with low birth weight (147) or for the infant immediately after birth, as in the case of the association between a rejected pregnancy and infanticide (144-45). And presumably the very experience of being inhabited by a fetus against one's will is a kind of violence against the self; on this point, Little makes an analogy to the violation involved in sexual assault (301-3). Thus, such situations are clearly bad for the women experiencing them.

Thus, what is well within the range of typical and not at all worrisome in the early stages of pregnancy—experiencing the fetus as wholly other, strongly desiring not to be pregnant, or failing to realize or acknowledge that one is pregnant—becomes less common and associated with moral worries, both on behalf of the pregnant woman and the fetus, by the end of pregnancy. The fact that early and late stages of pregnancy diverge in such radical ways is itself more evidence in favour of conceptualizing pregnancy and motherhood as well as maternal and pregnancy ambivalence as distinct, even if there are significant overlaps in the late stages of pregnancy.

The second and third differences between pregnancy and motherhood are deeply related and centre on the issue of moral status. Consider some of the darker, though rare, results of maternal ambivalence: violence as a channel for the mother's frustration that can lead to harm or even death for the child (LaChance Adams). One may attempt to make a parallel between this outcome in the case of ambivalence regarding one's infant or child and aborting one's fetus, but there are a number of glaring moral differences here. Consider first that although ending a relationship with a child or fetus is conceptually distinct from killing that child or fetus, fetal death necessarily accompanies all endings of gestational relationships for at least the first six months or so of pregnancy. In contrast, the social aspect of a parental relationship—if not the genetic or gestational aspect—can be ended through relinquishment of the child, with no direct relation to ending the child's life. Here, again, we find more reason to reject any tight analogy between pregnancy and motherhood inasmuch as what ending a parental versus gestational relationship involves can be massively different. (And again it turns out that the later stages of pregnancy seem to have more in common with motherhood than the early stage—for example, at least theoretically, one can end a gestational relationship after twenty-four weeks of pregnancy through live birth rather than abortion, which offers a somewhat closer parallel to relinquishment than abortion, in which the fetus is killed).

The second obvious difference between killing a child and terminating a pregnancy is the moral acceptability of these practices. There is nothing morally acceptable about the horrendous acts of violence that LaChance Adams takes up, yet feminists almost universally take contemporary U.S. abortion practices—including terminating for social or elective reasons—to be perfectly morally permissible.

Why such a stark difference in the feminist understanding of killing one's child versus one's fetus? One common way of drawing a moral distinction between abortion and the killing of infants and children is to point to differences in physical development and cognitive capacities. For instance, many analytic philosophical accounts associate personhood and moral status with various mental capacities, such as rationality, thought, communication, or consciousness. To the extent that fetuses lack such capacities through most or all of pregnancy, they are concluded to be quite distinct morally from most infants and children, and so they lack the kind of moral protections against killing that infants and children have.[13]

But many feminists, echoing some aspects of Arcana's view, eschew this almost complete denial of the value of fetal life and look to alternative ways of conceiving of fetal status that are nonetheless compatible with a moral defense of abortion. For example, Bertha Alvarez Manninen, drawing on related themes from a number of philosophers, argues that it is one thing to have a right to abort, but another thing for a particular exercise of that right to be morally good, decent, or virtuous. If fetal life is indeed valuable, then some terminations may be morally concerning even if the pregnant woman in question has every right to make that decision (176-78).[14]

In this vein of valuing fetal life, many feminists stress relationality as the basis of moral status. These accounts suggest a kind of inherent openness in pregnancy about what the fetus is. Discussing prenatal testing and selective termination as creating the "tentative" pregnancy Barbara Katz Rothman comments that "To abort an accident is one thing. To abort your baby, even your very imperfect baby, is something else again. And that is equally true of two fetuses who are identical in size, in ounces, in 'viability'" (5-6). On a relational account, what makes one fetus merely an accident and another a baby is the perspective of the pregnant woman and more specifically the particular relationship she does or does not engage in with the fetus, which is what constructs the fetus as a being with moral standing. Thus, Susan Sherwin and Linda Layne suggest that personhood must be understood as a social or anthropological phenomenon, such that beings are brought into personhood through social relations and engagement. But not every fetus is thought about or perceived by the pregnant woman as a baby. Fetuses then are unlike all other humans in terms of being extremely limited in the social relationships they can be a part of, given the biological reality of pregnancy; for this reason, Sherwin concludes that no fetus can fully be a person and the sole determinant of whether and how a given fetus matters morally is how the perspective of the woman gestating it is situated (Sherwin 355-56).

Such accounts have in common that they hold the morality of abortion in any given case to depend significantly on the woman's perspective on the pregnancy and the kind of social relationship (if any) she has engaged in with the fetus. This brings us to the third difference in moral consequences between pregnancy versus motherhood and pregnancy ambivalence versus maternal ambivalence. In great contrast to maternal ambivalence, pregnancy ambivalence as a phenomenon may actually be part of what determines the moral status of the fetus in the first place, at least according to feminist relational accounts of pregnancy and abortion.

How does this occur? Consider that ambivalence about the fetus in the early stages of unintended pregnancies will undoubtedly shape the contours of the relationship the pregnant woman engages in with the fetus. In particular, the negative side of ambivalence—experiencing the fetus as a parasite or invader, resenting it, hating it, etc.—may lead a woman to terminate immediately, leaving no possibility of engaging in a person-constructing relationship. Or a woman who is uncertain might continue the pregnancy for some number of weeks in order to decide what to do. Suppose she finds a few weeks later that negative emotions outnumber moments of affection; perhaps, she has begun just the most minimal kind of relationship with the fetus that may bring it into personhood over time. Yet she may reasonably decide upon assessing the situation at the end of the first trimester that she is not emotionally engaged enough with the fetus to want to continue the pregnancy. In both cases, a relational account of fetal status and abortion would judge these terminations morally permissible, given the lack of an engaged personal relationship between woman and fetus. Yet notice that such a relationship did not develop in part because of the women's ambivalent emotions towards their fetuses. In this way, ambivalence can prevent the development of a person-constructing relationship, which in turn ensures the fetus does not have significant moral status, which then means that killing the fetus is morally permissible.

But nothing of the sort is true about infants and children. Although maternal ambivalence sometimes does contribute to violence against infants and children, it does not alter the fundamental moral status of infants and children, which feminists generally do not take to be a relational matter. Nor does maternal ambivalence in any way morally legitimate such violence. Thus, if relationality about fetal status and abortion is correct, this is one more way in which maternal and pregnancy ambivalence have quite dissimilar moral consequences. We have all the more reason, then, to accept the provisional conclusion that although maternal and pregnancy ambivalence have some significant similarities, the two phenomena are conceptually and morally distinct and must be theorized as such, just as motherhood and gestation are distinct and must be theorized separately.

Conclusion

My discussion of pregnancy ambivalence as distinct from maternal ambivalence attempts to affirm the great diversity in how pregnancy is experienced and what it is taken to mean. Some pregnancies—or, at least, some parts of some pregnancies—are experienced in much the way motherhood (thickly construed) is. And in such cases, an individual's experience of ambivalence towards her fetus and ambivalence towards her child will have much in common. Yet inasmuch as pregnancy and motherhood remain conceptually and phenomenological different, I suggest we resist analogizing the two experiences, at least for now.

This conclusion is provisional in the sense that future work, and particularly empirical investigation and women's own personal narratives about the experience of pregnancy ambivalence, may further shape what we can and should say about pregnancy ambivalence.

Endnotes

1. Technically, maternal ambivalence may be defined a bit differently, as fundamentally a self-relation, in the sense in which women both lose and find themselves in motherhood and often experience their own interests as "directed against themselves" when in conflict with their child's interests (LaChance Adams 36). It still appears to me that even on this broader understanding, the sorts of cases I raised above would not fit.

2. This raises a number of questions about to what extent maternal ambivalence is tied to women as opposed to anyone who is fulfilling a mothering role, whatever their gender. What of, say, a gender nonconforming woman in a same-sex partnership who actively cultivates a nonmother role, identifying as a "papi" or a trans man who transitions after birthing a child and identifying as a mother for the first few years of the child's life? Such cases point to questions about how self-identity, social expectations, and pressures interact to produce or mitigate maternal ambivalence for those who do not fit within the enforced gender binary. Because the relation between maternal ambivalence and gender is complex in these ways, I generally refer to "women" throughout this chapter when referencing those who might be pregnant, be mothers, or experience

maternal ambivalence, but always with the implication that what is said will likely not apply to all women and will apply to some men and non-binary individuals.

3. Consider outlier representations, such as Olivia's abortion on *Scandal*, *Shrill*'s abortion storyline, and the film *Obvious Child*. In each instance abortion is portrayed as essentially a mundane aspect of women's reproductive lives, with little if any ambivalence or "will she or won't she" portrayed. These representations sparked great interest and commentary because they were so out of the ordinary.

4. Though, perhaps, we need to consider not rates of actual filicide but rates of serious contemplation thereof. I still suspect this would not make maternal ambivalence anything like a universal experience.

5. When *Friends*' Rachel is unable to make out the shape of the first-trimester fetus in the ultrasound as well as later when she views a photo of it, she worries that she will be "a terrible mother" (Kulka 73). Similarly, *Sex and the City*'s Miranda finds herself "faking an ultrasound" when she does not sincerely experience any excitement at learning the baby's sex in contrast to her friends, the baby's father, and the ultrasound technician; again, her lack of appropriate reaction leads her to cast doubt on her suitability to be a mother at all (Tropp 64-65).

6. A significant literature has sprung up in the last decade and a half among feminists who support the moral right to abortion while also holding that fetuses have significant moral value and/or while acknowledging women's grief and the possibility of regret after abortion (Ludlow; Layne). See also the recent special issue of *The Journal of Social Philosophy* on pregnancy loss, in which many papers touch on related issues.

7. See, however, Soren Reader for a feminist defense of filicide, at least in exceptional circumstances, such as in Morrison's *Beloved*, "in which a runaway slave kills her young daughter at the moment they are about to be recaptured ... [in order] to spare her daughter a life of slavery" (146) as one sympathetic example.

8. Here I am referring to justifications of abortion that claim any of the following: that the moral status of the fetus is significantly less than that of a child; that women's bodily autonomy rights justify their

removing fetuses from their body but are irrelevant to killing a being outside of their bodies; and that there is a substantial difference in the relationship one has with a born child compared to a fetus one gestates.

9. See Leslie Reagan's account of her miscarriage (356-58).

10. Following Lundquist's terminology, a denied pregnancy is one in which the woman is not consciously aware of gestating until delivery, whereas a rejected pregnancy is not only unwanted, but involves "an enduring perception of the unwanted fetus as hostile being, or invasive growth" (143). Lundquist's main example of the latter is the case of carrying a pregnancy that results from rape as a war crime during the Bosnian Civil War (141-42).

11. The recognition of thin parental relationships and the example of gamete donors raises an underlying difficulty with discussions of the nature of maternal ambivalence (or parental ambivalence more generally). Where is the boundary between a thin parental relationship and a relationship that is not parental at all? Although it is outside the bounds of this chapter, I would hold that gamete donors who have no social contact with their offspring are not parents even in a thin sense.

12. Even here though there may be room to wonder how similar the kind of love involved in such sacrifices is to the kind of love parents typically have for their children. So, for instance, when we love our children, we love them as another individual in their *full* particularity given who they are, and not simply as someone who happens to fill the role of being our child. But in pregnancy, there is perhaps less possibility to love the fetus in its full particularity inasmuch as there are limits to how much of a particular individual a fetus can be. It is one thing to take on a great burden out of the deep love and connection one feels for *this* child or fetus; it is a different thing altogether to take on that burden because one so badly wants to be or remain a parent and this child or fetus allows one to be a parent. Some cases in which women sacrifice greatly during pregnancy may have little to do with *this* fetus and more to do with the deep desire to be a parent to *a* fetus—*any* fetus. This surely seems to be what is occurring when women go to great lengths to conceive in the first place, for instance by taking on painful or risky fertility treatments.

13. Of course, one major objection to such views is that depending on what capacities are taken to make a moral difference, infants may also turn out to lack full moral status, and, thus, some such defenses of abortion also justify infanticide.

14. So, for instance, legally speaking historically separation from the mother's body has denoted the commencement of personhood (Hogan). This approach to the legality of abortion is perfectly compatible with the fetus having some degree of moral value.

Works Cited

Almond, Barbara. *The Monster Within: The Hidden Side of Motherhood.* University of California Press, 2010.

Arcana, Judith. "Abortion is a Motherhood Issue." *Mother Journeys: Feminists Write About Mothering*, edited by Maureen Reddy et al., Spinters Ink, 1994, pp. 159-65.

Bardos, Jonah et al. "A National Survey on Public Perceptions of Miscarriage." *Obstetrics & Gynecology*, vol. 125, no. 6, 2015, pp. 1313-20.

Ennis, Linda. *Intensive Mothering: The Cultural Contradictions of Modern Motherhood.* Demeter Press, 2014.

Guttmacher Institute. "Induced Abortion in the United States." *Guttmacher Institute*, www.guttmacher.org/fact-sheet/induced-abortion-united-states. Accessed 2 Dec. 2019.

Harman, Elizabeth. "Creation Ethics: The Moral Status of Early Fetuses and the Ethics of Abortion." *Philosophy and Public Affairs*, vol. 28, no. 4, 1999, pp. 310-24.

Hayes, Sharon. *The Cultural Contradictions of Motherhood.* Yale University Press, 1996.

Kjelsvik, Marianne, et al. "Women's Experiences When Unsure about Whether or Not to Have an Abortion in the First Trimester." *Health Care for Women International*, vol. 39, no. 7, 2018, pp. 784-807.

Kirkman, Maggie, et al. "Reasons Women Give for Abortion: A Review of the Literature." *Archives of Women's Mental Health*, vol. 12, 2009, pp. 365-378.

Kukla, Rebecca. "Measuring Mothering." *IJFAB*, vol. 1, no. 1, 2008, pp. 67-90.

LaChance Adams, Sarah. *Mad Mothers, Bad Mothers, and What a "Good" Mother Would Do: The Ethics of Ambivalence.* Columbia University of Press, 2014.

Layne, Linda. "Breaking the Silence: An Agenda for a Feminist Discourse of Pregnancy Loss." *Feminist Studies*, vol. 23, no. 2, 1997, pp. 289-315.

Little, Margaret. "Abortion, Intimacy and the Duty to Gestate." *Ethical Theory and Moral Practice*, vol. 2, no. 3, 1999, pp. 295-312.

Ludlow, Jeannie. "Sometimes, It's a Child *and* a Choice: Toward an Embodied Abortion Praxis." *NWSA Journal*, vol. 20, no. 1, 2008, pp. 26-50.

Ludlow, Jeannie. 'The Things We Cannot Say: Witnessing the Traumatization of Abortion in the United States." *WSQ*, vol. 36, 2008, pp. 28-41.

Lundquist, Caroline. "Being Torn: Toward a Phenomenology of Unwanted Pregnancy." *Hypatia*, vol. 23, no. 3, 2009, pp. 136-55.

Manninen, Bertha Alvarez. "The Pro-Choice Pro-Lifer: Battling the False Dichotomy." *Coming to Life: Philosophies of Pregnancy, Childbirth, and Mothering*, edited by Sarah LaChance Adams and Caroline Lundquist, Fordham University Press, 2013, pp. 171-92.

Marquis, Don. "Manninen's Defense of Abortion is Unsuccessful." *The American Journal of Bioethics*, vol. 10, 2010, pp. 56-57.

Morrison, Toni. *Beloved.* Knopf, 1987.

Parker, Rozsika. *Torn in Two: The Experience of Maternal Ambivalence.* Virago Press, 1995.

Reader, Soren. "Abortion, Killing, and Maternal Moral Authority." *Hypatia*, vol. 23, no. 1, 2008, pp. 132-50.

Reagan, Leslie. "From Hazard to Blessing to Tragedy: Representations of Miscarriage in Twentieth-Century America." *Feminist Studies*, vol. 29, 2003, pp. 356-78.

Rich, Adrienne. *Of Woman Born: Motherhood as Institution and Experience.* Bantam Books, 1977.

Rothman, Barbara-Katz. *The Tentative Pregnancy: Prenatal Diagnosis and the Future of Motherhood.* W.W. Norton & Co, 1986.

Sherwin, Susan. "Abortion Through a Feminist Ethics Lens." *Dialogue*, vol. 30, no. 3, 1991, pp. 327-42.

Sprenger, Stephanie. "Maternal Ambivalence." *Mommy for Real*, 17 Feb. 2015, stephaniesprenger.com/maternal-ambivalence/. Accessed 2 Dec. 2019.

Tropp, Laura. *A Womb With a View: America's Growing Public Interest in Pregnancy*. Praeger, 2013.

Weiss, Gail. "Birthing Responsibility: A Phenomenological Perspective on the Moral Significance of Birth." *Coming to Life: Philosophies of Pregnancy, Childbirth, and Mothering*, edited by Sarah LaChance Adams and Caroline Lundquist, Fordham University Press, 2013, pp. 109-19.

Young, Iris Marion. *Throwing Like a Girl and Other Essays in Feminist Philosophy and Social Theory*. Indiana University Press, 1990.

Chapter Four

The Unspeakables: Exploring Maternal Ambivalence through the Experience of Depression and Anxiety during Pregnancy

Aleksandra Staneva

In what ways can pregnant women be viewed as separate and unique subjects of interest, away from their temporary function in a culture obsessed with regulating and articulating a much corseted and uniform image of the mother-to-be? Is a pregnant woman entitled to a full range of embodied experiences, from absolute love and fusion with her baby to feelings of distress, resentment, anger, of even hate? Can she be both good and bad? Can we allow women to have complex stories?

Despite advances in feminist-informed research and a shift in cultural representations of what it means to be a mother, the ideology of the "good mother" is pervasive. Such a dominant concept operates within both social and individual levels (Staneva et al.). Moreover, the rightness of different mothering styles is being debated, judged, and assessed in obvious ways both publicly and privately. Such public messages around what it means to be a good mother can be experienced as coercive. As a result, genuine experiences of diverse maternal subjectivity remain muted. What do women make of this silence, of such absences? How do they find ways to articulate their experiences? If language fails them, how do they tell their story? Does this have implications on their mental health and wellbeing?

Drawing on my doctoral work with women who experience psychological distress during pregnancy, I present an exploration of maternal ambivalence during pregnancy. I consider the agenda of mainstream research when it comes to distress in pregnant women within the dominating discourses of pregnancy that are fetus, birth-outcome, and child oriented. A growing number of epidemiological studies suggest a link between maternal distress during pregnancy and adversities at birth, such as preterm birth, low birth weight babies as well as cognitive and developmental implications for the child and even for the adult (Stein et al.). However, there is insufficient research on the lived experiences of mothers-to-be who experience distress. I argue that stories of maternal ambivalence weave the fabric of maternal experiences, albeit in subversive and hidden ways.

To better illustrate my arguments I will use two data sources. One is interview data with eighteen Australian women who presented with different levels of pregnancy distress (anxiety and/or depression; self-labelled as well as measured by standardized screening tools). The second data source comes from online texts produced by twenty-two mothers from a social media group of which I am a member. I have been engaged in moderating and facilitating online spaces (i.e., Facebook pages on pregnancy, birth, and adjustment to mothering) as part of both my studies and as a form of social media presence and activism. This particular Facebook group facilitates discussions around mothering, pregnancy, and childcare under an explicit feminist framework. It is important to note that as part of my preparations for this chapter, I placed an invitation to women to share their thoughts on maternal ambivalence, which led to an overwhelming outpouring of responses. In contrast, similar Facebook groups on mothering practices, styles, and advice—but with less emphasis on feminist empowerment—did not garner any direct responses. I infer that this is evidence of censorship and active self-surveillance (both private and public) that occurs within women-shared online spaces, especially within the heated arena of motherhood.

Pregnancy and Maternal Ambivalence

Julia Kristeva's work offers a rich theoretical lens about the ways in which language is used to either express or hide stories of ambivalence. Kristeva, a French (and Bulgarian by birth) postmodern cultural theorist, explores the importance of language in the psychological understanding of the individual, especially language's relationship to identity. She identifies two separate but intertwined modes of being and of language: the semiotic and the symbolic. The semiotic is more emotive than logical, and it is expressive of the poetic discourse of dreams, the imaginary, and ambiguity. Conversely, the symbolic communicates authority, order, unity, repression, and control; it is associated with patriarchal culture. The symbolic embraces disciplined, coherent, and logical thinking, whereas the semiotic is associated with the maternal sphere and allows for imagined alternatives as well as an increased range of possibilities, disorder, displacement, slippage, inconsistency, and condensation. The semiotic is the ambiguous, and it is the core of écriture feminine (i.e., woman's or feminine writing), which constitutes the relationship between the cultural and psy-chological inscription of the female body and female difference in language with a woman's subjectivity. In the spirit of écriture feminine, I present an interpretation of pregnancy through Kristeva's under-standing of the semiotic. In Kristeva's own description of pregnancy, we can see an example of this style of writing:

> Cells fuse, split, and proliferate; volumes grow, tissues stretch, and body fluids change rhythm, speeding up or slowing down. Within the body, growing as a graft, indomitable, there is an other. And no one is present, within that simultaneously dual and alien space, to signify what is going on. "It happens, but I'm not there." "I cannot realize it, but it goes on." ("Motherhood" 237)

According to Kristeva, the maternal experience is a state beyond representation, beyond understanding at least within the realm of language. When we try to explain the maternal according to Kristeva, we face an enormous complexity that parallels pregnancy, as we are located on "the threshold between nature and culture, biology and language" (*Tales of Love* 297). The state of being a mother, which Kriteva believes to begin with pregnancy, taps into the visceral and poetic semiotic aspects of language.

The difficulty in speaking about pregnancy is reflected in my conversations with pregnant women who experience distress. Pregnancy is a time of liminality between one's past and future selves; of suspense; of confused and shared bodily boundaries; of transforming social roles, identity, and relationships; of forcefully confronting the present; and of and going back in time to face one's own mother. Pregnancy is a time for a woman to relive her self as her child self. However, apart from the taken for granted unspeakables, which pregnancy itself inherently evokes, another significant untellable was also present in these conversations of pregnancy distress: the unspeakable stories of experiencing maternal ambivalence.

Furthermore, Melanie Klein describes ambivalence as the simultaneous holding of both love and hate towards an object. She focuses on the infant's ambivalent attitude towards the mother, which she depicts through the split between the "good breast" and "bad breast." Roszika Parker considers the mother as the ambivalent subject who has to negotiate conflicting emotions towards the infant. According to Parker, maternal ambivalence in itself is not problematic because awareness of it serves to promote concern and responsibility for a child, enlarges one's capacity for self-knowledge, and helps to creatively problem solve one's own undesirable traits. Significant issues arise as women are faced with managing ambivalence within a culture that "is ambivalent about ambivalence" (Parker 56), inflating maternal guilt over one's ambivalence. This is further exacerbated as women's experiences are silenced and considered unacceptable; they become unmanageable and, thus, on the verge of the unspeakable.

Parker identifies two types of ambivalent feelings. Manageable ambivalence successfully protects against hate and serves as a positive, creative force (Parker). Parker does not pathologize this experience but instead accentuates its importance and the benefits for the mother in experiencing "the co-existence of love and hate that propels her into thinking about what goes on between herself and her child" (9). In contrast, intolerable ambivalence sits at the other end of the emotional spectrum and has a powerful destructive charge. Unmanageable maternal ambivalence involves intolerable guilt and stigma, which the mother turns inwards and becomes linguistically stuck, which makes her story unspeakable. Below, I illustrate these arguments through some of my work with women.

The Women

The eighteen women who participated in my research and who agreed to be interviewed on the experience of pregnancy were between twenty-two and forty-six years of age and were all within their second or third trimester of pregnancy. All of them were either married or in a de-facto partnership. Most resided in metropolitan cities across Australia; two lived in small rural towns. Twelve of the women did not have other children from previous pregnancies; the rest of the women had between one and three children of varying ages (from toddlers to teenagers), and two of the women had stepchildren. For eight of the women, this was an unplanned pregnancy. Eight of the women had experienced pregnancy loss, and one woman had undergone a selective termination. Although no information around background and demographics was available for the twenty-two women who participated through social media, overall they were part of a Australian and New Zealand private Facebook group, and all identified as mothers (either pregnant or with small children).

Dynamics

I found it both challenging and rewarding to recruit pregnant women for research that focuses on distress and maternal ambivalence. There is a narrow scope within which women seem able to engage in conversations that steer away from the "pregnancy-glow" narratives. Women lack a narrative space and adequate language to reflect experiences that contradict dominant assumptions. As Marjorie DeVault argues, there is a dominant language that represents a male-centred worldview and is often incongruent with women's lives. Although, understandably, language can never fully capture experiences, particularly ones related to motherhood and pregnancy as discussed above, other feminist scholars also draw attention to the lack of adequate language to reflect women's experiences, such as their leisure and pleasure (DeVault), or women's experiences in leadership positions (see Sheryl Sandberg's *Lean In* for such examples).

In my interviews, the women's speech was full of pauses, gaps, broken speech, and inconsistencies. When asked about their experiences of negative mood, distress, and ambivalence, women attempted to present a completely positive account or avoid the question. Sarah, a pseudonym,[1] said the following:

> I usually understand the reason why I am feeling low…. Life isn't that bad and I need to have a bit of a suck it up princess moment like "You are not that bad; you are alive; you've got a roof over your head, a house; there's a lot worse out there." And I have to have a bit of a pep talk … you know sometimes I just let it pass and just think, "Ah you will get over it, shut up [laughs]" like … sometimes it is just … I don't know … walk around, but I do try to say just as much as possible that this is just a passing phase and know that it is just your hormones and yourself or your mood or whatever, you know! … Tomorrow you wake up, and you are going to be happy, and you are gonna shut up and that's about it! So that's it! I guess it's … more … I am … I can go to work. I am healthy. You know, I've got everything … so there's nothing to be hanky [slang for being tearful] about except you've been spoilt you know and all you are having is a shit day and your body… and you are not full of beans today so … it is just the case of saying, you know, "where is this coming from?" And if you don't know where it is coming from, you just need to hurry up and deal with it because there is nothing to be sad about!

Although she struggled to make sense of her experience and tried to understand what was causing her sadness, Sarah was both internally punitive ("suck it up princess") and also spoke from a second-person perspective. I would argue that Sarah was attempting to distance her maternal identity from the unacceptable feelings of ambivalence.

Similarly, research calls looking at women's experiences of depression and anxiety during pregnancy were met with ambivalence at best and disbelief and denial at worst. Dominant scripts around good mothering are exceedingly narrow and situated within a happiness imperative; they exclude by default feelings of regret, inadequacy, hate, dislike, aggression, and ambivalence. Needless to say, all of the women in the study who were invited to take part in the interviews (and who had scored high on standardized self-measures of depression and anxiety in the pregnancy survey) began by telling me how wonderful they had been feeling and how excited they had been with this pregnancy. Only after the women felt safe within the interview space and only after I framed the conversations around the idea of the "mixed bag of emotions" that all women experience during pregnancy did women begin to open up and share their own stories of distress. It seems to me that the women needed a safety net, through which a nonjudgmental listener could provide a space to talk freely. In a study exploring individual experiences of depression during pregnancy, women shared feelings of emotional isolation that seemed to contribute largely to their experience of antenatal depression (Raymond 43). Partner support (or lack of it) seemed to be crucial to the women's psychological wellbeing during pregnancy. Similarly, for some of these women participating in the research interview, it was the first opportunity for them to talk about their needs and feelings during pregnancy. Connecting with other women via peer support during pregnancy was identified as central in women's stories.

Stories of Ambivalence

Conflict was present throughout women's stories of pregnancy and motherhood—conflicts around their responsibilities for care (self-care vs. baby care), their career, and their problematic relationships with their own mothers and partners. Importantly, a central struggle was around negotiating understandings of ideal motherhood. Emotional journeys of conflict and ambivalence encompassed a gamut of experiences from the tolerable through the unacceptable and the potentially repressed. Similarly, ways of dealing with these emotions lay in a continuum of psychological, embodied subjectivities—from liberating and creative empowerment through shame and isolation to guilt, distress, and depression. Marta, a participant on social media, shared her "pairs of contrasting feelings" that she noted she "could feel at once" (presented below verbatim):

- extreme loneliness/baby as my secret friend (early pregnancy, first days after birth)

- hunger/nausea

- wanting something desperately/being terrified of it (birth)

- concern for another/violent urges toward them (baby waking for 5th time after midnight)
- boredom/deep fulfilment (daily chores)
- tenderness/disgust (child puking!)
- feeling I'm flying/feeling I'm limping (being without kids for the first weekend alone)
- love paid work/hate paid work
- familiarity/awe (watching their personalities unfurl)
- frustration/pride (at toddler staunchness)

Through these binaries, Marta presents a rich story of her experience of conflicts and clashes, expectations and realities, concerns and awes. Such tactile and experiential stories served to open up powerful discussions of feelings of vulnerability and distress within the group; and many women joined in to share their similar realities. When the context and the linguistic space allow for such narratives to freely circulate, women express an immediate sense of connection and a relief: "How refreshing to read these experiences. I feel so guilty that I feel resentful" (Peta, social media).

Creative Conflict: Manageable Ambivalence

All of the women interviewed and on social media described ambivalent emotions. I argue that accepting the resentment and hostility towards the negative experiences related to pregnancy and motherhood enabled a level of manageability of their ambivalence. Such conflict was creative, and discussing it enabled women to tolerate and accept these parts of themselves that did not necessarily correspond to the so-called ideal mother:

> I absolutely loathed being pregnant: it was stressful (after four years of trying I was petrified that something would go wrong) and so uncomfortable (twins on board—horrific). My kids drive me mental sometimes, and I hate the way that I react to their infuriating behaviour, and I've definitely had moments when they make me so angry that I have to leave the room. But I don't think I've ever not felt love for them. Holy crap, they're good at

pushing my buttons, though. I don't always like them, but fortunately those feelings tend to pass relatively quickly. I do give myself a hard time about it, which is pretty stupid really. (Tina, social media)

Participants acknowledged that resisting the maternal ideal was liberating. It served to metaphorically break the levy of frustrated drives that needed to come to the surface of consciousness and to be faced in their fullness; Kristeva's "threshold between nature and culture, biology and language" was metaphorically crossed. Many found the voicing of negative experiences therapeutic, particularly in the context of a safety net and protected by a shared experience. For women with high levels of distress, it was particularly helpful to recognize that their experiences are common:

I'm no longer hung up on doing it right. I don't get hung up on the small stuff. A leaked nappy, a sleepless night, they just don't stress me anymore. I know that this is a short time, and then my job will be done, and I will have time for my next projects. I have a partner and friends and family supporting me. I have a partner who values my job, who tells me on a regular basis that what I do is important and valued. I have spaces where I can express myself without worrying that I am a horrible failure of a mother. Where I can say "hey, I'm sick of my kid today" and will be met with smiles of understanding and offers of cups of tea. I have many pairs of arms waiting to rock and cradle whilst I get a moment to myself. I'm learning to ask for help and accept. And I'm finally building community and feel like I belong. And I can see that reflected in how happy and secure my children are. And I'm not so hung up on being a good mother anymore. I'm good enough, which is massively liberating. (Emma, social media)

Normalizing such emotions helped women to reframe their situation; it had a positive impact on their sense of self-efficacy and increased their agency when it came to speaking up and seeking help. Instead of isolating themselves, they felt empowered to build a sense of belonging within supportive networks and communities, and ultimately to create their own safety nets of support"

All the parents posting only the happy moments, there is no honesty; there is nobody saying "hey, this is hard, and sometimes it really sucks." It's all rainbows and flowers and sensory baths with blue water and spaghetti worms in it, Pinterest worthy crafts and MasterChef meals, and here I am barely holding my shit together wondering where the fuck I went wrong. Love the shit out of my little rascals though. Just don't like them sometimes.... Pregnancy and motherhood feel like something I'm not cut out for. I often feel like a kid wearing mum's high heels and playing house, wondering when the adult is going to come along and do a better job for me. I had never intended on being a parent, and sometimes I really mourn for my freedom. It's hard not to resent my children and their neediness, and though I try not to let them see that and feel that, I definitely feel it sometimes. (Davina, social media)

In acknowledging her ambivalence towards the baby (both the newborn and the fetus), a mother is pushed into searching for solutions, and she displays an increased concern with knowing both herself and her baby. Maternal ambivalence signifies the mother's capacity to tolerate parts of herself and her experience that are not well accepted. By doing this, she is able to hold a more complete image of herself and of her baby. This is a painful process as seen in the examples of the women who "mourn their freedom" and "resent the children" and of those who feel they are "not cut out for pregnancy and motherhood." At the same time, it is also the reality of maternal responsibility that the mothers acknowledged. Once distress is allowed and accepted as a tolerable emotion, a mother can find ways to be creative and to find solutions, as Emma did in the above example.

To resolve or to face conflict creatively, women engaged in deep reflection; they renegotiated older patterns and reexamined relationships. The women I spoke with shared their experiences with their sisters, friends, and mothers, asking about their own birth and childhood. They reached out and connected with support groups, went to psychotherapy, kept personal diaries, decorated infant rooms, engaged in deep conversations with their unborn babies, and managed to both mourn the loss of their previous selves and welcome their future mother-selves. On social media, Jody, for example, said this: "I often feel very guilty that I'm not one of those 'love to be with my kid all the time' people. The more regular breaks I have from her (at part time work or when she goes to kindy) the more reserves I have and the better a mum I am."

Unmanageable Ambivalence

Women in the face-to-face interviews had a greater difficulty articulating the presence of negative and ambivalent emotions related to their pregnancy. Their experiences seemed rather precariously masked within nuanced stories, or they were hushed or completely avoided; hence, they were missing from their talk, despite my attempts to return to the topic of distress:

> But I don't necessarily use the word "depressed" ... I do say that I am feeling very down ... slacked you know? Those kinds of words ... kinds of words when you read them you go "Uh she is really not in a good way" ... and I ... and I think I do that ... like ... you ... you want to tell somebody what's going on, but you don't want to. So you kind of ... hope that you put through your message so in a way they would understand.... I just... to me it was I can't tell anybody that I've got depression cos this is just .... nobody can know ... cos I should be able to get over this. I should be able to just get out of it and get happy you know, which is something that people who don't really understand it they do this a lot cos they don't understand how could it be that bad and feel that down. So yeah I think that's one of the reasons why the messages get coded, trying not to mask it but trying to well so it doesn't look so obvious that oh no I am really quite depressed at the moment. Like I said, it is definitely not one the words that I use ... because part of me still doesn't like to admit that ... you know ... I get depressed. (Jade, individual interview)

Jade used a coded message to disclose how she felt. Even more so, she reflects that she does not like to admit these emotions even within herself. There is a sense of shame and guilt associated with admitting that one is depressed, particularly within the cultural context of motherhood and pregnancy when women are expected to glow with feminine satisfaction. When there was a clash between expectations concerning maternal bliss and experiences of resentment, regret, distress, or depression, women found it difficult to speak. This was evidenced by their gaps and long pauses, which seem to imply an internal censorship around expressing negative emotions.

A Mother's Mother: Generations of Trauma

Another strong source of ambivalent and conflicting emotions for pregnant women was their relationship with their own mothers. All of the women in the individual interviews shared a resurgence of unresolved issues from their childhood—things that some of the women thought were well forgotten and in the past. For these women, pregnancy was indeed a time of deeper reflection and reassessment of past experiences, especially those related to their own experiences of being mothered and cared for (Raphael-Leff). For some of the women, pregnancy involved reexperiencing childhood trauma and neglect; they simultaneously identified with both the child they once were and with their own unborn baby. A shared fantasy was the thought that mothering would heal the shortcomings of their own past and will enable women to be the good and benevolent mother they never had.

According to object-relations theory (Klein), an internal object is the mental and emotional image of the mother; internal objects are formed by the patterns in one's experience of being taken care of as a baby, usually by the mother. Klein provides a compelling theory to explain depression. She argues that it is because of the loss of the internal object (which is a deviation from classical psychoanalytic theory where the object is never lost but is rather inaccessible) as well as the mourning for that lost object that people experience depression. As a result, the depressed person feels an inexplicable "shield of sadness" (Kristeva) as a fundamental mood represented by the unshakeable feeling of something or someone lost.

> Not really not really ... she wasn't [her mother]... all that interested in us. She ... she left quite a few times cos she wasn't happy but she just left all of us? Sp I am hoping that I am not gonna be anything like her. [Voice breaks down] Sometimes I am worried that I am. But you know ... I worry ... that I just don't put enough effort into things ... that I am more interested in my own ... little ... you know... things that I do. You know hatching chickens and stuff like that, art projects, whatever ... that doing stuff for him [son]. (Susana, personal interview)

She's [her mother] not in my eyes someone to look up for guidance because I've always looked after her, and I have been in foster care since I was sixteen, and it was a big a big thing.... So my mum ... I just find it really hard to trust my mum. (Brooke, personal interview)

The issue with my mum is that she ... how do I say it? She ... I grew up really quickly. I basically feel like I've mothered my mum and my mum ... is ... she is not really a mother in my eyes; she is not the mother role. (Simone, individual interview)

Such accounts draw on unresolved issues that had direct implications on how the women seem to struggle to make meaning of their experience; they wonder whether they could ever be a good mother, as they themselves never had one.

Psychoanalytic literature has highlighted how pregnancy can reactivate a woman's ambivalent emotions towards her own mother—an archaic identification with both the powerful, life-giving force of the mother and her counter-image of the vengeful and murderous Medea (Rapahel-Leff). These past experiences are a source of ambivalence and internal conflicts, as they position the pregnant woman and her own needs (to be once more cared for and care-free) against those of the fetus inside (who could be experienced as an internal robber hijacking her body and frustrating her needs and identity). Such conflicts are not easy to tolerate and were unmanageable for some women, who as a result sank into further distress and depression.

"If You Don't Laugh, You Cry": The Either-Or Position and the Need for Complex Representations of Pregnancy

I feel so guilty that after years of being unsuccessful [in getting pregnant], I hate being pregnant so much. This is my fifth pregnancy and second child. Good grief!! And I'm looking forward to having another child ... Kinda! Mostly, I'm terrified. Don't know how I'm going to cope or deal with two busy boys and then guilty that I'm not thrilled and glowing. So complicated!"(Kate, social media)

In this example Kate shares her experiences of guilt, doubt, and regret in an open and vulnerable way. At the same time, however, Kate refuses to settle with a simple story of feeling negatively about this pregnancy, stating that the experience is complicated. In attending to a "both/and" type of expression—as in "I am both scared and looking forwards to motherhood—Kate, as with many of the women I spoke with, refuses to settle with a simple "either/or" story, as in "I am either a good or a bad mother. Instead, the women proposed richer, individualized, and specific descriptions of their own maternal experiences and of their own maternal ambivalence:

> Holding the space for our kiddos to be authentic also means modeling that, right? I am a glass half full kinda girl, but I am also working on being aware of my triggers and "hard feelings," for want of a better word. Hate is too strong for me personally, but I really struggle with self-care. My kids are now 18mo+ so those initial struggles I had with the complete upheaval of my world seem to have faded. The inability to find time for self-care continues though. For now, I'm at peace with my kids being my passion. It's such a short time. I loathe how I am constantly having to learn the same lessons about being calm when they are not. I wish I was a quick learner. I also loathe the pressures women put on ourselves and each other. We each have our own story. (Isabelle, social media)

> I think this is a great topic to get into the mainstream [ambivalence]. I read a great article on it when I was just getting out of a difficult time of transition into parenthood and wish I had read it sooner. It's incredibly complex, personal, and changing the thoughts, emotions, and actions we as mothers go through. It's often linked to our own upbringing, goals, priorities, peers, and support network. Mainstream media tends to only talk seriously about the loving part of being a mother and tries to laugh off the hard stuff. I guess people feel if "you don't laugh, you cry." If you dare to cry you're often labelled as having PND [Postnatal depression] when that's not always the case. (Fiona, social media)

Society inflates maternal guilt, which makes the experience of negative or less than positive emotions unmanageable, thus creating a taboo around maternal ambivalence. Therefore, stories of glow, bliss, and contentment during pregnancy prevail and are regularly reproduced by society and by mothers themselves, but with a price. Stifling and silencing stories that represent the multiplicity and complexity of pregnancy, including the negative ones, could have serious implications on maternal mental health and wellbeing, including depression, anxiety, and further social isolation. Whereas the larger culture continues to keep love and hate in distinct categories, motherhood will inevitably be seen only from the binary position of idealization or denigration, which are both equally abstract and unrelated to the day-to-day experiences of mothering.

We need representations of pregnancy and motherhood that enable the inherent conflicts—such as love and hate, care and irritability, awe and boredom—to be experienced simultaneously and constructively, instead of framing them as a failure. Pluralist narratives that are inclusive and form a plethora of both good and bad stories create space for women to tell their stories in helpful and meaningful ways. Such modes of speaking combine both of Kristeva's semiotic and the symbolic modes of language, and, hence, promote a revolt—an active and empowered maternal claim of being in the world.

Endnote

1. Pseudonyms are used throughout this chapter.

Works Cited

DeVault, M. L. "Talking and Listening from Women's Standpoint: Feminist Strategies for Interviewing and Analysis," *Social Problems*, vol. 37, no. 1, 1990, pp. 96-116.

Klein, M. *The Writings of Melanie Klein: Envy and Gratitude and Other Works*. Hogarth Press and the Institute of Psycho-Analysis. 1975.

Kristeva, Julia. "Motherhood according to Giovanni Bellini." Desire in Language: A Semiotic Approach to Language and Literature, edited by Leon S. Roudiez and translated by Thomas Gora et al., Columbia University Press, 1980, pp. 237-70.

Kristeva, Julia. *Tales of Love*. Translated by Leon S. Roudiez. Columbia University Press, 1987.

McAfee, N. *Julia Kristeva*, Psychology Press, 2004.

Parker, R. *Torn in Two: The Experience of Maternal Ambivalence*. Virago Press, 2005.

Raphael-Leff, J. *Pregnancy: The Inside Story*. Karnac Books, 2001.

Raymond, J. E. "Creating a Safety Net: Women's Experiences of Antenatal Depression and Their Identification of Helpful Community Support and Services during Pregnancy." *Midwifery*, vol. 25, no. 1, 2009, pp. 39-49.

Staneva, A. et al. "The Experience of Psychological Distress, Depression, and Anxiety during Pregnancy: A Meta-Synthesis of Qualitative Research. *Midwifery*, vol. 31, no. 6, 2015, pp. 563-73.

Staneva, A., et al. "The Effects of Maternal Depression, Anxiety, and Perceived Stress during Pregnancy on Preterm Birth: A Systematic Review." *Women and Birth*, vol. 28, no. 3, 2015, pp. 179-93.

Stein, A., et al. "Effects of Perinatal Mental Disorders on the Fetus and Child." *The Lancet* vol. 384, no. 9956, 2014, pp. 1800-19.

Chapter Five

On Ambivalence and Giving Birth: Reflecting on Labour through Beauvoir's Erotic

Sara Cohen Shabot

I reflect here on labour as a project, using Simone de Beauvoir's phenomenological premises. In *The Second Sex*, Beauvoir seems reluctant to consider childbirth as potentially empowering, whether because patriarchal concepts of childbirth have biased her or because she is describing labour under patriarchy.[1] She naturalizes labour:

> Giving birth for cows and mares is far more painful and dangerous than for female mice and rabbits. Woman, the most individualized of females, is also the most fragile, the one who experiences her destiny the most dramatically ... Childbirth itself is painful; it is dangerous. (*TSS* 38, 42; *LDS* 1: 41, 48)

Later, she adds: "*all women* fear the suffering of giving birth, and they are happy that modern methods free them from it" (*TSS* 412; *LDS* 2: 164, my emphasis). In fact, for many women, childbirth presents conflicting potentials—opportunities for both immense suffering and empowerment. Although it can be painful and exhausting, it can also be joyful and creative. Beauvoir's account in *The Second Sex* seems to miss this legitimate variability in women's attitudes towards labour. However, as I will demonstrate here, her accounts of ambiguity and authenticity in describing the erotic can shed light on women's ambivalence towards childbirth. I contend that in Beauvoir's own terms, childbirth can be reframed as an existential project. Like other such projects, it presents a chance to take up one's immanence in a transcendent fashion, but to seize this opportunity, one must approach childbirth in active recognition of the ambivalence it inspires.

What Are Feminist Critiques of Labour Missing?

Although a critical feminist discourse on childbirth has developed in recent decades,[2] the topic remains underexplored. Some women are increasingly dissatisfied with medical authorities' co-optation of the labour experience, reifying women by making childbirth a mechanical, teleological chore where the process is not valued;[3] the feminist response and critique understands labour as a highly significant event in itself that can dramatically affect how birthing women construe themselves as subjects. Research shows that large numbers of women find labour either deeply empowering (even if genuinely ambivalent) or profoundly oppressive, with important repercussions for their future lives (Charles; Goodman, Mackey, and Tavakoli; Gray; Hodnett).

The feminist literature tries to answer questions about the meaning of childbirth for birthing women and why they are so dissatisfied with its overmedicalization. How is labour important in itself (not just as an instrumental process)? Why is medical intervention such a serious threat to women's power and agency (even their perception of themselves as subjects)? Emily Martin and Adrienne Rich explore the disempowerment and alienation from their bodies that many modern (middle-class) women report after a highly medicalized labour. But there is also a feminist counter-critique of this essentialist counter-discourse: could this not be a reactionary message that once again ends in women's submission rather than liberation?[4]

Highly medicalized labour abandons the experiential body, constructing it as unimportant: the productive body, the medium for delivering the product (the healthy baby), is what counts. In this system, women learn to detach themselves from their bodies for their own good, since labour's only purpose is to deliver a healthy baby. The critique of industrialized labour points out that it in fact does not provide better childbirth outcomes. But the main feminist objection is that this medicalization turns women's bodies into delivery machines without agency and prevents women from experiencing birth as natural and/or feminine.

The counter-critique—the critique of idealized labour—condemns the first critique for essentializing women and nature and forcing women to go through a possibly painful, even dangerous, birth simply because it is what a natural woman should experience. This critique argues that the idealization of labour relies on oppressive concepts that though presented as being beyond culture also originated in culture and only subjugate women all over again. This critique points out that the naturalization of birth can be an essentialist trap, driving labouring women to reject the possibilities of liberation and agency offered by medicine and technology.

Both critiques neglect the *Leib*, the lived body: the experiencing body of a woman in labour, with its inherent possibilities for transcendence.[5] The critique of industrialization— arguing that the mechanization of the childbirth process and women's alienation from their own bodies push the fleshly body aside and tear it from the real self—operates primarily through an essentialist and sometimes highly prescriptive conception of how labour ought to be experienced: as natural and sublime, the epitome of an uplifting feminine experience. Ina May Gaskin, one of the most prestigious American theoreticians of midwifery, writes about the "*true capacities of the female body*" (emphasis in the original) during labour and birth: those that are "experienced by real women." She continues, "Even when women in my village experience pain in labor ... they know that it is better to keep their senses alive ... to experience the true wisdom and power that labor and birth have to offer" (xi–xii).

The lived body is utterly absent from Gaskin's scenario, not because it is regarded as a productive, functional (or dysfunctional) machine but because it is essentialized—turned into a feminine stereotype and surrounded by myths of inherent power and instinctive, even animal, knowledge. This body is no more concrete and no more connected to a particular self or authentic subjectivity than the one transformed into an instrument.

The Importance of Feminist Phenomenology in Thinking about Labour

Phenomenology's importance for feminist research—mainly for reflections on embodied subjectivities—is already well recognized.[6] In "Laboring with Beauvoir" I demonstrate how crucial feminist phenomenology is for dealing with the loss of embodied subjectivity in childbirth. Using Beauvoir's concepts of ambiguity, immanence, and transcendence and of the embodied and situated subject, I offer an alternative to the existing feminist critique of labour.[7] A woman's grief over her "dismembered" body after a Caesarean section, her anger at being treated like an instrument, is not usually about the loss of the natural or feminine body. This grief and anger are grounded, instead, in the pain of the body being stripped of its inherent transcendence and active character and the subject being turned into pure immanence. Beauvoir's phenomenological-existentialist perspective helps us to understand how the loss of the body in labour is the loss of an embodied, ambiguous subject as well as an ambivalent, potentially enriching experience; it also shows how recuperating this embodied subjectivity in labour can allow childbirth to be highly empowering.

Beauvoir

Readings emphasizing the phenomenological aspects of Beauvoir's philosophy[8] describe her ambiguous subject as constituted by elements that seem contradictory at first but are necessary aspects of a synthetic real subjectivity. Beauvoir's subject exists through a living body, completely different from the dead and/or mechanical body studied by science. This embodied subjectivity is not pure flesh (i.e., not voided of meaning and not totally available for shaping by historical and social conditions); it is rooted in a species, in the world of materiality and objects, and is imbued with intrinsic meanings and characteristics (sex included) from which it cannot completely escape. This subject, invested a priori with meaning and influenced by social and historical conditions, is also intrinsically free: "A man is at the same time freedom and facticity; he is free ... but free within a situation" (Beauvoir, *Pyrrhus et Cinéas* 279, my translation).

The lived body is, above all, ambiguous, simultaneously immanent and transcendent; it is part of the fleshed world of materiality while constituting a site of freedom from which the future-oriented project of subjectivity can be developed. The body is the subject's situation.[9] In Beauvoir's words, "if the body is not a *thing*, it is a situation: it is our grasp upon the world and the outline of our projects.... It is not the body-object described by the biologist ... but the living body of the subject" (*TSS* 66, 69).[10]This existentialist and phenomenological framework is crucial for resolving the tension between the critiques of idealized and industrialized labour. Childbirth, lived as embodied and painful but nonetheless allowing agency and movement, can be paradigmatically empowering—not in essentialist terms, but phenomenologically and existentially. Childbirth conjoins the immanent with the transcendent to create a moment of clear and forceful authentic subjectivity, the epitome of the perfect understanding of the ambiguous human condition. (This framework also explains why the labouring woman who is objectified, whether by technology or by essentialist ideals, may feel disempowered or even abused.[11]) The experience of childbirth can be perceived by the labouring woman as both inescapable and allowing agency and empowerment. This is ambivalence. And childbirth, then, is not a feminine experience (in the essentialist sense) but a human one—empowering, even potentially ethical, because of the ambivalence it offers.

What I propose is a novel philosophical analysis of the experience of labour and childbirth. Feminist phenomenology's robust theoretical apparatus allows us to develop a new, more profound, and conceptually accurate discourse on how labour affects subjectivity. At the core of the attempt to recuperate the agency and subjectivity so often lost to women during childbirth, there must stand a commitment to recognizing subjects as essentially embodied and provided with agency.

In "Laboring with Beauvoir," I propose Beauvoir's framework as a remedy to the absence of the experiential embodied subject from the discourse around labor, whereas in "Constructing Subjectivity," I examine the nature of labour pain; the results reiterate the ambiguity and intricacy of the question of subjectivity in childbirth and the need to investigate further. Here, I show how Beauvoir's ideas on the erotic, as central to the constitution of authentic subjectivity, illuminate labour and childbirth as well (Cohen Shabot, "Grotesque Phenomenology"). Phenomenology, thus, continues to be a crucial tool in the further meticulous analysis of the various aspects of labour.

Towards an Erotic-Ambivalent Understanding of Labour

Beauvoir's comments on labour itself yield no positive understandings of childbirth, which she could only imagine as experienced under oppression. I look instead to her descriptions of a kind of experience that she did conceive of as authentically lived: the erotic encounter. For Beauvoir, "my body may become a threat to subjectivity only if I experience immanence as objectification" (qtd. in Bergoffen, "Out from Under" 191). Beauvoir's subversive erotic allows embodied subjects gendered by patriarchy to disrupt the powers that construct them as immanent, docile, gendered, and sexed. Thus, a new feminist ethic arises: "In tracking de Beauvoir's muted voice we see her exploring the ways in which these erotic disruptions refigure our understanding of the existential-phenomenological subject and direct us to an ethic of the erotic" (Bergoffen, "From Husserl to de Beauvoir" 57).

Merleau-Ponty and Beauvoir both see eroticism as significant in making ourselves subjects—ambiguously immersed in the world through an erotic-cum-emotional bond—and differentiating ourselves from objects (Heinämaa, "The Body as Instrument," 63-64). Beauvoir's generous and open erotic is the perfect form for recognizing, locating, and embodying ambiguity, of which it fleshes out two kinds: the vague distinctions between subjects and the world and the ambiguity expressed through the intertwining of immanence and transcendence that characterizes all subjects (*TSS*, 402, 499). Through the erotic, we recognize both the otherness within us (our own flesh) and the irreducible freedom (and factual presence) of the other. Beauvoir gives a moving description of the kind of authentic erotic encounter that may take place when oppressive conditions are overcome:

This blossoming supposes that ... woman succeeds in overcoming her passivity and establishing a relationship of reciprocity with her partner.... *Each partner feels pleasure as being his own while at the same time having its source in the other....* In a concrete and sexual form the reciprocal recognition of the self and the other is accomplished in the keenest consciousness of the other and the self.... What is necessary for such harmony [is] a reciprocal generosity of the body and soul.... *The erotic experience is one that most poignantly reveals to human beings their ambiguous condition;*

they experience it as flesh and as spirit, as the other and as subject. (*TSS*, 377-78, my emphasis)

Beauvoir's erotic is granted the power of transcendence in at least two ways. First, it is as a rejoicing, embodied experience:

In order for the idea of liberation to have a concrete meaning, the joy of existence must be asserted in each one, at every instant; *the movement toward freedom assumes its real, flesh and blood figure in the world by thickening into pleasure, into happiness.* If the satisfaction of an old man drinking a glass of wine counts for nothing, then production and wealth are only hollow myths; they have meaning only if they are capable of being retrieved in individual and living joy. (*TEA*, 135, my emphasis)

And second, there is transcendence in the mere power of the erotic to make us recognize and experience our own and the other's ambiguity, a precondition for authentically and ethically being. Beauvoir's description of pregnancy testifies to the connection between experiencing ambiguity and reaching transcendence: "Specific to the pregnant woman is that the body is experienced as immanent at the moment when it transcends itself.... The transcendence of the artisan, of the man of action is inhabited by one subjectivity, but in the becoming mother the opposition between subject and object is abolished" (*TSS*, 512).[12]

Here, Beauvoir describes a gendered transcendence, the specificity of pregnancy, as well as the ambiguity lived between a woman's body and the other inside her, which allows women to transcend differently than does "the man of action." Thus, the erotic encounter—which does not incarcerate us inside our armoured selves but dissolves our boundaries, taking us out to meet the other—may also have an important meaning for the flourishing of an authentic and intercorporeal subjectivity (*TSS*, 410-11).

For many women, childbirth shares the empowering, creative features Beauvoir places at the core of the authentic erotic encounter. Martin's *The Woman in the Body* emphasizes labour's erotic character and the importance, for an empowering experience, of recognizing that eroticism: "Birth is fundamentally a creative act, as is the act of sexual union. The quality and intensity of the energy present and the ultimate surrender during both events are closely related" (Baldwin in Martin,

157-58). When labour is interpreted as sexual or erotic, it is usually to portray it as inherently active and rewarding (159). This association is also used to justify independent birth practices, such as unassisted childbirth:

> When genital sex is chosen as the key metaphor for what birth is, a number of consequences for action follow. Husband and wife will give birth alone, in private, just as they would when engaged in other sexual behavior. To help the process along, just as in other forms of sexuality, lovemaking, fantasizing, hugging, kissing, caressing are the most relevant means. (159)[13]

For Beauvoir, identifying ourselves as free as well as corporeal is the first step towards an ethics that identifies the other, too, as ambiguous, free, and immanent. Here, the erotic encounter is a priceless resource.

Although an ambivalent childbirth—both painfully erotic and empowering—might have been unimaginable to Beauvoir, her philosophy offers resources for developing this vein of thinking. We must oppose both reactionary and romanticizing childbirth discourses; it is not only overmedicalized childbirth but also the midwifery model of childbirth that can disempower women. (Sonya Charles reflects on the feelings of incompetence and shame that many women experience after failing to give birth without medical intervention.)

Feminist theory and politics (including Beauvoir's accounts of labour) have already helped to deromanticize labour and demystify it as the epitome of femininity—an experience that must be lived naturally and painfully for a woman to be feminine or moral. But feminist phenomenological accounts, while deromanticizing labour, must also examine its empowering possibilities and attend to the voices of those who find labour (and other feminine embodied experiences, such as pregnancy and breastfeeding) ambivalent, both strenuous and powerful, and of critical meaning to the construction of authentic subjectivities. Otherwise these experiences will be co-opted by essentialist, romanticizing discourses that consider them necessary to femininity rather than one possibility to be freely chosen in the process of becoming an authentic subject.

Conclusions

This chapter's basic assumption is that feminist discourses on childbirth have lacked a phenomenological perspective. Elsewhere, I demonstrate how phenomenology enriches our understanding of labour and its consequences for women's subjectivities ("Laboring with Beauvoir"; "Making Loud Bodies 'Feminine'"). In future projects, I shall shed new light on further aspects of labour and the embodied subject experiencing them.

The relatively new but abundant feminist research on motherhood and the mothering subject often ignores labour and childbirth in favour of such themes as reproductive technologies (Harwood; Martin; Sawicki), pregnancy (Heinämaa, "An Equivocal Couple"; Young, "Pregnant Embodiment") and the practice of mothering (LaChance Adams; Rich). This is not accidental: labour's shocking importance and lasting effects, combined with its short duration and enormous intensity, makes it difficult to grasp and express. I hope that this chapter has brought us closer to a thorough examination of the potential ambivalence of labour through the lens of feminist phenomenology.

Endnotes

1. Notable exceptions are her mention of women enjoying pregnancy and childbirth (even erotically) and discussion of childbirth's powerful, creative potential in certain contexts (Beauvoir, *The Second Sex* [hereafter TSS] 549, *Le deuxième sexe* [hereafter LDS] 2: 319). Heavily influenced by Marxist theory, Beauvoir proposes that one precondition for developing freedom and transcendence is the absence of major material constraints and oppression (Beauvoir, *The Ethics of Ambiguity* [hereafter EA] 82, 83; *Pour une morale de l'ambiguïté* [hereafter PMA] 104; Arp 122, 123). This implies that we must provide mothers with such conditions. See Beauvoir in Schwarzer, 72–76; Fischer; and Johnson.

2. Canonical texts include Rich; Martin; and, more recently, Brand and Granger; Fox and Worts; Gleisner; Heyes; Johnson; Jones; Katz Rothman, "Laboring Now" and "A Lifetime's Labor"; Lintott; Mullin; Pollock; and Thomson.

3. Fisher, et al.; Lobel and DeLuca. This reaction is grounded, of course, in material and social plenty; while more privileged women

protest this medicalization, poorer populations lack proper medical attention at all, in childbirth and otherwise. See also Johnson.

4. On backlash discourses and the romanticization of labour, see Baker; Charles; Johnson; and Jones.

5. Husserl recognizes the embodied subject not as pure materiality provided with a mind but as a living subject in itself, immediately experienced and expressed by way of its kinesthetic embodied consciousness. Merleau-Ponty and Heidegger, among others, develop this into an ontological concept; see Behnke. Beauvoir and the feminist phenomenologists following her use the concept of the *Leib* (see, for instance, Beauvoir, *TEA*; Young, "Pregnant Embodiment" and "Throwing Like a Girl").

6. Some of the most illuminating items in this vast literature include Alcoff; Al-Saji; Fisher; Heinämaa, *"An Equivocal Couple*; Heinämaa, *Toward a Phenomenology*; Weiss, "The Abject Borders"; Weiss, *Body Images*; Weiss, "The Body as a Narrative Horizon"; Weiss, *Refiguring*; and Young, "Throwing Like a Girl."

7. Lisa Guenther similarly uses Beauvoir's ethics to show how childbirth can be seen as constitutive of an ambiguous ethics mainly because of the unclear limits between mother and baby and the responsibility this confers on mothers. My analysis, however, deliberately avoids the meanings arising from the mother-baby relationship in order to address the less popular philosophical subject of the mother's own experience and subjectivity.

8. Bauer; Cohen Shabot, "How 'Free'?"; Cohen Shabot, "On the Question of Woman"; Cohen Shabot, "Grotesque Phenomenology"; Cohen Shabot and Menschenfreund; Gatens; Gothlin; Heinämaa, "The Body as Instrument"; Heinämaa, *Toward a Phenomenology* 64-79; Heinämaa, "What Is a Woman?"; Horton; Kruks; Mackenzie; and Moi.

9. On Beauvoir's concept of the body as already in itself expressing life and transcendence, see, for example, Bergoffen, *The Philosophy of Simone de Beauvoir* 154-60; Heinämaa, *Toward a Phenomenology*; and Scarth 81-84.

10. On the phenomenological nature of Beauvoir's position, see Bauer; Cohen Shabot, "On the Question of Woman"; Gatens; Heinämaa, "The Body as Instrument"; Heinämaa, *Toward a Phenomenology*;

Heinämaa, "What Is a Woman?"; and Moi.

11. Labour may also objectify women simply because it is unwanted or not reflected on. Here, however, I address only welcome labours.

12. This is the translation as modified by Heinämaa ("An Equivocal Couple"), emphasizing the gendered transcendence granted specifically to pregnant women.

13. On childbirth as erotic and on orgasmic birth, see Gaskin, 150-66.

Works Cited

Alcoff, Linda Martin. "Phenomenology, Post-Structuralism, and Feminist Theory on the Concept of Experience." *Feminist Phenomenology*, edited by Linda Fisher and Lester Embree, Kluwer Academic Publishers, 2000, pp. 39-56.

Al-Saji, Alia. "Bodies and Sensings: On the Uses of Husserlian Phenomenology for Feminist Theory." *Continental Philosophy Review*, vol. 43, no. 1, 2010, pp. 12-37.

Arp, Kristana. *The Bonds of Freedom: Simone de Beauvoir's Existentialist Ethics*. Open Court Publishing Company, 2001.

Baker, Jen. "Natural Childbirth Is for the Birds." *Motherhood–Philosophy for Everyone: The Birth of Wisdom*, edited by Sheila Lintott, Wiley-Blackwell, 2010, pp. 154-66.

Bauer, Nancy. *Simone de Beauvoir, Philosophy, and Feminism*. Columbia University Press, 2001.

Beauvoir, Simone de. *The Ethics of Ambiguity*. Translated by Bernard Frechtman.

Philosophical Library, 1948. Originally published as *Pour une morale de l'ambiguïté*. Gallimard, 1947.

Beauvoir, Simone de. *Pyrrhus et Cinéas*. Gallimard, 1944.

Beauvoir, Simone de. *The Second Sex*. Translated and edited by Howard M. Parshley. Vintage Books, 1989. Originally published as *Le deuxième sexe*, 2 vols. Gallimard, 1949.

Behnke, Elizabeth A. "Edmund Husserl: Phenomenology of Embodiment." *The Internet Encyclopedia of Philosophy*, Aug. 2011, www.iep.utm.edu/husspemb/. Accessed 4 Dec. 2019.

Bergoffen, Debra. "From Husserl to de Beauvoir: Gendering the Perceiving Subject." *Metaphilosophy*, vol. 27, no. 1&2, 1996, pp. 53-63.

Bergoffen, Debra. "Out from Under: Beauvoir's Philosophy of the Erotic." *Feminist Interpretations of Simone de Beauvoir*, edited by Margaret A. Simons, The Pennsylvania State University Press, 1995, pp. 179-92.

Bergoffen, Debra. *The Philosophy of Simone de Beauvoir: Gendered Phenomenologies, Erotic Generosities.* State University of New York Press, 1997.

Brand, Peg, and Paula Granger. "The Aesthetics of Childbirth." *Philosophical Inquiries into Pregnancy, Childbirth and Mothering—Maternal Subjects*, edited by Sheila Lintott and Maureen Sander-Staudt, Routledge, 2012, pp. 215-36.

Charles, Sonya. "Disempowered Women? The Midwifery Model and Medical Intervention." *Coming to Life: Philosophies of Pregnancy, Childbirth and Mothering.* Ed. Sarah LaChance Adams and Caroline R. Lundquist. New York: Fordham University Press, 2013, pp. 215–240.

Cohen Shabot, Sara. "Constructing Subjectivity through Pain: A Beauvoirian Analysis of Pain in Childbirth." *European Journal of Women's Studies*, vol. 26, Nov. 2015, pp. 1-15, doi: 10.1177/ 1350506815617792.

Cohen Shabot, Sara. "How 'Free' Is Beauvoir's Freedom? Unchaining Beauvoir through the Erotic Body." *Feminist Theory*, vol. 17, no. 3. 2016, pp. 269-84, doi: 10.1177/1464700116666254.

Cohen Shabot, Sara. "Laboring with Beauvoir: In Search of the Embodied Subject in Childbirth." *A Companion to Beauvoir*, edited by Nancy Bauer and Laura Hengehold. Blackwell, 2017, pp. 134-45.

Cohen Shabot, Sara. "Making Loud Bodies 'Feminine': A Feminist-Phenomenological Analysis of Obstetric Violence." *Human Studies*, vol. 39, no. 2, 2016, pp. 231-47.

Cohen Shabot, Sara. "On the Question Of Woman: Illuminating de Beauvoir through Kantian Epistemology." *Philosophy Today*, vol. 51, no. 4, 2007, pp. 369-82.

Cohen Shabot, Sara. "Towards a Grotesque Phenomenology of the (Ethical) Erotic." *Women: A Cultural Review*, vol. 24, no. 1, 2013, pp. 1-10.

Cohen Shabot, Sara, and Yaki Menschenfreund. "Is Existential Authenticity Unethical? De Beauvoir on Ethics, Authenticity and Embodiment." *Philosophy Today*, vol. 52, no. 2, 2008, pp. 150-56.

Fischer, Sally. "Becoming Bovine: A Phenomenology of Early Motherhood, and Its Practical, Political Consequences." *Philosophical Inquiries into Pregnancy, Childbirth and Mothering*, edited by Sheila Lintott and Maureen Sander-Staudt, Routledge, 2012, pp. 191-214.

Fisher, Jane, et al. "Adverse Psychological Impact of Operative Obstetric Interventions: A Prospective Longitudinal Study." *Australian and New Zealand Journal of Psychiatry*, vol. 31, 1997, pp. 728-38.

Fisher, Linda. "Phenomenology and Feminism: Perspectives on Their Relation." *Feminist Phenomenology*, edited by Linda Fisher and Lester Embree, Kluwer Academic Publishers, 2000, pp. 17-38.

Fox, Bonnie, and Diana Worts. "Revisiting the Critique of Medicalized Childbirth: A Contribution to the Sociology of Birth." *Gender and Society*, vol. 13, no. 3, 1999, pp. 326-46.

Gaskin, Ina May. *Ina May's Guide to Childbirth*. Bantam Dell, 2003.

Gatens, Moira. "Beauvoir and Biology: A Second Look." *The Cambridge Companion to Simone de Beauvoir*, edited by Claudia Card, Cambridge University Press, 2003, pp. 266-85. Gleisner, Jenny. "The Good and Normal Pain: Midwives' Perception of Pain in Childbirth." *Dimensions of Pain: Humanities and Social Sciences Perspectives*, edited by Lisa Folkmarson Käll, Routledge, 2013, pp. 107-17.

Goodman, Petra, et al. "Factors Related to Childbirth Satisfaction." *Journal of Advanced Nursing*, vol. 46, no. 2, 2004, pp. 212-19.

Gothlin, Eva. "Reading Simone de Beauvoir with Martin Heidegger." *The Cambridge Companion to Simone de Beauvoir*, edited by Claudia Card. Cambridge University Press, 2003, pp. 45-65.

Gray, Jennifer A. "Implications of Perceived Control for Recovery from Childbirth for Unplanned Cesarean, Planned Cesarean and Vaginal Deliveries." *Journal of Prenatal and Perinatal Psychology and Health*, vol. 19, no. 3, 2005, pp. 251-67.

Guenther, Lisa. *The Gift of the Other: Levinas and the Politics of Reproduction*. State University of New York Press, 2006.

Harwood, Karey. *The Infertility Treadmill: Feminist Ethics, Personal Choice, and the Use of Reproductive Technologies*. The University of North Carolina Press, 2007.

Heinämaa, Sara. "The Body as Instrument and as Expression." *The Cambridge Companion to Simone de Beauvoir*, edited by Claudia Card, Cambridge University Press, 2003, pp. 66-86.

Heinämaa, Sara. "'An Equivocal Couple Overwhelmed by Life': A Phenomenological Analysis of Pregnancy." *PhiloSophia*, vol. 4, no. 1, 2014, pp. 31-49.

Heinämaa, Sara. *Toward a Phenomenology of Sexual Difference: Husserl, Merleau-Ponty, Beauvoir.* Rowman & Littlefield Publishers, 2003.

Heinämaa, Sara. "What Is a Woman? Butler and Beauvoir on the Foundations of Sexual Difference." *Hypatia*, vol. 12, 1997, pp. 20-40.

Heyes, Cressida J. "Child, Birth: An Aesthetic." *Dimensions of Pain: Humanities and Social Sciences Perspectives*, edited by Lisa Folkmarson Käll, Routledge, 2013, pp. 132-41.

Hodnett, Ellen D. "Pain and Women's Satisfaction with the Experience of Childbirth: A Systematic Review." *American Journal of Obstetrics & Gynecology*, vol. 186, 2002, pp. S160-72.

Horton, Stephen. "Reading, Resistance and Disempowerment." *Simone de Beauvoir's The Second Sex, New Interdisciplinary Essays*, edited by Ruth Evans, Manchester University Press, 1998, pp. 159-79.

Husserl, Edmund. *Ideas Pertaining to a Pure Phenomenology and to a Phenomenological Philosophy: Second Book, Studies in the Phenomenology of Constitution.* Translated by Richard Rojcewicz and André Schuwer, Kluwer, 1989.

Johnson, Candace. "The Political 'Nature' of Pregnancy and Childbirth." *Coming to Life: Philosophies of Pregnancy, Childbirth and Mothering*, edited by Sarah LaChance Adams and Caroline R. Lundquist, Fordham University Press, 2013, pp. 193-214.

Jones, Jane Clare. "Idealized and Industrialized Labor: Anatomy of a Feminist Controversy." *Hypatia*, vol. 27, no. 1, 2012, pp. 99-119.

Katz Rothman, Barbara. "Laboring Now: Current Cultural Constructions of Pregnancy, Birth and Mothering." *Laboring On. Birth in Transition in the United States*, edited by Wendy Simonds, et al., Routledge, 2007, pp. 29-96.

Katz Rothman, Barbara. "A Lifetime's Labor: Women and Power in the Birthplace." *Laboring On. Birth in Transition in the United States*, edited by Wendy Simonds et al., Routledge, 2007, pp. xi-xxii.

Kruks, Sonia. "Gender and Subjectivity: Simone de Beauvoir and Contemporary Feminism." *Signs*, vol. 18, 1992, pp. 89-110.

LaChance Adams, Sarah. *Mad Mothers, Bad Mothers, & What a "Good" Mother Would Do. The Ethics of Ambivalence.* Columbia University Press, 2014.

Lintott, Sheila. "The Sublimity of Gestating and Giving Birth: Toward a Feminist Conception of the Sublime." *Philosophical Inquiries into Pregnancy, Childbirth and Mothering—Maternal Subjects*, edited by Sheila Lintott and Maureen Sander-Staudt, Routledge, 2012, pp. 237-50.

Lobel, Marci, and Robyn Stein DeLuca. "Psychosocial Sequelae of Cesarean Delivery: Review and Analysis of Their Causes and Implications." *Social Science & Medicine*, vol. 64, no. 11, 2007, pp. 2272-84.

Mackenzie, Catriona. "A Certain Lack of Symmetry: Beauvoir on Autonomous Agency and Women's Embodiment." *Simone de Beauvoir's The Second Sex, New Interdisciplinary Essays*, edited by Ruth Evans, Manchester University Press, 1998, pp. 122-58.

Martin, Emily. *The Woman in the Body: A Cultural Analysis of Reproduction.* Beacon Press, 1987.

Moi, Toril. *What Is a Woman?* Oxford University Press, 1999.

Mullin, Amy. *Reconceiving Pregnancy and Childcare: Ethics, Experience and Reproductive Labor.* Cambridge University Press, 2005.

Pollock, Della. *Telling Bodies Performing Birth.* Columbia University Press, 1999.

Rich, Adrienne. *Of Woman Born: Motherhood as Experience and Institution.* Norton, 1986.

Sawicki, Jana. "Disciplining Mothers: Feminism and the New Reproductive Technologies." *Feminist Theory and the Body: A Reader*, edited by Janet Price and Margrit Shildrick. Routledge: 1991, pp. 190-202.

Scarth, Fredrika. *The Other Within: Ethics, Politics, and the Body in Simone de Beauvoir.* Rowman and Littlefield, 2004.

Schwarzer, Alice. *After the Second Sex: Conversations with Simone de Beauvoir.* New York: Pantheon Books, 1984.

Thomson, Gill. "'Abandonment of Being' in Childbirth." *Qualitative Research in Midwifery and Childbirth: Phenomenological Approaches*, edited by Gill Thomson et al., Routledge, 2011, pp. 133-52.

Weiss, Gail. "The Abject Borders of the Body Image." *Perspectives on Embodiment. The Intersections of Nature and Culture*, edited by Gail Weiss and Honi Fern Haber, Routledge, 1999, pp. 41-60.

Weiss, Gail. *Body Images: Embodiment as Intercorporeality.* Routledge, 1999.

Weiss, Gail. "The Body as a Narrative Horizon." *Thinking the Limits of the Body*, edited by Jeffrey Jerome Cohen and Gail Weiss, State University of New York Press, 2003, pp. 25-38.

Weiss, Gail. *Refiguring the Ordinary.* Indiana University Press, 2008.

Young, Iris Marion. "Pregnant Embodiment: Subjectivity and Alienation." *Journal of Medicine and Philosophy*, vol. 9, no. 1, 1984, pp. 45-62.

Young, Iris Marion. "Throwing Like a Girl: A Phenomenology of Feminine Body Comportment, Motility and Spatiality." *Human Studies*, vol. 3, 1980, pp. 137-56.

Chapter Six

A Healthy Baby Is Not All That Matters: Exploring My Ambivalence after a Caesarian Section

Bertha Alvarez Manninen

"That night, in a dream, the first girl emerges from a slit in my stomach.
The scar heals into a smile."
—Warsan Shire

Very little of how conception and pregnancy are supposed to work happened for me. Both my daughters were planned conceptions that took, on average, a year to attain. For my second daughter, I was only able to conceive after two rounds of Clomid failed and sent me into a deep depressive state and I was prescribed Femara instead (which is traditionally used for breast cancer treatment). Both of my children were big babies—my firstborn was nine pounds, eleven ounces, my second was two ounces heavier. Consequently, my doctor suggested that I undergo a scheduled Caesarian section (a "C-section") with both of them; although he was open to my having a VBAC (vaginal birth after a Caesarian) for my second daughter, he withdrew his consent after she measured over nine pounds towards the end of my pregnancy. Neither of the C-sections was a pleasant experience, but my first was significantly worse than my second. Whatever medication I was given the first time resulted in my losing consciousness immediately after my daughter was born, followed by hours of throwing up and being unable to hold or bond with her until the next day. (Things were slightly different for my second daughter— more on that later). Needless to say, then, that my birthing experiences did not approximate the idealized version so often portrayed in the media and popular culture. Instead of in nice, warm, and comforting room and on a soft bed, my babies came into the world in a cold and sterile operating room. Instead of my labouring to release them into the world, seeing them gradually emerge and embracing them as soon as they were outside, I was numbed and cut open. My babies were taken out of my body through the labour of others, and I was only able to briefly glimpse at them over a paper curtain.

When I tell people how badly I feel that I missed labouring and birthing my babies, they often look at me like I am insane, since I should feel grateful that I circumvented the pain of childbirth altogether. But I did want to experience that pain; I wanted to work to bring my children into the world. Everyone's well-meaning attempts to comfort me in the aftermath concentrated on how healthy and beautiful both my daughters were, and they repeated that in the end, that was all that mattered. As a new mother, holding a healthy baby (who might have not been healthy had she gotten lodged in the birth canal), how are you supposed to argue with that? But I will indeed argue against that sentiment in this chapter, for while I agree that what primarily matters is that my children and I made it through pregnancy and childbirth alive and well, that is not all that matters. The loss I have felt over what I perceive was an absence of me giving birth continues to haunt me.

The purpose of this chapter is three fold. First, I will explain the subjective feelings of loss I have experienced because of my failure to labour and give birth in the traditional way (i.e., a vaginal birth) by appealing to Karl Marx's theory of alienated labour. Although Marx himself does not apply the concept of alienation to reproductive labour, his description of the worker estranged from the products of his labour due to the intrinsically oppressive nature of the capitalist economic system captures many aspects of the phenomenology of my C-sections. I have also found that Marx's description of the role technology plays in alienating the worker from his labour is relevant. Although I am incredibly grateful that the technology existed and helped ensure my children were born safely, it is also that very technology that substituted for me, my body, and what should have been my labour in bringing them into the world.

Second, although I will defend my mourning using a Marxian lens, I will also subject my reactions to critical scrutiny. There are many women who experience C-sections in joyful and rewarding ways. I see nothing wrong with this. I do not think the procedure is intrinsically alienating. However, somewhere deep within I have the preconception that giving birth the traditional way is also the right way; experiencing a vaginal birth is part of the essence of pregnancy, birth, and motherhood and by failing to have this experience, I am somehow less of a mother. This is not a belief I defend; rationally, I know that this is an absurd conclusion. Yet that feeling persists—not just for me but for many women who have had similar birthing experiences. So I believe it is imperative to ask where such a belief comes from and what questionable social mores it betrays.

Finally, I will turn a critical eye towards how we tend to comfort women who do not have the birthing experience that they idealize and desire. Although it is true that the welfare of mother and child are paramount in the birthing process, when we tell a woman that this is all that matters, we are dismissing the value that she gives to her embodiment as a pregnant woman; we are telling her that her views about the fate of her body and herself in this regard do not matter to us. This is an attitude about pregnancy that has been concerning feminists for some time when discussing reproductive ethics in many of its incarnations. Woman and fetus are often described in relation to each other in a way that does violence to the sui generis intimacy that is an essential component to pregnancy. Some prolife literature, for example, paints women and fetuses as essentially adversaries and of the womb as a prison rather than a sanctuary.[1] Fetal surgery, itself a technology that has incredible beneficial effects for both children and their families, has also contributed to the dehumanization of pregnant women. Regarding fetuses and women as wholly distinct subjects ignores the unparalleled enmeshment and intimacy that is intrinsic to pregnancy. This contributes to the dismissive attitude that we have towards women when their birthing experiences end up not according with their beliefs, values, and desires.

Marx and the Alienation of Labour

Karl Marx's theory of alienation of labour begins with a fundamental assumption about human nature; human beings' *Gattungswesen* (their species-essence) is intimately connected to their work and labour. It is through their labour that humans can express their creativity and take control over nature and their surroundings. Human labour is substantially different than the labour produced by animals because the latter only produces the bare minimum it needs for survival, whereas humans create even that which they do not need. Human production is indicative of our nature as free and conscious beings. In his *Economic and Philosophical Manuscripts of 1844*, Marx writes the following:

> The practical creation of an objective world, the fashioning of inorganic nature, is proof that man is a conscious species-being, i.e. a being which treats the species as its own essential being or itself as a species being. It is true that animals also produce. They build nests and dwellings, like the bee, the beaver, the ant, etc. But they produce only their own immediate needs or those of their young; they produce one-sidedly, while man produces universally; they produce only when immediate physical need compels them to do so, while man produces even when he is free from physical need and truly produces in freedom from such need.... Man also produces in accordance with the laws of beauty. (328-29)

Marx notes that humans are essentially social animals and must inevitably build relationships with each other in order to thrive in society. One vital way human beings' relationships are built is through the creation and exchange of the products of their individual labour, as work reflects their individuality and personality. In the *Excerpts from James Mill's Elements of Political Economy*, Marx explains it thusly:

> Let us suppose that we had produced as human beings. In that event each of us would have doubly affirmed himself and his neighbor in his production. (1) In my production I would have objectified my specific character of my individuality and for that reason I would both have enjoyed the expression of my own individual life during my activity and also, in contemplating the object, I would experience an individual pleasure, I would

experience my personality as an objective sensuously perceptible power beyond all shadow of doubt. (2) In your use of enjoyment of my product I would have the immediate satisfaction and knowledge that in my labour I had gratified a human need ... in the individual expression of my own life I would have brought about the immediate expression of your life. (277)

In a capitalist system, where the means of production and therefore the labour of the workers is not owned by them (but is owned, rather, by the capitalist), the workers become alienated from their labour, which is best understood as a "loss of control, specifically the loss of control over labour" (Cox). In precapitalist society, workers labour for themselves. They own the products of their labour and choose when to work, the conditions in which they work, and how long they work. They have final say over the disposition of the product they create (they can keep it, sell it, or barter with it—whatever they wish). In a capitalist society, none of this is the case. Workers labour for another who owns the means of production and the product they create. Workers, therefore, become estranged from their labour.

Marx describes four ways in which humans experience estrangement, or alienation, from their labour under a capitalist system. First, the worker is alienated from the objects they produce. The objects they produce as a result of their labour should be a meaningful or creative expression of their individuality. In a capitalist system, where workers fail to own the means of production and anything that they create, and have little control over the conditions in which they work, the products they make have little significance for them:

The worker is related to the product of his labour as to an alien object. For it is clear that, according to this premise, the more the worker exerts himself in his work, the more powerful the alien, objective world becomes which he brings into being over against himself, the poorer he and his inner world become, and the less they belong to him. (Marx, "Economic and Philosophical Manuscripts" 324)

In this kind of alienation, as Lanny Ace Thompson explains it, "the product the worker claims is not his, but is appropriated by the capitalist" (25).

Second, the worker is alienated from the process of labour itself, for the process, again, fails to expresses the worker's personality or essence:

> Labour is external to the worker, i.e. does not belong to his essential being; that he therefore does not confirm himself in his work, but denies himself, feels miserable and not happy, does not develop free mental and physical energy, but mortifies his flesh and ruins his mind. Hence the worker feels himself only when he is not working; when he is working he does not feel himself. (Marx, "Economic and Philosophical Manuscripts" 326)

Consider the differences between writers who are so engrossed in their work that they do not mind spending long hours on their craft versus workers who regard their job as simply a means for survival—one that fails to reflect anything about their personality or character (say at a factory). For the writer, the final product (a book, or a poem, or a piece of academic literature) is significant to them in a way that a created product is not for the factory worker. Moreover, the process of creating that final product is inherently meaningful to the writer in a way that the working day simply is not for the factory worker. Writers are not estranged from their product or their labour, whereas factory workers are. When humans fail to see themselves in the objects they create, when they fail to feel at home in their work, they succumb, according to Marx, to their baser, more animalistic side, as they are denied the creative process essential to their human nature: "the result is that man (the worker) feels that he is acting freely only in his animal functions— eating, drinking and procreating ... while in his human functions he is nothing more than an animal" (Marx, "Economic and Philosophical Manuscripts" 327).

Third, the worker is alienated from themselves qua worker and therefore qua their species-essence. Labour is no longer regarded as an activity with intrinsic worth and individual expression but rather purely as an instrumental method for continual survival. In this sense, labour begins to resemble the basic labour of animals (who work only as a means towards survival) rather than creative labour:

> Estranged labour therefore turns man's species being—both nature and his intellectual species powers—into a being alien to

him and a means of his individual existence. It estranges man from his own body, from nature as it exists outside him, from his spiritual essence, his human essence. (Marx, "Economic and Philosophical Manuscripts" 329)

Finally, because humans relate to one another other through mutual labour, capitalism also alienates them from themselves:

An immediate consequence of man's estrangement from the product of his labour, his life activity, his species-being, is the estrangement of man from man. When man confronts himself, he also confronts other men. What is true of man's relationship to his labour, to the product of his labour and to himself, is also true of his relationship to other men, and to the labour and the object of the labour of other men. In general, the proposition that man is estranged from his species-being means that each man is estranged from the others and that all are estranged from man's essence. (Marx, "Economic and Philosophical Manuscripts" 330)

Because the worker has become nothing more than another cog in the great machine of capitalism, because their work is reduced to mindless activity rather than a creative or intellectually challenging endeavor, humans begin to see themselves, and others, in this impersonal and dehumanizing manner. Cox explains it in the following way:

Our lives are touched by thousands of people every day, people whose labour has made our clothes, food, home, etc. But we only know them through the objects we buy and consume.... We are related to each other not as individuals but as representatives of different relations of production, the personification of capital, or land or labour.

In one of his most substantial writings, *Capital*, Marx explains how the introduction of machines and technology in the work environment only served to exacerbate the workers' estrangement from their labour. In precapitalist society, tools were utilized by humans in their work as an extension of their bodies; the paint brush, for example, is an extension of the painter's hand and helps realize her creative powers. After the Industrial Revolution, however, machines were introduced into the capitalist system, and those tools subsumed whatever creative power the worker had remaining. Instead of creating a whole product themselves, the worker now only created a portion of a product or did nothing more than control the machine itself. Far from reducing the pressures on the worker, the introduction of machinery only served to lengthen the working day and increase the demands on the worker to produce even more capital. It also paved the way for the exploitation of child and female labour, since machines could be easily run by individuals with (as Marx perceived it) less muscular power.

Producing objects via machinery adds yet another layer of separation between worker and product: "labour becomes automatic, things moving and working independent of the workman (Marx, *Capital* 440). Workers are reduced to little more than the "conscious linkages" of the machine (Marx, *Grundrisse* 692). Because machinery can create many more products in a fraction of the time it used to take when humans did all of the work, the value of individual labour power is diminished. Thus, machinery has served to further rob labour of any creative or intellectual challenge, which turns working into a mindless chore rather than a creative representation of the worker's *Gattungswesen*:

> In manufacture the workman are parts of a living mechanism. In the factory we have a lifeless mechanism independent of the workman, who becomes its mere living appendage. "The miserable routine of endless drudgery and toil in which the same mechanical process is gone through over and over again, is like the labour of Sisyphus." (Marx, *Capital* 462).

It is important to note that technology need not be intrinsically oppressive. It is only so under a capitalist system in which the worker owns neither the means of production nor the fruits of their (now watered down) labour. In a fully idealized communistic society, technology can be used to create material abundance, which can then be freely dispersed to meet the needs of all citizens. In a society where the means of production are owned collectively by the workers, technology can be used to do the "grunt" work, so to speak, resulting in a reduced need for physically taxing labour and opening up time for more leisurely and intellectually stimulating activity (Marx, *Grundisse* 711-12).

Although Marx's explanation of estranged labour does give us a window into the phenomenology of the oppressed working class, it is not only an explanation of a subjective mental state. For Marx, estranged labour is an objective part of a capitalist system. Even if a worker does not feel oppressed or alienated, this does not mitigate the fact that they are, indeed, oppressed and alienated. Nevertheless, it is true that Marx managed to successfully capture the drudgery and boredom of labour that so many working-class people report feeling. The endless social media memes that celebrate the weekends and lament the start of the work week is a modern-day illustration that Marx gets it right. In general, so many of us are "at home when [we are] not working, and not at home when [we are] working" (Marx, "Economic and Philosophical Manuscripts" 326).

Alienation, Reproductive Labour, and Caesarian Sections

Despite being concerned about the exploitation of female labour in a postindustrial capitalist society, Marx does not extend his analysis of alienation into the realm of reproductive labour. As Donna Dickenson puts it, for Marx, "the oppression of married women is not, strictly speaking, a form of alienation, which is characteristic only of relations under capitalism; domestic work is instead a non-capitalist anomaly" (207). When it comes to reproductive labour, Marx holds that women's work in this regard is "natural, not social ... alienation cannot apply to women's reproductive labour, because women's reproductive labour lies outside the realm of productive work" (208). Dickenson repudiates Marx's perspective here, arguing that it "radically undervalues labour in childbirth, or labour in labour" (208). Nevertheless, she further notes that many feminists have sought to extend Marx's theory of alienation into the realm of marriage and reproduction, and Dickenson herself expands it into the realm of bioethics, where women can indeed sell their labour as surrogate mothers and ova providers.

With this all this in mind, I would now like to analyze the phenomenology of my C-section experiences through the lens of Marx's theory of estranged labour. To varying degrees, three of Marx's four kinds of alienation (alienation of the worker from his product, his labour, and his species-essence) apply to how I was affected by my birth experiences.

Marx argues that what makes labour such an integral part of our species-essence is that we, as humans, create in ways that animals do not. Whereas animals work to satisfy their most basic needs, we work beyond this. We create not just what we need to survive but what intellectually and creatively fulfills us as well. Pregnancy and childbirth, I submit, can be subject to a similar analysis. Whereas many animals reproduce and care for their young as a matter of pure instinct, most (with the exception, perhaps, of higher-ordered mammals) do not attach the psycho-social significance human women do to gestation, childbirth, and mothering. (The chapters in this very anthology illustrate the depth with which women regard their relationships with their children.) Margret Olivia Little emphasizes the deep physical, mental, and emotional intimacy inherent in the pregnant woman-fetal relationship, and argues that because pregnancy can affect a woman's body and mind in such drastically significant ways, it is a state of bodily enmeshment that she must always assume voluntarily (301-304). In this way, it is possible to understand how reproductive labour qua pregnancy and childbirth can be part of a mother's species-essence for the same reason Marx argues labour is part of humanity's species-essence: women attach significance to pregnant embodiment in ways most other animals do not. For women, pregnancy is not just a physical state; it is also, as Julie Piering aptly puts it, "an embodied and lived phenomena" (180).

While pregnant, a woman has privileged access to her child, and her body is intertwined in a way that results in an existential paradox—they are simultaneously distinct and identical beings. Childbirth represents the cessation of this most intimate and unique relationship. Iris Marion Young describes the birthing experience as follows:

> The birthing process entails the most extreme suspension of the bodily distinction between inner and outer. As the months and week progress, increasingly I feel my insides, strained and pressed, and increasingly feel the movement of a body inside of me. Through pain and blood and water this inside thing emerges between my legs, for a short while both inside and outside of me. Later I look with wonder at my mushy middle, and at my child, amazed that this yowling, flailing thing, so completely different from me, was there inside, a part of me. (49)

For me, labouring to give birth was important because it involved me working to release my child into the world. The reason I wanted to experience childbirth is not because I take pleasure in what many women describe as the worst pain they have ever experienced but because of the labour that this pain represents. Sheila Lintott poetically describes the significance many women attribute to the pain of labour and birth:

> The pain of labour and birth can be excruciating and both, involving the beginning of life, are closely associated with the other side of life, with death. Yet, in spite of, or perhaps because of, the complex associations with pain and death, there is room for distinct pleasure, reflection, and learning in childbirth. In many cases, labour and birth are time consuming and rhythmic, affording a birthing woman the opportunity, not always a welcome one, to reflect on the experience during it. The temporal extension of labour and birth may actually invite intellectual reflection on the nature and extent of the pain.... After all, the pain of giving birth is not simply something to endure because one has to; the situation is something much more than this. (244)

Lintott notes that for some women, the pain of childbirth not only can cause great terror but can also allow for the contemplation of something sublime.[2] This makes sense to me. It is the process through which the person a woman has created—one who was simultaneously a wholly other life yet fully "embodied within a woman's person" (242)—is now permanently physically severed from her. During the birth process, the child leaves the body through the birth canal, and her mother pushes and works through her pain to bring her into the world, dissolving their unique connection in a way that will never exist again. In childbirth, a woman pours herself into her child's introduction to the world. The baby comes into the world because of her work, her will, her effort, and her pain. In pregnancy, a woman's body and mind work together to create the infant; in childbirth, a woman works to present the infant into the world.

My children are my creation; they are my most treasured Marxian product. There is nothing that I can create that is as significant to me as they are, and their existence will forever be marked by my creative powers. But, in my eyes, my C-sections robbed me of the opportunity to work to bring them into the world and to experience the unique sublimity of childbirth. The last moments of this wonderful embodied journey were taken from me, and technology came and did the work for me instead. My children were taken from within me, not brought into the world by me. In this way, I was estranged from my labour in that I experienced none of it.

To be estranged from one's species-essence is to "no longer produce in a way characteristic of the human species" (Thompson 27). Because I consider the experience of labour and childbirth integral to my species-essence as a mother, I feel alienated from that essence and, therefore, alienated from (what I take to be) an essential aspect of motherhood because of my C-sections. Moreover, being deprived of any experience having to do with childbirth (both of my C-sections were scheduled and I had not yet experienced any contractions), I was not just alienated from my labour qua childbirth—I had no labour at all to speak of. According to Marx, a worker is estranged from his labour when it is external to him, when it "does not belong to his essential being; that he therefore does not confirm himself in his work, but denies himself" ("Economic and Philosophical Manuscripts" 326). By not working to bring my children into the world and by my labour being eradicated altogether, the birthing process became utterly separable and external to me, and, therefore, my children's entrance in the world was in no way confirmed by me or my creative powers.

Sonya Charles emphasizes that the kind of birth experience a woman desires for herself can form an integral part of her personal narrative and personal identity qua pregnant body and motherhood. When a woman has a birth experience that was not the one she invested, it can do damage to that narrative and her personal identity. As an example, Charles discusses a woman who "identifies with natural birth stories" and, therefore. chooses to have her child via midwifery rather than in a hospital setting. What happens in cases where such a woman is forced by circumstances to have a hospital birth instead?

If the midwifery script is both a significant component of your personal identity and your interpretative framework for making sense of your experience of labour, then what happens when you are unable to enact that script? You are left with insufficient interpretative tools (your script no longer fits) and you are an outside to your chosen community.... Your story is aberrant, but you also do not fit with the obstetrical model of adherents because your persona is still committed to the midwifery model....

Women who identify with the midwifery model, but need medical intervention, do not have tools to make sense of their experience. (Charles 219)

The same kind of phenomena may happen to women invested in a narrative involving a vaginal birth but who had a C-section instead. In both these cases, the emphasis on the health of the baby abandons the women, who are left mourning a radical, often unwanted, change in their self-perceived identities as pregnant bodies and mothers. It leaves them with little support and no conceptual tools to makes sense of their loss.

Was I also estranged from my product—the baby herself? I am not sure. With my first daughter, I did, initially, regard her with less emotion than I was anticipating. I had tried for so long to become pregnant and had relished every single moment of my pregnancy. I was eager to hold her and meet her from the moment my pregnancy test was positive. I do not remember her birth; the drugs rendered me unconscious, and I spent hours later violently throwing up and being unable to hold her. I was also unable to immediately breastfeed, and after receiving bottles for two days, she never wanted to nurse directly from my breast. (I spent fourteen months pumping milk to ensure she received breastmilk, but she never nursed directly from my body—yet another way I was alienated from what my body was supposed to do for her.) I do feel, therefore, that my initial bonding time with her was severely compromised because of my post-Caesarian experience and recovery and that this might have influenced my initial feelings of detachment from a baby I had spent years desiring.

I also experience feelings of ambivalence about the medical and technological advancements that made my C-sections possible. I believed my physician when he told me that my daughters stood a high chance of becoming lodged in the birth canal if I attempted to give birth to them vaginally. I am grateful for the skilled physicians and the medical facilities that ensured that my babies and I survived childbirth. Yet it is also that technology which did the work for me, the work I wanted to do myself. You do not need a huge industrialized machine in a factory in order to rob the worker of the experience of labouring—sometimes all you need are scalpels, anesthesia, and an operating room. Medical technology saved my children, but it also allowed external hands to do for them what I should have been able, and wanted, to do myself.

My feelings of estrangement from my body, my labour, and my children after my C-sections are not uncommon. Consider these testimonials from other women who had unwanted C-sections:

> I feel I have missed something by having my first child by emergency C-section in 2006. But I would have died if I hadn't had it done. Even if I was awake during the surgery, I did not feel that joy you are supposed to feel when you give birth to your own baby. This was one of the causes that triggered my postnatal depression. ("Birth Writes")

> I suffered from severe post-partum post-traumatic stress disorder. Which is not often diagnosed! The trauma of my emergency c-section and the loss of my desire and dream to have a vaginal birth was too much. I felt like a failure even though I had this beautiful healthy baby. I felt nothing like a woman. I felt as if my body failed to do the one thing it was made to do. (Lynne)

> I was awake during my caesarean, but I really didn't feel like I "was there." The doctor brought my baby to me, but I really didn't have any connection to this baby. It's been twelve weeks, but it's still difficult to associate him with the caesarean. I had no euphoria, didn't feel much joy. For many weeks after I kept dreaming that I was on my way to the hospital to give birth to him. (Jukelevics)

Although they do not use Marxian language, all of these women express some feelings of ambivalence and alienation. They felt betrayed by their bodies and sensed that failing to experience the joys of giving birth compromised their essence as women and mothers. They felt alienated from their babies after they were born yet still felt grateful that their babies were alive and healthy. Now, to be sure, there are many women who have had C-sections and do not report an estranged phenomenology. I do not regard their positive experiences as any less legitimate than my negative ones; I do not regard C-sections as intrinsically alienating. This is where my analysis parts ways with Marx, since he does regard estranged labour as intrinsic to the capitalist system. My estrangement is largely a product of my foundational assumption that my species-essence as a woman and mother is tied into my ability to give birth in the traditional way, but I recognize that this assumption needs to be called into question.

In popular culture, pregnancy and childbirth are almost always portrayed the same way: a woman becomes pregnant rather easily (sometimes unintentionally, but infertility is not a topic often addressed), experiences morning sickness as well as cravings, and relies on her partner (almost always a man) to satisfy her desires and needs. Her water breaks unexpectedly, and she is rushed to the hospital, where she pushes for a while (often unaided by medicine), and then a baby slides right out with little complication. She is embraced by her delighted partner, and then a perfectly healthy baby is placed immediately on her chest as she stares at it with rapt love and awe. This is how it is supposed to go. A medicine-free vaginal birth is a badge of honor, and that anything that deviates from this is abnormal and less than the ideal. This sets up not only women who experience C-sections for disappointment and estrangement but also women who opt to take pain killers during birth, and even mothers who do not gestate or birth their babies at all.

I admit to having been taken in by this picturesque story about how my body is supposed to function, about how I should endure the pain of childbirth as a sign of my femininity and courage, and about how giving birth is a magical wondrous experience that ushers in the equally magical and wondrous experience of motherhood. I have been a mother long enough now to know that parenting is not always wonderful and transcendental. Yet I still mourn my inability to give birth. I do not know whether I should regard such mourning as simply a by-product of being successfully manipulated by the social mores that pressure women and their bodies to always live up to unrealistic expectations and ideals or that there really is something to the labour involved in birthing a child in the traditional way that is significant for the reasons Marx contends— it is important for the worker to remain intimately connected to his labour. Like so many things in life, I suspect the answer lies somewhere in between.

De-estranging Nontraditional Methods of Childbirth

In this final section, I would like to propose some to support women whose birth experiences deviate from their own desires and ideals (even while at the same time keeping a critical eye on the questionable social pressures that may influence those ideals). First, we should not try to comfort a grieving woman by telling her that all that matters is a healthy baby. Of course, mothers are happy that their children are in the world alive and well. But when we regard the health of the infant as the only thing that matters, we are cavalierly dismissing the legitimacy of a woman's embodied pregnancy experience. Her pregnant phenomenology matters to her, and it should therefore matter to us as well.

In general, once the baby is born, a women's pregnancy, childbirth, and postpartum experiences are often pushed to the backburner and become secondary to the welfare of the child. Jennifer Benson and Allison Wolf explore how lay literature about pregnancy and childbirth often pays little attention to a woman's postpartum needs, especially her physical healing, and focus instead on the needs of the infant and even her partner. As an example, they note that while reading through various popular books about pregnancy and childbirth, only 3.6 per cent of the content of these books focus on "the mother's recovery from birth." One book "dedicated only 5 of 613 pages to postpartum care" (Benson and Wolf 39). And, often, even these sections focus more on the mother's care vis-à-vis successfully caring for the new baby or for her partner (e.g., reintroducing sexual intercourse while healing). Throughout their analysis, Benson and Wolf repeatedly note that once the infant is born, the postpartum woman all but disappear from public consciousness. The pregnant woman's needs matter "only until the baby is born, at which point the focus is firmly shifted to the infant and the mother is as best of secondary importance.... The postpartum woman herself is erased as someone whose needs and interests exist apart from her baby and her partner" (34, 42).

If a woman is suffering from a loss because her pregnancy, birth experience, or postpartum experiences are not what she originally desired or intended, solely focusing on the health of the baby as a way to help allay her disappointment will only further contribute to this erasure. This also happens to many women who wanted to breastfeed and are unable to— their disappointment at missing out on the nursing experience is typically met by affirmations that as long as the baby is fed, that is all that matters. The focus on the baby's health and welfare may be well intended, but it simultaneously serves to "deemphasize the postpartum experience" (Benson and Wolf 39), and, condescendingly, it treats the woman as someone who should be focusing primarily on the health of her child rather than legitimately mourning the loss of the experiences she desired. Julie Piering highlights the many ways pregnant women are judged when they engage in behaviours that are perceived to be harmful to the fetus (e.g., a woman who indulges in a single glass of alcohol while being visibly pregnant). Strangers may feel it acceptable to comment on that behavior in the interests of protecting fetal life and health; however, "mean-spirited finger wagging and demeaning disapproval by poorly behaved strangers may have the best interests of the child in mind, but it is hard to imagine that it achieves its goal" (Piering 184). The same applies to the issue at hand. Reminding women that they should focus only on the health of their baby and not on the loss of their invested birthing experience may mean well, but not only does it fail to assuage their sorrow, it also tacitly criticizes them for mourning it at all. In failing to legitimize their grief, such actions rob them of the social recognition needed in order to help their healing process (Charles 218).

Feminists have, for a long time, criticized the medicalized birth experience for being concerned only with the welfare of the fetus or infant and dismissing the woman as a pregnant subject.[3] For example, Young writes the following:

> The pregnant subject's encounter with obstetrical medicine in the U.S. often alienated her from her pregnant and birthing experience.... A subject's experience or action is alienated when it is defined or controlled by a subject who does not share one's assumptions or goals.... A woman's experience in pregnancy and birthing is often alienated because her condition tends to be defined as a disorder, because medical instruments objectify internal process in such a way that they devalue a woman's experience of those processes, and because the social relations and instrumentation of the medical setting reduce her control over her experience from her. (55)

One need only look towards cases in which women have been

compelled into having a C-section because it was believed to be best for the baby. In 2014, a Florida hospital threatened to report Jennifer Goodall to child welfare authorities for her decision to try to labour first before agreeing to a C-section. That same year Rinat Dray sued the Staten Island University Hospital and Dr. James Ducey, who blatantly overrode her wishes and forced her to undergo a C-section. One of the most infamous cases of a forced C-section occurred in 1987, involving twenty-seven-year-old Angela Carder. Carder was suffering from an aggressive form of cancer and had decided to undergo treatment despite being twenty-six weeks pregnant. Physicians at George Washington University Hospital sought to deliver the fetus via C-section against her and her family's consent while refusing to administer any treatment to Carder while she was still pregnant. Both she and the baby died shortly after the procedure was performed.

Susan Bordo notes that the rising tendency to regard the fetus as an entity independent from the mother effectively serves to erase the pregnant woman from moral consideration: "increased empathy for the fetus has often gone hand-in-hand with decreased respect for the autonomy of the mother" (86). In her book about advancements in fetal surgery, Monica Casper notes a similar phenomenon. Viewing fetuses as patients independent of the women who carry them correlates with the increased dehumanization of those same women by "transforming them into environments or containers for the unborn patient" (89). Casper compares two sketches meant to illustrate the position in which a female is supposed to be placed while undergoing fetal surgery: one sketch illustrates a human female, whereas the other features a nonhuman primate. What is telling in these sketches is that both females, human and nonhuman, are drawn in a similar manner with similar instruments attached to their bodies. The images portray "women and monkeys ... as interchangeable work objects" (97). Casper also quotes a fetal surgeon who admits his lack of concern for the pregnant woman: "We tend to view the fetus as independent. We're not looking at the mother; we see her as a carrier for the fetus" (144).

The point here is not to minimize the concern for a fetus's or an infant's welfare but to draw attention to the fact that too often in pregnancy and childbirth "pregnant women are not subjects at all... while fetuses are super-subjects. It is as though the subjectivity of the pregnant body were siphoned from it and emptied into fetal life" (Bordo

88). Being told that having a healthy baby is all that matters when mourning the loss of my desired birthing experience did not help me feel better. Rather, it was condensing, and it tacitly questioned my priorities as a mother. (I do not need to be told that my children's health is of paramount importance.) Essentially, it told me that my desires about my pregnant embodiment amounted to naught.

My particular physician was, thankfully, not one of those kinds of doctors. The day of my second planned C-section, he came to my room early, and I made a crack about hoping he would be caught in traffic so I could try to deliver vaginally. Instead of laughing at my joke, he sat down next to my bed, took my hand, and gently reiterated to me that there was no way my baby could be born without a C-section and that my health and the baby's health were paramount. Nevertheless, he promised me he would do all he could to have the experience approximate a vaginal birth as much as possible. I received strong antinausea medication and was not as sick this time around. He ensured that I receive another kind of anesthesia to try to guard against my losing consciousness. The moment my second daughter was cleaned up, he instructed that she be placed on my chest right away so I could start to nurse, and she followed me into the recovery room rather than being whisked away. He simultaneously affirmed the need for a C-section while also helping me approximate the birth I so desperately desired. When counselling women who have felt loss over not having their desired birth experience, it important to simultaneously affirm their feelings of grief as legitimate while helping them confront and stand up against the societal preconceptions, pressures, and prejudices that have led so many women (including myself) to believe that it is part of their species-essence as women and mothers to experience childbirth in the right way. By internalizing that there is one right way to be pregnant or give birth, a woman who experience this "deviation from the 'norm' becomes a resource for further psychological oppression in which she cannot find herself or her narrative. Her experience is an aberration: she is an aberration." As a result, "women see themselves as abnormal and cannot see the social and cultural assumptions that actually construct them as abnormal" (Benson and Wolf 43). One helpful way to do this is highlighted by Charles: women need to share their stories. The social recognition that is found in public narratives and a receptive audience goes a long way towards healing. By sharing stories, "women make sense of their stories and regain a significant aspect of their personal identity. Our stories tie us to (or isolate us from) others.... We need a greater diversity of birth stories to accommodate a greater range of birth experiences" (Charles 220, 237).

These stories do not always have to be told in traditional verbal ways. One recent photograph that is circulating online helps challenge these social and cultural assumptions in a breathtaking manner. The black and white picture shows a naked woman's torso, her C-section scar new and still raw, while her newborn infant sleeps peacefully below it and over her vagina. The newborn is simultaneously blocking the place from where it was supposed to emerge while highlighting the scar from where it did emerge. The background story behind the photograph is that the woman did not want a C-section. She too wanted to have birth the natural way but had to undergo one nevertheless when both she and her baby were experiencing signs of distress. The photograph affirms the gift of having a healthy child and highlights a scar that is indeed indicative of a kind of labour and bodily sacrifice. For women who have experienced an unwanted C-section, the picture has been therapeutic:

I had a c-section and felt so guilty, like I had failed and hadn't technically "given birth" to my son. It took a long while to get through the depression that followed. This photo is absolutely stunning and a beautiful symbol of the magic of new life.

I had to have an emergency c-section with my first. It took a long time to come to terms with it, I read too many comments on stupid blogs ... saying that women like me hadn't given birth, we'd had our babies surgically removed, and other bull**** like we don't bond with our babies as well as women who'd had natural births.

Birth, scars, a new baby and a woman's body are all NORMAL parts of life. Beautiful photo and a cherished memory for this mother and child.

At first I had to admit, I was a bit surprised by the picture. But, then as I continued to look at the precious baby, I focused more on the beauty and sheer amazement of how incredible our bodies are to give life to these little gifts. (Aller)

For me, the photo has also helped me in my journey to heal from my loss. Even if I have never pushed a child out of my womb, the picture reminds me that I too gave over my mind and my body to bring two beautiful girls into the world. My body still created and nurtured new life; two beautiful children were released from my womb.

In other words, I may have indeed laboured differently, but in the end, I laboured no less—and I have the scar to prove it.

Endnotes

1. For instance, Rachel Roth notes that fetal rights advocates typically refer to pregnant women as "maternal hosts" or the "fetal environment" and that a woman's uterus has been described as the "'maternal abdominal wall [that serves as a] fortress against fetal health care (25).

2. A sublime experience does not always have to be a pleasurable or enjoyable one. Rather, as Lintott writes, it is one that allows us to "find meaning in difficult places ... the sublime captures a woman's struggle to understand and confront the intensity, for good and for bad, of these experiences" (246-47). Pregnancy and childbirth, no matter how painful, can be sublime because it is an experience "in which a person finds a thread of meaning that holds personal significance for him or her. A feminist sublime explains how some women might find such a thread to follow during gestation and birth" (Lintott 249). For another account concerning how labour and childbirth can be sublime or transcendent experiences through a feminist lens, see Sara Cohen Shabot's essay "On Ambivalence and Giving Birth: Reflecting on Labour through Beauvoir's Erotic" in this book.

3. However, as Charles points out in her essay, the midwifery model of birth, though meant to empower women to take control of their birthing experience, may unwittingly result in alienating and shaming women in the event medical intervention becomes necessary. This is especially true for women who have had C-sections, since there already exists in the natural birth community a predisposition to think that most C-sections are medically unnecessary. In these cases, Charles argues that "sharing medically justified cesarean narratives can help rebuild a sense of personal identity that was lost" (219).

Works Cited

Aller, Helen. "How My Photograph Inspired Thousands of Mothers to Share their Stories of C-section Childbirth." *Independent*, 2015, www.independent.co.uk/life-style/health-and-families/how-my-photograph-inspired-thousands-of-mothers-to-share-their-stories-of-c-section-childbirth-10460135.html. Accessed 4 Dec. 2019.

Benson, Jennifer and Allison Wolf. "Where Did I Go? The Invisible Postpartum Mother." *Philosophical Inquiries into Pregnancy, Childbirth, and Mothering: Maternal Subjects*, edited by Sheila Lintott and Maureen Sander-Staudt, Routledge, 2012, pp. 34-48.

"Birth Writes." *The Guardian*. 9 Jan. 2016. Web. 31 May 2019. www.theguardian.com/society/2008/oct/26/caesarean-section-experiences. Accessed 7 Dec. 2019.

Bordo, Susan. *Unbearable Weight: Feminism, Western Culture, and the Body*. University of California Press, 1993.

Casper, Monica. *The Making of the Unborn Patient: A Social Anatomy of Fetal Surgery*. Rutgers University Press, 1998.

Charles, Sonya. "Disempowered Women? The Midwifery Model and Medical Intervention." *Coming to Life: Philosophies of Pregnancy, Childbirth, and Mothering*, edited by Sarah LaChance Adams and Caroline R. Lundquist, Fordham University Press, 2013, pp. 215-38.

Cox, Judy. "An Introduction to Marx's Theory of Alienation." *International Socialism*, 1998, www.marxists.org/history/etol/newspape/isj2/1998/isj2-079/cox.htm. Accessed 4 Dec. 2019.

Dickenson, Donna. "Property and Women's Alienation from their Own Reproductive Labour." *Bioethics*, vol. 15, no. 3, 2001, pp. 205-17.

Jukelevics, Nicette. "The Emotional Scars of Caesarean Birth." *Babybelly*, 8 Dec. 2014, www.tabs.org.nz/pdfdocs/emotionalscars.pdf. Accessed 4 Dec. 2019.

Lintott, Sheila. "The Sublimity of Gestation and Giving Birth: Toward a Feminist Conception of the Sublime." *Philosophical Inquiries into Pregnancy, Childbirth, and Mothering: Maternal Subjects*, edited by Sheila Lintott and Maureen Sander-Staudt, Routledge, 2012, pp. 237-50.

Little, Margaret Olivia. "Abortion, Intimacy, and the Duty to Gestate." *Ethical Theory and Moral Practice*, vol. 2, no. 3, 1999, pp. 295-312.

Lynne, Sarah. "Birth Story: Emergency C-section, Post-Partum Post-Traumatic Stress Disorder and Type 1 Diabetes." *Unexpectant: Exploring the Story of Modern Motherhood*. 10 Oct. 2013, www.unexpectant.com/. Accessed 7 Dec. 2019.

Marx, Karl. *Capital: A Critique of Political Economy*. Modern Library, 1938.

Marx, Karl. "Economic and Philosophical Manuscripts of 1844." *Early Writings*, edited by Rodney Livingstone and Gregor Benton, Penguin Books, 1975, pp. 279-400.

Marx, Karl. "Excerpts from James Mill's Elements of Political Economy." *Early Writings*, Edited by Rodney Livingstone and Gregor Benton, Penguin Books, 1975, pp. 259-78.

Marx, Karl. *Grundrisse*. Penguin Books, 1973.

Piering, Julie. "The Pregnant Body as a Public Body: An Occasion for Community, Care, Instrumental Coercion, and a Singular Collectivity." *Philosophical Inquiries into Pregnancy, Childbirth, and Mothering: Maternal Subjects*, edited by Sheila Lintott and Maureen Sander-Staudt, Routledge, 2012, pp. 178-90.

Shire, Warsan. "Nail Technician as Palm Reader." *Poem Hunter*. www.poemhunter.com/poem/nail-technician-as-palm-reader/ Accessed 9 Dec. 2019.

Thompson, Lanny Ace. "The Development of Marx's Concept of Alienation: An Introduction." *Mid-American Review of Sociology*, vol. 4, no. 1, 1979, pp. 23-38.

Young, Iris Marion. "Pregnant Embodiment: Subjectivity and Alienation." *The Journal of Medicine and Philosophy*, vol. 9, 1984, pp. 45-62.

Section II

Seeking Perfection, Finding Despair

Chapter Seven

"I'm So Tired": The Labour of Care, Infant Sleep Management, and Maternal Ambivalence

Patricia MacLaughlin and Gwen Scarbrough

The past two decades have seen an increasing interest in the experience of motherhood and the often intensive labour that women carry out to provide care for their children (Arendell). Although the changing nature of the family has led to shifting dynamics in the labour of care and the emergence of a "new fatherhood," women continue to be positioned as the primary caregivers for children (Craig; Doucet). This research is concerned with the invisibility of "motherwork,"—a term that Patricia Hill Collins describes as the unacknowledged labour that mothers do, including care work. Specifically, this discussion is focused on the practice of motherhood and the labour of care that occurs throughout the night as women attempt to manage the quality of their infant's sleep. Even though the experience of nighttime mothering and the management of infant sleep has been examined from a number of perspectives—including maternal mental health (Goldberg et al.), nighttime parenting strategies (Volpe et al.), the impact on family relationships (Medina et al.), and maternal wellbeing (Lam et al.)—the lived, everyday experience of motherwork and the way in which it is perceived by women as they labour throughout the nighttime hours has yet to be explored. In particular, the emotional, physical, and psychological challenges that occur when nighttime is characterized by, albeit normative, frequent night waking in infancy will be explored. This work also provides a deeper understanding of the emotional work involved in mothering and discusses the ambiguity that may arise as a result of the intensive care work that takes place during the nighttime hours.

I have a one-year-old baby. She is my first child, and although I had anticipated the forewarned "sleepless nights" of early parenthood, I did not fully comprehend what this meant or have any sense of the intensity of the experience. My life has become all about sleep. Did I get enough? Was it of quality? Did I wake up feeling generally well rested? Did I dream? Or was I awakened countless times throughout the night because of my back and hips were sore from nursing continuously while lying on my side, trying to keep my child from waking completely and wanting to play at 3:00 a.m.? Nights of deep sleep are a surprise and lead into days of surprising clarity. I can think a little clearer and move my body faster. Nights of frequent waking slowly and painfully turn into mornings of rising before the sun is up, facing a new day already exhausted. Although my offspring is cheery and full of energy, I feel like I am moving through molasses and can barely move my limbs or keep my burning eyes from closing without copious cups of coffee. I am comforted by sleep research and online support groups that proclaim my experience is within the range of normal as well as magazine articles, family and friends, and even random members of the public who say my baby should have been able to sleep solidly through the night by three months. I appreciate the support of my partner, but resent it when he snores right through our infant's tossing and turning while I gently pat her back and silently pray she does not wake up. I tell myself that babies are only babies for a short time and it will not be long before I cannot even remember the tiredness I am feeling now, yet it feels never ending. I am amused by the little rituals and superstitions I have developed in the evening to ensure a better night of sleep, and when the night does not go so well, I am convinced I somehow performed them incorrectly and failed to appease the baby sleep gods. More than anything, I love the closeness, the holding and rocking, the intimacy, and the physical relationship that continue to develop between me and my baby, so much so that at times I feel like we are one. But there are moments when I cannot stand for one second more to have her nursing or lying asleep on top of me, leaving me unable to move for fear of waking her up. These feelings are complex, ambiguous, intense and ever changing. I often feel joy, love, frustration, anger, and loneliness all at once as I work to manage the sleep of my baby at three in the morning. However, little information exists in the public domain describing this experience from the mother's perspective beyond the seemingly infinite amount of advice, instructions, as well as critiques of parenting and, more specifically, mothering methods.

The Trouble with Sleep(lessness)

Humans have a basic need for sufficient sleep. In young families, sleep, or rather sleeplessness, in the form of just a few hours or sleep fragmentation is considered a challenging and sometimes stressful occurrence. An increasingly medicalized view of infant sleep asserts that frequent night waking is problematic, and past a particular age of infancy, it becomes pathologized (Williams and Crossley). Parents are presented with conflicting information and advice on how children should sleep as well the best ways to achieve the desired outcome of a solid night's sleep for the household.

Yet even well into toddlerhood, one third of parents describe sleep as a "significant problem" (Armstrong et al.). However, research indicates that night waking can be normal infant behaviour (Goodlin-Jones et al.; Scher; Weinraub et al.), and periods of night waking have been found to be common for longer periods into infancy and toddlerhood than have been previously recognized (Scher et al.; Weinraub et al.). Nonetheless, while wakeful patterns of sleep may be biologically normal, prolonged sleeplessness and sleep fragmentation can lead to parents becoming chronically exhausted, experiencing stress, and, in mothers, feeling depressed (Hiscock and Wake; Sadeh et al.).

Understanding women's experiences of the nightshift is significant to mothering research as they are more often responsible than their male partners for infant feeding, nighttime soothing and its related care work (Burgard). This research is concerned with the invisibility of motherwork. Drawing on feminist theories of mothering, this chapter explores the experiences of women as they labour throughout the nighttime hours and discusses the subsequent impact of prolonged sleep disruption on mothers due to this care. In particular, this work is concerned with the ways in which ongoing care work that occurs outside of the daytime hours is physically and emotionally intensive and reflects broader social conceptualizations of gendered responsibility within the household. Furthermore, this chapter will discuss how the labour of nighttime child care, as primarily performed by women, is framed within a context of "intensive motherhood" (Hays), which promotes practices of good mothering that are child centric, requires willing maternal sacrifice, and often poses the needs of the mother against those of the child and family. Burgard aptly notes that "inadequate sleep due to child care needs is also the greatest example of women putting their needs secondary to their child's and family's needs" (3). However, the prioritization of the needs of others during the nighttime hours and the exhaustive practices that mothers carry out in order to manage infant sleep requires intensive and ongoing emotional work (Venn et al.) that is often ambivalent and challenging.

Methodology

A qualitative phenomenological approach was selected to best explore women's experiences of nighttime motherwork. Phenomenology attempts to ascertain the lived experience of a shared phenomenon (Jackson). In doing so, through an interpretative process, researchers seek to identify the essence of an experience and present this experience from an insider's point of view. Phenomenology is an apt method to gather data on mother's experiences of the nightshift, as care work in the nighttime hours is labour intensive and is often characterized by tiredness and frustration; it is physically, psychologically, and emotionally challenging.

Seven women with infants who were experiencing night waking and sleep fragmentation due to the care needs of their children, aged between four and eighteen months, participated in this research. The mothers, who were cohabiting with male partners, were asked to document their sleep and wake experiences over a period of three consecutive days and nights. The participants kept written diaries describing what they were doing, thinking, and feeling. Once this documentation was gathered and an initial analysis carried out, each mother participated in a semi-structured interview. Questions focused on their self-reported experiences while managing their baby's sleep. The primary research findings were informed through each participant's interview transcripts and their day-to-day narratives in the form of journals. The following section explores the mothers' experiences of care work during the nighttime hours.

Motherwork and the Nightshift

The limited sociological research exploring the ways in which household labour and childcare is carried out during the nighttime hours indicates that women take on a greater responsibility of care work than male partners, resulting in sleep disruptions, sleeplessness, and waking early to tend to others in the household (Hislop and Arber; Maume et al.; Burgard). For this small qualitative sample, participants detail the immense workload necessary in ongoing infant sleep management and the physical, psychological, and emotional impact of the work. In her journal, for example, Mary[1] describes the exhaustive practices that she engages in to manage her baby's sleep:

> Took baby upstairs for bed around 7:00 p.m.; it was 7:50 before he finally went off to sleep, carried him around the room for a further fifteen minutes to wind him ... 9:00 p.m. awake, whimpering, a sign of wind, picked him up and he did a few little burps ... 10:05 p.m. awake again and cries a bit more this time. Try to burp him, but he doesn't settle until I feed him ... 11:00 p.m. awake ... [partner] takes him, but he just cries for boobie. I feed him, then change his nappy and feed him a little more.... I get some sleep.

She continues to labour throughout the night as primary carer, and by morning she notes the following:

> I'm wrecked. I let him lay on me as I remain propped up with pillows. It's comfy enough, and I know I will get some sleep. When I lay him down, he is very unsettled, and I am too tired to do the walk around the room. He settles perfectly when on me and has a good sleep. I sleep with an aching neck and a full bladder, damn. But if I put him down he is just going to cry.

After a difficult night, Elaine's baby eventually succumbs to sleep, but her work is not yet finished:

Yeah, he's finally asleep now; course there's no chance I'm going to move now that he's asleep…. Well that didn't last long. Two minutes and he's awake again … so, I sleep beside him with my shirt up so that he can access my breasts when he needs them. It's not very comfortable or dignified for me 'cause I'm actually up on my elbow now. And I'm thirsty, and this isn't comfortable…. I feel like I'm doing the plank now.

As the labour of the day merges into the work of the night, the night permeates the daytime. Ongoing sleep deprivation creates a sense of an overwhelming burden that is constant and relentless, with a subsequent difficulty in everyday function. One mother describes how her "body has given up relaxing" and the relief she experiences knowing the night is coming to an end. She is "happy to wake up as the night is over" but has a constant sense of being pulled in all directions—"all feels a struggle" (Deirdre interview).

The end of the day is not viewed as a time to wind down and rest. Instead, these mothers ready themselves for more work: "Throughout the day, the thoughts of the night ahead keep popping into my head and I start feeling anxious" (Deirdre journal).

Some of the participants report feeling at times broken by the relentless interruptions to their sleep. Yet the women rally and tell themselves "it's only for a short time." They find ways to persevere:

Baby wakes at 4:00 a.m. That's a grand total of four hours for me, [so] I feel great, well I don't feel like I am about to die. This is all manageable, even getting out of bed to walk the floor with him to wind him. He doesn't settle back in the bed, so I walk the floor with him again. Oh and I have changed his nappy at this point also. So I walk some more with him and lay him down. He is a little scratchy but, with rubbing his back and his cheeks for a little while he settles. 6:00 a.m., feeds for a few minutes, moves around the bed a little and then settles. 7:00 a.m., feeds same as before moves a bit but settles. 8:00 a.m., feeds, moves about a bit more than last time, and gets up on all fours and turns over and sits up wide awake and a big smile on his face. (Mary journal)

Some of the women fluctuate between anxiety over how they are performing as mothers and a fear that something is wrong with their children due to the frequency of their night waking. One mother admits to constant worry: "what is wrong with Lisa? She's been fed, she's got a clean nappy. She's in her bed. What am I missing? Am I doing something wrong?" She describes this process as follows:

Frustrating, emotionally and physically draining, the anxiety ... like sometimes I feel I can't handle even the smallest of things, and everything is on top of me. My mind feels kind of hazy as well 'cause I'm so drained that I can't even think of the smallest tasks. It all seems to be larger than it is; it just seems to be a lot of work because I'm so tired, and your mind is constantly thinking it over and over again what could be wrong with her. (Ann interview)

The pressure to perform mothering successfully and to have restful nights of sleeping children compound the distress that mothers already experience as they are going through periods of sleeplessness:

I've been to some toddler and parenting groups, and there's an awful lot of pressure.... There's never any real honest discussion. Someone might say "I had a terrible night," but really, they usually say, "it's great." It's nearly a competition about who's got the most perfect children. (Ann interview)

Overall, the participants are reticent to speak about to their lack of sleep with others. Several of the women will only discuss their situation with people they know will be sympathetic, as they believe the resulting conversation will usually contain unsolicited advice or criticism of their parenting. "Of course everyone has a solution," notes Niamh.

As well, the participants are constantly searching for ways to improve the sleep of their children. They read about sleep, have discussions on online mothering forums, confide with other mothers, and sometimes seek medical advice. This, in turn, helps the women to feel less helpless and to potentially find a solution to their difficult nights. Deirdre, for example, has worked painstakingly to determine why her infant is so restless, since no medical problems were identified. She has experimented with the use of a dehumidifier, tried turning on or off the heating at strategic times, used different types of lighting, changed sleep location (bed share, cot, car seat, and buggy), initiated dietary changes, administered medications, explored alternative therapies, and tested out various experimental sleep routines.

In addition to worry, the experience, complexity, and logistics of ongoing maternal practice when caring for an infant during these hours involve extensive emotional work. These emotions involve a range of feelings, often ambiguous, in regards to family relationships. During these moments, feelings towards the infant as well as the partner are particularly complex.

The mothers in this research have mixed emotions. Love and intimacy are reported as being a special benefit of caring for their children through the night, especially once their babies have fallen back asleep, and they are able to finally relax, stroke their baby's heads, listen to their breathing, and gaze at their faces. Elaine describes how her "[sleeping baby] is yanking my hair so it's uncomfortable, but he's very cute and adorable, so right now I'm feeling very tolerant and loving and lucky, blessed to have such a cute thing. But I don't always feel like that."

But they also describe the wakefulness in the nighttime as lonely and oppressive. Ann experiences "a sort of claustrophobic feeling; at times, you know, there's that intense love because you sit with them and have a bond ... sometimes it can feel very restricting as well." This mother also feels that because of the constant physical contact, and in her case breastfeeding, her frustration arises from a sense that "your body is not your own" (Ann interview).

Both Nancy Chodorow and Sara Ruddick argue that women are socially positioned to be the primary carers of children, which leads to emotional intimacy and attachment to their offspring and the subsequent identity work of motherhood. The emotional experiences of mothering, however, are broader and more complex than presented in intensive mothering discourse. Women not only experience an array of emotions in relation to their children (Rich; Arendell): "mother's emotions can vary within the course of a day, and certainly over time, depending upon the behavior of her children, the space, time, and services available to her, and myriad other desires and frustrations" (Ruddick 34). For the women in this research, periods of extreme fatigue often coincide with negative emotions, and some admit to feelings of anger and frustration, often directed towards their children:

When it was really bad, I'd actually be very angry with [the baby] because I could just not figure out what was wrong with her, and I felt like she was doing it more with me than [husband]. It got strange where I actually thought she was doing it to me on purpose. I would have all the boxes ticked. Her nappy would be changed. She wouldn't be hungry, and she'd just start crying ... I actually would have felt very angry towards her during the night. Her cry used to really get to me at nighttime; it used to really go through me, and I couldn't handle it. Her cry would really trigger me feeling angry, but if I did have a good night's sleep I'd be fine. I would be able to handle the cry. (Niamh interview)

In her journal Deirdre describes "holding [the] baby, going *shhhh* and getting angry. It's my night, and she doesn't do this with husband." The frustration and sense of unease builds during the night in anticipation of the baby waking: "It takes me a while to fall asleep because I am there listening and waiting and wondering is she going to start." At times, the anger for some of the participants becomes overwhelming:

I love being a Mam so much; my heart would explode with the amount of love I have in it, but if I am exhausted, I have snapped and shouted at her. I remember hitting the wall one day when she wouldn't go to sleep. I had one night pacing around the spare room with her, rocking her, burping her—trying everything I could to get her to go to sleep. I thought about throwing her out the window. I just wanted to sleep and the crying to stop. I wanted to feel like I could calm her. Thankfully, I was still lucid enough to know that this wasn't ideal, and I went to my husband and woke him up and told him to take her. (Niamh interview)

Feelings of ambivalence are compounded by what Arendell describes as the "paradoxical character of experience [of mothering] ... intensified by the uncertainty of the likely outcome of the work" (19). The women in this study often find that their babies sometimes sleep better or worse despite their best efforts.

The gendered nature of nighttime childcare can also give rise to negative emotions towards cohabiting fathers. Several sociological studies indicate that within families, men's sleep is prioritized, leaving women primarily responsible for the nightshift (Venn et al.; Maume et al.). However, this privileging has an emotional cost. Women in this study are overwhelmingly responsible for the care of their infants at night and experience chronic exhaustion. As a result, mothers describe feelings of impatience, resentment, and, at times, intense anger towards their male partners:

> There is definitely a reason sleep deprivation is a form of torture.... I've cried and screamed and raged at times. Myself and my husband have fought a lot, especially in the first year.... No one had told me it would affect my relationship either. I've hated him for getting more sleep than me. I especially hated him when he tells me he was tired after a night of me up with my daughter. It's terrified me how much I've hated him. I lashed out with him for leaving the nappy on top of the bin rather than put[ting] it in the bin, for not being as tired as me, but still being tired.... Tiredness has made me mean and angry.... I didn't think I was capable of that much rage. (Niamh interview)

As well, mothers report an acute awareness of the total hours spent caring for children, hours of rest, and "alone time" in comparison to their male partners. These perceived inequalities often lead to negative feelings toward the partner: "I'm just envious of him that he gets a break during the day. If [partner] ever says that he had a bad or busy day that really gets my wick up; it's kind of like does he really understand the type of day I've had to do? They can walk out of the front of the house and go off and won't think of [the baby]" (Deirdre interview).

However, despite the physical and emotional challenges of the nightshift, women report their confidence growing and evolving as they accumulate mothering experience. With this growing confidence, they tend to reconceptualize mothering practices and forge their own strategies for the nighttime hours. Participants also describe renegotiating the nightshift with their male partners as their babies grow older, especially as the demands of feeding in the night decrease. Deirdre, for example, organized a night on and then a night off system to share the load of nighttime care work, which resulted in improved sleep for her. Additionally some of the mothers are less influenced by discourses of intensive mothering and find that they are more able to integrate the work they perform with their identity as a mother. Ann describes how after the birth of her third child she has become easier on herself: I am not as concerned about housework." In her journal, she reflects, "I keep reading these books that tell me to get her on a schedule as she, and I will be happier, but we are both quite happy as it is and then there is my instinct."

Conclusion

The experiences of mothers when managing infant sleep on a nightly basis are intensive, challenging, and emotionally complex. Mothers typically take on a greater responsibility of the nightshift when compared to their male partners. While infant sleep is often characterized by periods of restlessness and frequent night waking, the distribution of care work involved suggests that "gendered social role responsibilities" are at play (Burgard 3). As a result, women endure chronic tiredness and experience frustration and ambivalence towards motherhood, their male partners, and their children. Negative feelings can emerge during these intensive periods of inadequate sleep. However, ideologies of intensive motherhood hide much of the real work, or motherwork, that mothers carry out. In particular, the physical and emotional care that occurs outside of the daytime hours by mothers is largely invisible and unacknowledged. Furthermore, as women struggle to help their infants to sleep through the night they report feeling pressure to perform mothering successfully. As a result, women are reluctant to share the experiences of their physical and emotional challenges when on the nightshift and are concerned that their performance of mothering may be viewed as poor or inadequate. Yet with time, women find themselves more able to resist these restrictive ideologies. Mothers begin to forge their own understandings and practices of mothering to encompass the work carried out during both the daytime and the nighttime hours. It is from this position that some women are able to find new ways to manage infants during the nighttime hours, to renegotiate the distribution of care on the nightshift, and to finally get some sleep.

Endnote

1. Pseudonyms have been used to protect the identities of the participants.

Works Cited

Arendell, Teresa "Caregiving and Investigating Motherhood: The Decade's Scholarship." *Journal of Marriage and the Family*, vol. 62, no. 4, 2000, pp. 1192-1207.

Armstrong, K.L., et al. "The Sleep Patterns of Normal Children." *The Medical Journal of Australia*, vol. 161, no. 3, 1994, pp. 202-6.

Burgard, Sarah. "The Needs of Others: Gender and Sleep Interruptions for Caregiving." PSC Research Report No. 10-697, 2010.

Chodorow, Nancy. *The Reproduction of Mothering*. University of California Press, 1978.

Collins, P.H. "Shifting the Center: Race, Class and Feminist Theorizing About Motherhood." *Representations of Motherhood*, edited by D. Bassin et al., Yale University Press, 1994, pp. 56-74.

Craig, L. "Does Father Care Mean Fathers Share? A Comparison of how Mothers and Fathers in Intact Families Spend Time with their Children." *Gender and Society*, vol. 20, no. 12, 2006, pp. 259-81.

Doucet, A. *Do Men Mother? Fathering, Care, and Domestic Responsibilities.* University of Toronto Press, 2006.

Goodlin-Jones, B.L., et al. "Night Waking, Sleep-Wake Organization, and Self-Soothing in the First Year of Life." *Journal of Developmental and Behavioral Pediatrics*, vol. 22, no. 4, 2001, pp. 226-33.

Goldberg, W., et al. "Eye of the Beholder? Maternal Mental Health and the Quality of Infant Sleep." *Social Science and Medicine*, vol. 79, no., 2013, pp. 101-108.

Hislop, Jenny, and Sara Arber "Sleepers Wake! The Gendered Nature of Sleep Disruption Among Mid-life Women." *Sociology*, vol. 37, no. 4, 2003, pp. 695-711.

Hays, S. *The Cultural Contradictions of Motherhood*. Yale University Press, 1996.

Hiscock, Harriet, and Melissa Wake "Infant Sleep Problems and Postnatal Depression: A Community-Based Study." *Pediatrics*, vol. 107, no. 6, 2001, pp. 1317-22.

Jackson, Barbara M. "The Lived Experience of Mothering During Incarceration." University of Lousiville Electronic Thesis and Dissertations. ThinkIR: The University of Louisville's Institutional Repository. 2011, ir.library.louisville.edu/etd/667/. Accessed 5 Dec. 2019.

Lam, P., et al. "Outcomes of Infant Sleep Problems: A Longitudinal Study of Sleep, Behavior, and Maternal Wellbeing." *Pediatrics*, vol. 111, no. 3, 2003, pediatrics.aappublications.org › content › pediatrics › e203.full.pdf. Accessed 5 Dec. 2019.

Maume, D., et al. "Gender, Work-Family Responsibilities, and Sleep." *Gender and Society*, vol. 24, no. 6, 2010, pp. 746-68.

Medina, A., C. et al. "Sleep Disruption and Decline in Marital Satisfaction across the Transition to Parenthood." *Family Systems Health*, vol. 27, no. 2, 2009, pp. 153-60.

Rich, Adrienne. *Of Woman Born: Motherhood as Experience and Institution*. W.W. Norton Company, 1976.

Ruddick, Sara "Thinking Mothers/Conceiving Birth." Ed. D. Bassin, M. Honey, & M.M. Kaplan. *Representations of Motherhood*, edited by D. Bassin et al., Yale University Press, 1994, pp. 29-46.

Sadeh, A., et al. "Why Care about Sleep of Infants and Their Parents." *Sleep Med Review*, vol. 15, no. 5, 2011, pp. 335-37.

Scher, A., et al. "Stability and Changes in Sleep Regulation: A Longitudinal Study from 3 Months to 3 Years." *Journal of Pediatric Psychology*, vol. 33, 2008, pp. 396-405.

Scher, A. "A Longitudinal Study of Night Waking in the First Year." *Child: Care, Health and Development*, vol. 17, 1991, pp. 295-302.

Venn, S., et al. "The Fourth Shift: Exploring the Gendered Nature of Sleep Disruption among Couples with Children." *British Journal of Sociology*, vol. 59, no. 1, 2008, pp. 79-98.

Volpe, L., et al. "Nighttime Parenting Strategies and Sleep-Related Risks to Infants." *Social Science and Medicine*, vol. 79, 2013, pp. 92-100.

Weinraub, M., et al. "Patterns of Developmental Change in Infants' Nighttime Sleep Awakenings from 6 through 36 Months of Age." *Developmental Psychology*, vol. 48, no. 6, 2012, pp. 1511-28.

Williams, Simon, and Nick Crossley "Introduction: Sleeping Bodies." *Body and Society*, vol. 14, no. 4, 2008, pp. 1-13.

Chapter Eight

Maternal Guilt and the First-Time Mother

Claire Steele LeBeau

How does a woman become a mother? How does she experience the radical transformation of her basic orientation, her priorities, her worldview, her sense of identity, her body, her time, her relationships, and, indeed, her entire life as she moves from living for herself to living for herself and her child? When she feels guilty for not being the mother or the person she wants to be in any given moment or circumstance, what does that mean and what does that teach her about herself, her child, and the world she lives in? The experience of guilt related to motherhood can be entirely unprecedented for a new mother because her relationship to herself, her child, her community, and her world has been transformed in the wake of this monumental developmental transition. Guilt is one aspect or one expression of a vast and multifaceted field of potential maternal experiences of ambivalence for the first-time mother. Her experiences are unique to her and her relationship with her child, yet they are also in many respects quite common and shared among mothers. This chapter presents the findings gathered from phenomenological research—which includes focusing exercise in the interview itself—with five first-time mothers who describe instances of their early experiences of maternal guilt.[1] The interpreted analyses of their stories revealed seven major themes: physical and emotional connection to their babies, intense feelings of responsibility, feelings of being divided, the multidimensionality of feelings of guilt as well as other emotions, preverbal miscommunication, anxiety over the unknown, and social expectations and comparisons.

Each of these themes relates to the vulnerability and poignancy of a time of radical transformation in a mother's basic orientation in the world, as she moves from living exclusively for herself towards living for herself as well as her child. Far from being merely an unpleasant emotional experience or simply what is often perceived as "the inevitable accompaniment of motherhood" (De Vaus 37), maternal guilt is a complex and important part of the constantly unfolding process of changing relationships to self, others, and world.

Physical and Emotional Connection: Maternal-Infant Bond

It may perhaps often be taken for granted that a mother and her infant child can be deeply connected on physical and emotional levels. Each of the mothers in this study—Meg, Cam, Beth, Ann, and Xena[2]— experienced guilt related to motherhood from a desired pregnancy. Each mother welcomed the new life she shepherded into the world through her body, and each expressed a profound and abiding love for her child.

Meg described this deep connection in terms of how the mother knows what to do for her child as "a mother's intuition." This connection, for Meg, was a primary recognition and relatedness between a mother and her child, through which communication was instantaneous and not dependent on verbal expression. She described this familiar connection as something that continued to grow for her from the time her son was a newborn: "But as they get older and you are able to realize, like OK, I'm the mom. I have the complete mother's intuition. I know what my child wants even though he can't tell me. I know him. And I know all he has to do is put his hand on me, and I'll know, OK, he wants his sippy cup, you know. I'm in his mind too." Meg described this period of time from newborn to age four and five as "that period of time when you are bonding so much." This bonding occurs on many levels, but even before verbal language, there is a great physical and emotional communication at play. This knowledge of what her child is saying and what he needs she calls "a mother's intuition."

In exploring her felt sense of her memory, Xena felt a strong sensation of ache in and around her heart. In our discussion after focusing, Xena felt this ache, which stemmed from her feeling a sense of guilt, as a strong "visceral bond" between her and her son, Wesley: "You know, so the ache was from the connectedness. You know, so it's like if I weren't connected, I wouldn't have this ache. So ... the ache is a good thing in a sense because it's one of many ways of feeling how close I am to my child. So it's actually really good." Xena was pleasantly surprised by this realization of a deep physical and emotional connection, which highlighted something that had previously felt quite negative to her.

Responsibility: "High Stakes"

Although each of the mothers talked about different experiences of anxiety or fear, each seemed to connect this experience to a heavy awareness of the enormity of their responsibility for caring for a new life, especially in the early stages. This sense of overwhelming responsibility was linked, on the one hand, to the complete dependency and helplessness of the newborn and, on the other, to the mother's ever-increasing awareness of how much work and effort is involved in trying to care for a baby and themselves at the same time. Wanting to do the very best and to give commensurate care to the love they experienced for their babies also played a major part in this heavy awareness.

Ann described herself as a consummate perfectionist, whose standards she acknowledged were impossible to attain. Yet when it came to the love and devotion she felt for her daughter, she said, "when you are in the moment, it's very high stakes, like you're looking at this sort of blank slate, new life. And it does matter very much what you do." Even thinking about how many environmental factors are at play for a new baby was overwhelming. Ann said, "even from the first moments of a baby's life, you are making choices about what kinds of, like what their environment is like, and how your interactions with them are and how your interactions with your partner are. They're observing all of those things." The stakes can indeed feel high for the mother who always wants to do the best for her child. The questions about "what kind of life do I want for my child?" and "what kind of world do I want my child to live in?" can become an ever-present backdrop to daily interactions and carry the weight of the future in terms of what the child is learning. As Meg wrote, "I have the most important responsibility now, being a parent." As a mother, she felt the enormity of her son's dependency on her.

CLAIRE STEELE LEBEAU

Feeling Divided: Guilt for Wanting Separation

Each of the mothers described an experience of feeling divided or torn in some way between the needs and demands of taking care of their babies and taking care of themselves. This division played out in various ways—from divided time and divided attention to an overall sense of feeling torn between the demands of the world and the demands of the baby. This division was not described as being torn between two negative options. On the contrary, each mother wanted to be the best mother she could be and to attend to all of her baby's needs herself while also meeting her own needs to be herself in the world. The calls of work, career, school, chores, and sleep (to name a few) were more than obligations that needed to be kept. They were calls for separation from their babies and time for themselves. Although this may seem to be an obvious and a reasonable necessity, it was not always easily implemented because each mother also wanted to be the one taking care of her baby at the same time. The feeling of being estranged from oneself at some level as a result of this division emerged as a subtheme in these narratives as well as the mother's solutions to this division, as in her need for balance and forgiveness. Obviously, these experiences were highly particular to each individual and experienced in unique ways.

The experience of wanting two separate things simultaneously is often deeply disturbing and guilt inducing, especially when one of the things is experienced at absolute odds with the other one. As the mother with the youngest baby, Cam's struggle with this feeling of wanting to be productive with a newborn stood out: "I felt guilty for wanting to do other things than take care of my baby because she needs me so much—how selfish of me to want to be productive instead of take care of this helpless child." At the same time, Cam also wanted to be the one to provide care and love to her daughter: "I stared at her and thought how wonderful she is. I thought of how I want to do everything possible to make her comfortable and happy." In focusing, Cam's struggle to negotiate the extreme conflict she experienced left her head spinning with a "black swirl" because it was all simultaneously too much.

Both Ann and Xena felt the division and the need for separation, especially with regard to having time to think and do creative work. When Xena returned to work, she acutely felt the division of her time and attention between her baby and her job. Naptime became a critical opening for her to meet her own needs and do her own work. When those naps became interrupted, she found herself insisting and "setting [her] jaw" in her resolve to try to reclaim them. Ann valued the weekly three hours she had carved out for herself to think and be creative. She wanted to have the opportunity to "think complete thoughts" and "be creative in a way that you can't be creative when you're distracted." This time to think and do work was more than simply their duty to fulfill their obligations in the world. It was a time to return to themselves and to come back to an awareness of who they are as separate from the all-encompassing responsibility of the mother role.

Several mothers articulated a sense of not knowing who they were anymore or estrangement from themselves after having a baby. The process of becoming a mother requires a great adjustment not only in time management and attention but also in understand the self. In talking about all of the responsibilities she had juggled the previous year, Ann said, "I've often felt like I am not, not just since P was born, but with the combination of P and losing my dad, like I have been surprised that I am not always the person that I had hoped that I was. Like I'm not necessarily doing things as well as I could."

Beth also experienced a great deal of pain and anxiety because she did not know or recognize herself after coming home from the hospital. She described a three month period of "going through the motions" and of feeling distant and removed from her family, the world, and especially herself. From a real state of despair, when she was convinced that she was dying, she remembered that she "prayed to God to help me so I could be myself again."

As a part of this sense of feeling divided, each mother articulated a clear desire and need for balance in her life. The struggle to find balance seemed to be an ongoing process but one that seemed to get easier the older their children became. Ann acknowledged that her own standards for herself both professionally and as a mother were "quite high," and she felt the need to find at least an intellectual and practical balance between her ideals of perfection and the acceptance of limitations. Meg found a sense of balance in the quiet acceptance of the fact that there were times when she would need to leave her son to do things "in order to live." Even so, this struggle to find this acceptance "broke her heart" when she needed to be away from her son. Cam, in particular, talked about a need to balance the time she spends with her daughter and the time she spends away from her in order in to meet her own needs: "I have to go to school so I can better take care of her, and somehow, I have to find a balance between being productive, loving her, and taking care of myself."

There are times when every mother must be separate from her child, and there are times when every mother makes mistakes, especially in negotiating the transitions between togetherness and separation. It is sometimes difficult not to push away too fast or too hard to try to hasten the departure or the return. When this happens, it can be important to be able to find ways to forgive one's own mistakes, misunderstandings, preoccupations, and limitations. That forgiveness may come in many forms from many different places.

For Cam, this need for forgiveness came in the form of a need for permission to let herself and her daughter experience the pain of separation as well as the joy of discovering oneself. For Beth, forgiveness meant being able to let go of missed time and truly enjoy the process of being a mother. If guilt calls us to find ways to repair places of rupture in our connection with our children, then forgiveness not only allows us to gently accept our own limitations but teaches us how to model that gentleness for our children as well.

Guilt Does Not Live by Itself: Guilt Is Multidimensional

A major theme that emerged in the course of all of the interviews was the clear sense that guilt is not an emotion that tends to be experienced in isolation of other emotions. The experience of guilt consistently seemed to be proceeded by and give rise to a myriad of different emotions. The speed of the emotional shifts often left the mothers feeling overwhelmed and overcome with intense and seemingly contradictory feelings. Guilt is so often considered to be what is called a negative emotion. Parcelling the emotional repertoire into valences and polarities can have dramatic consequences on what emotions a mother allows herself to pay attention to and on how each emotion, including guilt, is connected to the others. In the process of exploring their emotional lives as new mothers, they discovered a complex and rich tapestry of feelings that taught them a great deal about how they were relating to themselves, other people, and the world.

A few of the emotions, in addition to guilt, that were mentioned in the course of the interviews were as follows: joy, love (or a state of being in love in particular), frustration, anger, resentment, intense anxiety and fear, contentment, excitement, pride, sadness or sorrow, devotion, grief, and ambivalence. In her written description and our conversation, Meg made it clear that her happiness and joy in being a mother far outweighed the moments of guilt she experienced. She emphasized that love was a stronger emotion than guilt. Yet in our conversation, she also talked about how joy and happiness were "interconnected" with sadness and guilt:

> I feel like maybe it's a play off the emotions working off of each other ... a little bit of good with a little bit of bad. But I feel like what makes you wise is learning how to contain and control, and to make sure, in the end, the happiness weighs more than the guilt.... So, I definitely feel like that helps you grow as a mother, as a wife, as a person.

The priority of joy is clear in Meg's description, although she also acknowledged that sadness, heartbreak, and guilt also have a role to play in teaching something.

Ann described her "mixed feelings" about the "enormous change in every aspect of your day-to-day life." Part of her experience of guilt was her feelings of resentment that she was unable to do her other work to her satisfaction while taking care of and accommodating a new and utterly dependent life. At the same time, Ann experienced great love and devotion towards her daughter while she was also going through a considerable amount of grief in losing her father—a grief that she had had to put aside in order to do both the professional work in her career as well as the personal work to make room for her daughter in her world.

In the focusing work, Xena felt her guilt experience as a sense of heartache and, in so doing, highlighted an experience of a "visceral bond" with her son. Guilt was one aspect or presentation of a deep connection and communication that she called "the bond." The focusing also brought forwards feelings of tenderness, resolve, and compassion along with the "heartache" of guilt.

Beth also mentioned that she wished someone would have told her that having a baby was not just about joy. Aside from Beth's intense feelings of anxiety and fear, she mentioned that there were some days of feeling really "proud of myself as a new mom" and other days where she just felt "depressed and exhausted." Guilt arose from places of not "loving" breastfeeding as well as the disparity between what Beth was feeling and what she thought she should be feeling.

As mentioned previously, Cam experienced such a wide range of emotions through the course of a single day that it left her head spinning. For Cam, it was the conflicting nature of her emotions that seemed to give rise to strong feelings of guilt. Her desire to both be with her daughter and away from her at the same time left Cam feeling alternately frustrated and angry to joyful and content. Her feelings of guilt seemed to mark the transitions or in between states of being called away from and back to her daughter.

It is difficult to experience such a wide range of emotions that are all quite new, or regarding a relationship that is quite new, while so many of the emotions seem to be in conflict with one another. Even more difficult to reconcile is that this emotional kaleidoscope can exist simultaneously from one moment to the next. Cam felt deeply in love and wanted the very best for her baby at the same time as she felt frustrated, angry, and exhausted. Cam was deeply in love and frustrated, not deeply in love but frustrated. This may seem like a minor or inconsequential change in phrasing. However, it may be experientially significant for the first-time mother in particular. The word "but" seems to suggest a cancelling or negating of something that came before. The word "and" suggests that it is at the same time as something that came before. Guilt often arises when one emotion is experienced as cancelling or negating another. Yet what guilt seems more likely to do, especially in these examples, is mark or instigate the transition or the shift between emotional experiences.

Miscommunication: Negotiating the Preverbal

In this research, all of the first-time mothers had infant children who were two or younger. Language development in babies occurs at varying rates, but, typically, a one-year-old is able to form one-word utterances, and an eighteen-month old is able to begin to form two-word combinations in increasing sophistication through the second to third year when grammar and complete sentences often begin to increase exponentially. Mothers and babies are deeply attuned to one another through increasingly complex preverbal levels during infancy.

A mother begins to notice differences in her baby's cries quite early in the first few weeks of development. Yet it is not always easy to know for certain what is causing a baby to cry. In many of the mother's examples, a significant source of guilt arose during times when they had misunderstood the nature of their baby's cries. A mother of an infant or toddler is also not able to verbally explain her thoughts and feelings to her child, especially in transitional times of separation, such as dropping off at daycare or leaving to go to work. Nevertheless, significant communication occurs between a mother and baby through touch, smell, eye contact as well as through crying and talking. Perhaps it is because this physical preverbal communication was usually so effective that these mothers felt so guilty during those times they misunderstood what their babies had been trying to communicate.

Both Xena and Ann felt terrible that they had missed something in the cries of their babies because they had been preoccupied with their own needs and projects.[3] Ann wrote the following: "she was trying to tell me what was wrong, and I ignored her. She had been uncomfortable and in distress, and I'd been too wrapped up in my own work to take care of her." It was not exactly true that Ann had ignored her daughter's cries. In fact, she had attended to them faithfully, but she had misunderstood the nature of P's cries because she had been preoccupied.[4] In her example, it was the misunderstanding due to her preoccupation that caused her to feel guilty. For Xena, a v similar situation occurred: "I felt awful. Here I was, focusing so much on the nap that I was refusing to hear his call for food." Here again, misunderstanding alone does not produce the feelings of guilt but rather the reason for not hearing— namely, being preoccupied with one's own needs. Xena felt terrible because something she needed seemed to take priority over something so essential to her child.

In a slightly different example, Meg described her feelings of guilt when she had to leave her son to go to work while listening to him cry out for her. She felt intensely the limits of her ability to "explain it to him" in language. If words could have sufficed, she would have left him with words of constant love and promises of return. She herself was comforted by the fact that "one day he will be older and will understand that his mother will never leave him." In our conversation, Meg talked in detail about the profound physical and tactile communication that she and her son shared in his drifting off to sleep while feeling the contours of her face with his hand. Meg believed that her son would increasingly be able to understand their connection in verbal language and then remember the feeling of these experiences while holding these images of his mother's love, even when they were physically separated.

Fear of the Unknown: In the Beginning

When a baby is born to a first-time mother, the experience is entirely unique and novel to her. Although it is true that many mothers have had extensive experience in caring for babies—for example, in caring for younger siblings, as was the case for Meg—there is something very different about being the mother of your own child. Several of the mothers described a real sense of fear and anxiety about quite suddenly being in a situation where they felt powerless to control what would happen. When they brought their babies home from the hospital, they did not know what to expect and, therefore, could not predict or control their own time, habits, or even their own body responses the way they had before. These early experiences of not knowing what their child needed or how to adjust their lives to what was going to happen were described by several of the mothers as the stage through which their feelings of guilt of emerged.

Cam, whose daughter was only two-and-half-months old at the time of our interview, expressed a strong sense of outrage that she had not been informed about how difficult breastfeeding could be. Her first experiences of guilt were related to the exhaustion and pain involved with the physical demands of breastfeeding. She was truly upset that she did not know that "it doesn't just easily happen" and that she had "to work at it." At the time of our interview, Cam's milk supply was just beginning to even out so that she was not painfully overproducing. Cam felt that she would still have elected to breastfeed her baby but would have liked to know in advance how difficult it could be and how much she would have to work at it.

Xena described strong feelings of anxiety when her son was a newborn and she could not predict any of her son's eating and sleeping patterns. When her son was a newborn, Meg described these unknowns about what her baby needed as a kind of vastness, which felt to her almost like an "enemy." Ann joked that for her this experience of early motherhood was something like being thrust into a new job without any training yet still possessing a ranging desire to be the best at it.

For Beth, whose anxiety and fear were the most extreme, the unknown meant something far more terrifying—the possibility of death. Beth's trauma related to her birth experience left her in a state of first shock and then, subsequently, a state of near constant terror for her life, as expressed increasingly through panic attacks.[5] The chest pain and numbness in her arm (possibly related to nerve damage from a back injury suffered earlier in her life) were two known variables in a vast horizon of unknowns that she felt certain was far more deadly. Beth's guilt meant not as much that she would do something wrong but that she would not live to be there for her son and family.

Social Expectations and Comparisons: Images of Motherhood

If we go to a new town where we have never been before or attend a party with people we have never met, what do we do to figure out how get around or how to fit in? We look to the people who have lived there and know the terrain, and who can make introductions. In this sense, new mothers are particularly inclined to make social comparisons with other mothers and are particularly prone to internalizing perceived cultural expectations of motherhood. This can be both helpful in terms of practical guidance and hurtful in terms of damaging a new mother's self-confidence. Each of the new mothers I spoke with talked in some way about the influence of books, media, family members, and the stories of mothers about their experience of becoming mothers themselves.

Cam had felt largely prepared for becoming a mother, as she had read many books about the subject, But she was upset that none of the books had prepared her for how difficult breastfeeding could be: "I mean I read books and books about pregnancy and labour, and they tell you all these things to prepare yourself for delivering a child, and then they ... talk about latch and ... talk about soreness, but that's about it. I mean, it's painful!" It is true that most references prepare new mothers for the pain of childbirth but do not delve into the potential pain and complications of breastfeeding. Cam felt as if the reason for this was to not scare mothers from wanting to try it: "They just say, 'oh breastfeeding; it's the best thing to do.' I mean maybe they don't tell you because they don't want you to not try it. But I would have done it anyway. I just needed to know."

Beth talked about the social pressures related to the number of items sold for babies:

Even just preparing, you know, when you register, you think you need everything in the store. You think, "Well if I don't get that, is that bad?" Then I would like have to tell myself, "OK, how did people do it a hundred years ago? They didn't have all this fancy stuff. Do I really need this? But all my other friends or the other moms have it, so maybe I do need it." You know, I kind of felt overwhelmed in the sense of the pressures of having, you know, a perfect nursery, or a perfect wardrobe, just the safest car seat, everything.

Meg talked about how the uncertainty of becoming a mother made her want to read as much as possible and to know everything. Once she had her son, she realized that "there's no book that just tells you what to do." Her experience in becoming a mother and learning to trust what she called her "mother's intuition" astonished her in ways that she could never have prepared herself for: "you really have no idea [about] a mother's love until it really happens."

Who do new mothers respect and admire? The moms who make it look easy. The images of these powerful mothers leave indelible imprints on the psyche of the new mother. They are the mothers who juggle eight bags with a baby on the hip; they are multitaskers extraordinaire; they are well kempt and happy; they have clean houses and clean clothes and know all of the relevant resources for other mothers to access for help. For each mom, there may be some variability to the exact image of the supermom "who makes it look easy," but for the most part, the above list is a somewhat close approximation to the internalized image of the ideal mother—the mother who is confident and capable, and even more so, when the new mom does not feel that way herself.

In Ann's story, she described feeling guilty about being impatient with her babysitter after losing most of the time she had paid her for. Ann described feeling embarrassed about what kind of mother she looked like in comparison to her friend, whom she saw as a "really calm and unflappable mother who makes it look easy." Beth also described seeing mothers who seemed to have complete command of mothering:

"some people just make it look so easy, you know. It's like, 'I have one kid and I feel overwhelmed; you have, like, four, and you seem like you have everything together.'" Quite often, these extraordinary mothers, when asked how they do it, will say that they do not always have complete command. But in the imagination of a new mother, they can hold a power and a mystery because of her own vulnerability and uncertainty.

Having a baby can be a joyful and truly wonderful experience. For families who can welcome and have the emotional, financial, and physical resources for bringing a new life into the world, there could be no greater joy. Yet even if a new baby is more than welcome and there are optimal resources for him or her, there is still an enormous amount of adjustment necessary to accommodate this radical shift in focus. Socially and culturally, if the pregnancy is either planned or desired, the new mother often rightly perceives an overall expectation of joy. Although this joy may be real and true, it is also only one part of the story.

Beth talked about a real absence of information regarding some of the other possible experiences of having a new baby.

> And I think a lot of times when you find out you are pregnant it is a miracle and it's a wonderful thing and everyone congratulates you, but no one really warns you ... but sometimes in a positive way. You know, everyone's like "Oh, you're having a baby, you're having a baby. It's so great, it's so great!" But it's also terrifying and it's the stress on the marriage. My husband he's just wonderful, but I don't think he knew what to do sometimes.

For the first three months after her son was born, Beth felt real disconnect between what she was feeling, terror, and what she thought she should be feeling, unmitigated joy. This disconnect was not something that could be easily negotiated or rationalized: "I had so many 'What ifs?' ... 'What if this? What if that?' I mean, people just want you to stop and are like, 'just live every day like it is [laughs]. Don't sit there and worry about what I did.' I just couldn't help it." Beth felt a real sense of helplessness and fear that something was wrong. It was not helpful her to be told not to feel that way. It made her feel even less in control and more certain that things were not alright.

Before becoming a mother, a woman may have many ideas about what kind mother she wants to be. These ideas usually grow from how she was parented and what worked for her and what truly did not work. As a child, she might have recalled saying to herself, "when I grow up, I'm never going to treat my kids like that." These images can often be deeply ingrained and may not surface again until she actually does become a mother herself and until she is confronted with the same situations in reverse and she remembers, often painfully, what it was like for her growing up.

For Xena, this question of what kind of mother she wanted to be came from her reflections about the experience of stubbornly "setting your jaw" that she had while standing by Wesley's crib. In her description, she asked herself, "Why would I keep doing this to him?" She continued: "I even felt guilty about being so intent on the naps, complaining about it, getting upset when he would wake up, yet again, after twenty-five minutes.... Why did I need to focus on the one thing that was not working? ... I don't want to be one of those moms—or one of those people—who always focus on the negative."

In our conversation, Xena spoke about her own struggle to clearly define and separate her own identity from her mother's. The question of what kind of mother she wanted to be was a central one because of the focus in her adolescence on what was not working. In focusing, Xena discovered a different kind of "heartache" connection to Wesley, different from the kind of guilt she had known, which was dependent on manipulation. This kind of guilt felt more positive and productive for Xena because it was not a coercive means to change her son to fit her needs but rather a way to highlight her ability to be responsive to his needs.

Conclusion

Mothers in general and new mothers in particular bear the weight of vast expectations about what a mother is. Becoming a mother represents one of the most sudden and dramatic developmental shifts that anyone can experience. Because there is no way to truly prepare, experience and emotions become the first real on the job training. Guilt has an important place in the human emotional repertoire, but it is often difficult to talk about. It is not something to be merely overcome, ignored, or dismissed; rather, it is as an emotion that teaches us something about who we are in relationship to ourselves, to others, and to the world. Mothers tend to live their guilt in isolation, as they are worried how other people would see them and how they would be judged as mothers. The mothers in this research courageously explored their vulnerability in order not only to face own guilt but to create understanding and solidarity with other mothers who often have feelings of ambivalence.

Endnotes

1. All quotes and data in this chapter reflect the work of the author's dissertation research (LeBeau). The overall approach of this research was collaborative in nature, and the primary data of the study consist of first-person experiential written accounts and individual interviews with the participants. The interviews involved three stages: a reading aloud of the participant's written description, a modified embodied reflection stage based on Gendlin's focusing technique, and an open-ended conversational interview. The protocols and the transcribed interviews were interpreted using the procedures outlined by Colaizzi, Giorgi and Giorgi, and Todres.

2. At the time of the interviews, Meg was a partnered twenty-three year-old with a thirteen-month-old son. Beth was a partnered twenty-seven-year-old, with a two-and-half-year-old son. Cam was a partnered twenty-three-year-old, with a two-and-half-month-old-daughter. Xena was a single forty-three-year-old, with a seven-and-a-half-month-old-son. And Ann was partnered thirty-three-year-old, with a one-year-old daughter. All the names for the mothers and the babies are pseudonyms that the mothers chose.

3. Interestingly, both mothers were preoccupied with their babies taking naps in order that they may accomplish their own projects. Naptime is a critical period of separation between mothers and babies,, and it often becomes a point of resistance and impasse throughout childhood. As mentioned in the previous section, separation is both necessary and also very difficult for both mothers and children. A mother's insistence on naptime highlights the importance of this separation as well as the guilt that it inspires.

4. It is possible that Ann's guilt made her feel as though she had completely ignored her daughter's cries. Perhaps, anything but full, undivided attention has an experiential quality of neglect to it.

5. It is important here to note that although Beth's experience of guilt seems dramatic, many women do suffer through immense complications and trauma related to birth experiences, which, in turn, can influence their postpartum experiences with their babies as well.

Works Cited

Collaizzi, Paul. "Psychological Research as the Phenomenologist Views it." *Existential-Phenomenological Alternatives for Psychology*, edited by Ronald Valle and Mark King, Oxford University Press, 1978, pp. 48-71.

De Vaus, June. *Mothers Growing Up: Understanding the Heartaches of Motherhood*. Allen & Unwin, 1992.

Gendlin, Eugene. *Focusing*. Bantam Books, 1981.

Gendlin, Eugene. *Focusing-Oriented Psychotherapy: A manual of the experiential method*. New York: The Guilford Press, 1996.

Giorgi, Amedeo, and Barbro Giorgi. "Descriptive Phenomenological Psychological Method." *Qualitative Research in Psychology : Expanding Perspectives in Methodology and Design*, edited by Paul Marc Camic et al., American Psychological Association, 2003, pp. 243-273.

LeBeau, Claire. "Maternal Guilt: An Existential Phenomenological Study of the Early Experiences of First-time Mothers." Dissertation. Duquesne University, 2013.

Todres, Les. *Embodied Enquiry: Phenomenological Touchstones for Research, Psychotherapy, and Spirituality*. Palgrave Macmillan, 2007.

Chapter Nine

Meta-Helicopter Parenting: Ambivalence in a Neoliberal World

Talia Welsh

It has become commonplace to attack helicopter parenting as producing an endless array of social and individual woes. Young children who are coddled and scheduled all day fail to learn to play on their own and do not develop the basic cognitive skills to master self-control. As college-aged students, they are anxious, depressed, and afraid of basic life decisions because of their overinvolved parents. In an article in *The Atlantic*, helicopter parents are even to blame for individuals taking offense too easily and using their emotion, instead of reason, as sufficient grounds for lawsuits against teachers and professors (Lukianoff and Haidt).

This chapter challenges the story that helicopter parenting is a result of a loss of a mythical bygone past when parenting was easier and natural. It examines what is prescribed as antihelicopter parenting and finds it is just as intensive and historically situated as helicopter parenting. The solution offered to helicopter parenting is a rigorous disciplinary project on the part of the parents—what I term "meta-helicopter parenting." This task of correct parenting falls largely to mothers who are encouraged to make the right choices for the child's success. In academic and popular discussions on parenting, one finds little consideration of parental ambivalence and how to discern between existential and situational ambivalence. Existential ambivalence is inherent in parenting; parenting styles are different means of reaching provisionary and incomplete solutions, whereas situational ambivalence is due to unjust social structures that cannot be ameliorated by individuals choosing the right choice. The "best choices model" of human success embodied in contemporary neoliberal thinking obscures situational ambivalence by encouraging the view that by making the right parenting choices, parents can produce good futures for their children. Such a view obscures how our lives are always deeply shaped by institutions who can only be meaningfully changed at the social and political level—such as the quality of public education—and not at the individual choice level. To address situational ambivalence in parenting requires forgoing the model of "best parenting" and opting for cooperative, political solutions.

Helicopter Parents

The term "helicopter parent" can be attributed first to Haim Ginott's *Between Parent & Teenager,* in which a teenager describes her parents as "hovering" over her "like a helicopter." It is most commonly cited as originating in the parent training text by Foster W. Cline and Jim Fay—*Parenting with Love and Logic: Teaching Children Responsibility*—in which the authors directly use the term "helicopter parent." Subsequently, the term helicopter parenting has become synonymous with the term "overparenting"; I use the term "helicopter parenting" in this chapter.

Helicopter parenting is understood to be parents who are highly involved their children's lives to the point of planning the vast majority of their time, following and controlling all schoolwork and activities, and even continuing such intrusive care when their children go to college. Helicopter parents see their behaviour as beneficial and caring for the child and, hence, are often resistant to restraining their involvement. Of particular interest for this chapter is the discussion around emerging adults. The developmental stage called "emerging adults" is attributed to the delayed onset of fully independent living in industrialized countries for a variety of economic and social reasons (Arnett). Spanning roughly from eighteen to twenty-five, emerging adults would be young adults who were often in college or recently graduated but who are still not fully independent.

The press has reported variations on the problems of helicopter parenting. One example of a fairly typical, dire proclamation regarding its effects can be found in Kathleen Vision's article:

> An epidemic is running rampant in schools—helicopter parents landing on higher education institutions. "Helicopter parenting" is a term used to describe a phenomenon of a growing number of parents, obsessed with their children's success and safety, who vigilantly hover over them, sheltering them from mistakes, disappointment, or risks, insulating them from the world around them. (424)

These texts are addressed to those who may be inclined to helicopter parenting or who are self-consciously concerned with their children's performance and wellbeing (Lahey et al. Tabatsky; Lythcott-Haims). In the next section, these texts against helicopter parenting are analyzed to be merely different styles of overparenting rather than books about the cessation of helicopter parenting as promised.

Despite the vague but insistent fear that contemporary parenting styles are too involved, academic research regarding intensive parenting styles typically demonstrates a positive correlation between the wellbeing of children and emerging adults, and a high level of parental support, responsiveness, and involvement. The question becomes, as Laura Padilla-Walker and Larry Nelson ask, "Given that involvement, protection, affection, etc. tend to be aspects of 'good' parenting, it leads to question of when and whether a parent can give too much of a 'good' thing" (1178). What they have found is that helicopter parenting does often include involvement but also involves the parents permitting their children few autonomous activities. It is the lack of autonomy—not involvement—that is negatively correlated with healthy development. Various studies on the emerging adults of helicopter parents have found that autonomy-limiting parenting is related to lower wellbeing, lower performance, lower success in school, and higher drug use (LeMoyne and Buchanan 412-15). Daniel van Ingen et al. found that low self-efficacy was common for emerging adults with helicopter parents. The idea of the importance of self-efficacy comes from Albert Bandura's work and is defined as an individual's ability to execute behaviours that are tied to specific kinds of performance—say, in the case of an emerging adult, the capacity to organize one's time and effort in order to do well in a university course.

Establishing productive social bonds is also seen as a challenge for children of helicopter parents. Van Ingen et al. also discovered that emerging adults with helicopter parents had more difficulty with peer attachment. Padilla-Walker and Nelson argue that their studies and others indicate that the involvement of helicopter parents is a cautionary tale—a theory that dovetails with the alarming anecdotal stories filling the pages of popular press works on overparenting.

Overall, the concern with helicopter parenting is that emerging adults are poorly prepared to take up their independence due to smothering parents, whose concern for their children's happiness actually makes it more difficult for children to find fulfilling independent lives. Thus, the concern and care have an inhibiting effect on development rather than, as one may assume, a positive effect. Although Kayla Reed et al. point out that sometimes it is, of course, beneficial to monitor and aid one's children, they also highlight the importance of self-efficacy and autonomy. They argue that one wants "autonomy supportive parents," which are parents who "are involved in their child's life, but consider the child's perspective and act in ways that encourage the child's independence and ability to solve their own problems" (3137).

Academic research on helicopter parenting is in its infancy and has failed to provide clear definitions of what helicopter parenting is, how to track it, and whether or not its negative impact is similar across racial, gender, and class lines. Important nuances have yet to be discerned. For instance, Larry Nelson et al. found that "lower levels of self-worth and higher levels of risk behaviours" (284) were found in children with helicopter parenting styles, but only in those who reported low maternal warmth. They further report that "increased helicopter parenting was associated with lower levels of risk behaviour for those who reported that their mothers exhibit higher levels of warmth" (284). Such a study makes it unclear if overinvolvement is really a problem or only a certain kind of helicopter parenting. In a supporting study, Reed et al. affirm the idea that maternal overparenting in emerging adult males was correlated with wellbeing and success (3146). They also found that overall helicopter parenting was not associated with depression or directly predicative of mental health and life satisfaction, even if it did seem to negatively affect self-efficacy (3144).

Many of these studies appeal to the idea that such parenting styles do not begin with the emerging adult but starts early in upbringing. One common discussion is to suggest that serious developmental disorders may results from overparenting. Studies on "executive functioning" in young children demonstrate that self-efficacy seems to be related to children's ability to learn how to regulate their play and moods independently (Barker et al.). The less time young children are permitted to spend with unstructured time, the less they develop higher-order executive control. That is, young children whose parents monitor every moment and provide structured adult-led activities to develop young children produce young adults who struggle with the most basic of life skills—self-regulation. Self-regulation is essential to delaying pleasure, surviving discomfort, and organizing behaviour to achieve the complex, long-term projects of adults.

Popular parenting manuals conjecture that emerging adults need more self-directed experiences, prior to college, through which they can succeed and fail without parental interference. These manuals start with a smattering of research, such as those referenced above, provide many anecdotes, and then conclude with general guidelines for better parenting. Julie Lythcott-Haims' *How to Raise an Adult: Break Free of the Overparenting Trap and Prepare Your Kid for Success* is filled with stories: "Take, for example, the mother of a Beverly Hills high schooler who insisted her son text her hourly on his way to and from a beach outing with his friends.... Or the Stanford parents who contacted the university to say he thought his daughter was missing because he hadn't heard from her in over a day" (14). Lythcott-Haims argues that overparenting produces adults who function like children, who are unable to solve basic problems or negotiate stressful interpersonal situations without help. In another example, she writes the following" "Bruce is from Chicago. His son Nicolas is a college junior at a private college in the Big Ten. Bruce is a finance executive in Chicago whose phone often buzzes multiple times a day with texts from Nicholas" (48). We, the reader, subsequently find out that this parenting style has produced a seemingly dysfunctional man-child. Nicholas, who has managed to make it to a "Big Ten" university, goes to New York City, exits a subway, and finds himself lost. Instead of independently problem solving this pretty simple issue, he texts his father who exits a meeting to look up a map and help him figure out where he is (48).

One of the most important features of such texts is the theme of a halcyon past, in which parenting was simple and natural, and children were permitted freedoms they no longer are today. This lost past, though, can be recovered: children can relearn tools, such as grit, self-determination, and importantly, the ability to do things independently if one applies the ideas the various books present. For example, Sam, in George S. Glass and David Tabatsky's *The Overparenting Epidemic*, waxes nostalgic about his childhood of minimal supervision, how he rode his bike and played sports with his friends unattended: "From what I gather, my childhood was similar to my parents, and their parents' too. It was simple and real and uncomplicated" (1).This is a common trope of such books. After we enjoy some Schadenfreude reading about parents who are bizarrely overinvolved in their children's life and then the attendant guilt wondering if we engage in similar, if a little less dramatic, behaviours, we are reminded of a better past and encouraged with a series of usually quite mild suggestions about how to achieve a less-involved parenting style.

For instance, Jessica Lahey's *The Gift of Failure* largely focuses on pre-college-aged children and provides helpful guidelines about how to "praise for effort, not for inherent qualities" (68). She argues that the American obsession with talent tends to deemphasize work and struggle, thereby leading children (and adults) to assume that failure is a sign of "not having it" rather than part of normal progress. She also gives advice at negotiating with a child's teacher to avoid the kind of manic, intrusive parenting that makes teachers exhausted and children anxious (181-221). This includes being aware that the truth "is slippery" even if one trusts one's children (200). Lythcott-Haims gives us a checklist for skills eighteen-year-olds should be able to master before entering college:

1. talk to strangers
2. find his way around a campus
3. manage assignments, work-load, and deadlines
4. contribute to running of household
5. handle interpersonal problems
6. cope with ups and downs of courses, workloads, competition, tough teachers, bosses and others
7. earn and manage money
8. take risks (172)

As a university educator, I often find my students unwilling to do a modicum of investigation, such as looking at the syllabus, before asking for my aid. I too wish they would acquire more independence in problem solving. However, why do such books appeal to a past? Why not simply point out the value of independent problem solving or free play? The next section discusses how the past is required for the rhetoric of antihelicopter parenting to make sense.

Meta-Helicopter Parenting

The ancient Chinese thinker Mencius has a famous parable to illustrate that humans are innately good. He points out that if a child falls in a well, we will feel distressed without thinking, indicating that we naturally care about the suffering of others. In a parallel example, when holding a friend's baby who suddenly starts to cry, we feel a similar alarm at needing to do something. However, unlike in Mencius's example, what to do is not obvious. Trying to prevent a child from falling in a well or attempting to rescue it is the logical and caring response. When a baby begins to cry the question is—what do I do now? If you have experience with this baby, you may have a sense of what she or he needs. And, of course, there are those who are better at solving the mystery of crying babies, but it is their experience, not simply being human, which guides them. It turns out being human provides one with little inherent knowledge of how to soothe crying babies even if, arguably, being human does provide one with a desire to comfort them. In communal societies with large families living under the same roof, this instruction comes from others. I, like many other contemporary Western parents, spent a good amount of time on the Internet trying to figure how to best parent my baby in the middle of the night. Reading parenting advice seems to provide some help to negotiate the endless unclear situations that arise.

At the beginning of *The Overparenting Epidemic*, after we are reminded of Sam's past, when things were "simple and real and uncomplicated," the authors pick a series of locales in which such real parenting still exists:

Today, in small towns and communities across America, in places such as Bainbridge Island near Seattle, Washington, or L'Anse, Michigan, on the Upper Peninsula, or Cape Cod,

Massachusetts, kids still live like that. Their parents do not have afterschool programs for their kids. Those children go home after school and play for hours, like kids have been doing for decades, largely unsupervised and left alone to be children, surviving on their own devices and left to think for themselves. (1)

As a fictional nostalgic narrative, this move works nicely. We learn not only that was life once simple and real but that there are some places where it still is. One can almost see the Hallmark movie introduction with a soft, folksy song playing while we see rural, white children playing baseball unattended, the mom baking apple pies, and the dad driving his pickup truck home from the farm. Factual it is not. One has to do only a minimal amount of research to find that these locales have numerous organized sports, tutorial services, after-school clubs, and the usual organized activities that populate most middle- and upper-class neighbourhoods. The contemporary omnipresence of video games makes it seem unlikely that the children left on their own to play for hours are always out bike riding like in Sam's past. One cannot fail to be struck by the white, gender-normative, and suburban mythologies of these untroubled days of good parenting and the isolation of exactly such areas as where such good parenting still occurs.

The role of this nostalgia helps fuel the idea that parenting is somehow actually easy and conflict free, and we have lost this capacity in our contemporary situation. If this is so, my ambivalence in parenting and my experience of it being a great amount of confusing effort is a result of something askew in my attitude or behaviour. Once I can get the right approach, then my son can enjoy the real and simple childhood of Sam, and I will enjoy parental freedom. However, the irony of such tales is that what the books actually prescribe is not at all natural or simple but rather a program of parental discipline to provide educational opportunities for children.

As noted above, the term "helicopter parents" originated in the Bible of Montessori education—*Learning with Love and Logic* by Foster Cline and Jim Fay. As parents of a child who has been in strictly run Montessori school for two years, we are constantly encouraged to run our households according to this book. Although it is true that this education does encourage independence and does structure its curriculum around developing natural interests rather than mandated tests, it is by no means part of this nostalgic past where children ran around unattended.

It requires an exhausting amount of effort on the part of the parents and teachers.

Foster and Fay encourage parents to get their eighteen-month-old toddlers to already start participating in chores and attending to basic household tasks, such as taking a plate to the dishwasher. Our son started at three, at which time he was supposed to be able to dress himself, use the potty, wash his hands, put on his coat, zipper it, and participate in household chores. Children should eat well-rounded nonsugar diets and should not have white bread. Children should not spend any more than thirty minutes on tablets or watching TV per day. Children should put away all their own toys. Bedtimes should be rigorously followed. You should not sleep with your child or fall asleep with your child. While many of these guidelines can be defended, and even celebrated, they are quite taxing to enact. Would you like to add an additional, stressful hour to your morning before you squeeze in everything that must be done in a work day? Monitor, but not too closely, a toddler dressing himself. Then if he fails to do so, take him crying to school in his pajamas, with his clothes in his bag after telling him kindly, but clearly, that there will be no more time. Do not give in even if the child turns red with frustration and cries like his heart will break. This is what is called "natural consequences." I see nothing particularly natural or even traditional about such an upbringing. What is more natural than co-sleeping? Why wouldn't I naturally want to stop the distress of a child I love more than anything? If I'm late to work, what comes naturally is to put the dishes in the dishwasher myself and dress my child, not patiently stand by while a three-year-old puts his plate in the dishwasher and dresses himself making me late and him frustrated.

Like many other parents, I undergo a certain amount of ambivalence at such discipline on my part. I understand the value of such an education, but it requires constant self-control and an extensive amount of time. Not to mention Montessori is expensive. My husband and I have schedules (as we do not need second jobs) and an income that permit us, on most days, to work towards a home where we all participate in chores, eat largely healthy food, and obtain regular sleep. I cannot imagine doing so with an additional job, a job with longer hours, as a single parent, with more children, or on a more limited budget. The cruelty of the past myth is the idea that if it isn't simple and natural for you, you are doing it wrong. The discipline required by parents to provide worlds where children learn healthy, independent life skills are indicative of what I term "meta-helicopter parenting." If the helicopter parent is giving in to an uncritical desire for their child's betterment emboldened by current parenting norms and social class, meta-helicopter parents are strictly regulating our behaviour to provide artificial situations in which our children—because we care—can learn the skill of independence.

Sometimes the depictions of the past evoke a time in which kids were unsupervised and parents were free to enjoy themselves with adult time. But, of course, they were unsupervised in safe environments. If the parent left them at home while he or she worked, in a place where drugs were being dealt, or when there wasn't sufficient food to eat, we wouldn't consider this "simple and real and uncomplicated," we would consider it neglect. In terms of child mistreatment, 695,000 cases average occur each year in the U.S. (Pecora et al., 321). Of this, 78.3 per cent suffered neglect. One wishes to ask, when is leaving children alone "simple and real and uncomplicated" and when is it child abuse? If one reads the proposals, it is clear that one isn't advocating a return to a past of benign or harmful neglect but rather a pattern of management of parental behaviour to produce successful children. These breezy mythical pasts of children figuring out their own battles and riding bikes are not the children figuring out their own battles in a meth home or figuring out how to deal with not having enough to eat or not having clean clothes for school. So one can allow for natural consequences in the good neighbourhood by letting them play on the playground unsupervised but not in the bad neighborhood, where they are hurt on the way home.

After all, the subtitle of Lythcott-Haims's book is *Break Free of the Overparenting Trap and Prepare Your Kid for Success.* Note the importance of the verb "prepare." This is a book of activities for parents—not a book about not paying much attention to your children. The book's advertisement clearly stresses that she was former dean of freshman and undergraduate advising at *Stanford.* She writes consolingly to parents obsessed with university rankings and their children's grade point averages. The second half of the book is filled with information on having a better take on the admissions craze, some guidance on the problems of the *U.S. News and World Report*'s ranking of universities, and suggestions for universities that don't make rank and test scores central. Thus, what we are being taught by her isn't to just let our children, and now emerging adults, do whatever but to cultivate the right understanding of true measurements of success and then engage in the right behaviours. As a training manual, its core argument is that helicopter parents produced the wrong product—sad, unsuccessful, dependent adults. It does not claim that hypermanagement itself is problematic, just that a certain kind of hypermanagement is wrong.

Blaming Mothers

What is clear in these texts is the idea that it is the parents who need management in order to provide the proper care for children. The meta-helicopter parenting myth suggests if your child is on drugs, anxious, or unsuccessful, you didn't create a world of independent learning and now your failure of a child has no self-efficacy. As our Montessori principle tells us in parent-teacher meetings—these years are the ones in which the brain is developing, so we must work to make sure we create a world in which it develops properly. I never fail to leave these meetings worrying about how we, with some frequency, eat pizza and ice cream and watch TV instead of spending time at night teaching independent life skills. Am I ruining my child's brain? What about when I gave in and fell asleep with him violating the "he must learn to sleep on his own" principle?

The industrialized West, wherein increasingly children are luxury goods for the wealthy, has a long set of narratives in which parents create success. Of course, if we create successful children, we must likewise be to blame for unsuccessful ones. Sigmund Freud wrote extensively on how loving gestures in mothering—such as fondling, hugging, and kissing—form the basis of future psycho-sexual development. He argues that mothers should not be upset at such a "sexual" future for these innocent gestures. They should see it as part of normal development: Moreover, if the mother understood more of the high importance of the part played by the instincts [Triebe] in mental life as a whole—in all its ethics and psychical achievements—she would spare herself any self-reproaches even after her enlightenment" ("Three Essays" 125). I should, therefore, be happy in my loving attitude towards my son. However, I should not underestimate the importance of performing this role correctly. Freud also argues, in a discussion of Daniel Paul Schreber, that paranoid delusions are a result of homosexual fantasies that arose in early childhood that have not been properly rechanneled ("Psycho-analytic").

Perhaps the most devastating attack on bad mothering took place when Leo Kanner and Bruno Bettleheim argued that autism was the result of highly educated intellectual parents who were emotionally distant. Bruno Bettleheim's *The Empty Fortress: Infantile Autism and the Birth of the Self* blamed mothers of autistic children, likening them to Nazi guards. We can see contemporary versions of this discussion in discourses that emphasize mothers should breastfeed, should not smoke, and should avoid alcohol; in its most extreme form, such discourses advise incarcerating pregnant women who fail to care properly for their fetuses. Contemporary versions of mother blaming find their fuel largely upon scientific studies about care for the child in utero as well as in developmental studies. Although Bettleheim's work is dismissed as harmful and simply inaccurate about autism's origins, the basic formulation—children's problems must be due to problem parenting— still pervades many of our cultural ideologies.

The belief persists that mothers in particular are to blame for bad outcomes (Richardson et al.). After all, if science says you should breastfeed, what kind of perverse and amoral monster are you if you fail to do so simply because you don't like it? As parents, we are inevitably ambivalent in some of our decisions. This ambivalence springs both from the situation in which mothers find themselves and from existential difficulties that may be inherent to parenting. Understanding ambivalent feelings that pervade mothering requires reflection, not simply more research to determine what the right behaviour is. Sarah LaChance Adams evocatively discusses how maternal ambivalence is not something that is a sign of perversity but a sign that one should reflect upon the ambivalence itself and what it may indicate about the need to care for parents as well:

> These mixed feelings—passionate rage, love, profound boredom, ecstasy, and so on—are not mere reactions. They contain wisdom of their own that tells us what is going on in a given situation and they act as forces that can bind as well as liberate.... Rather than suppressing these lessons, we need to turn them over in our minds and conversations. It is time we realized, on a broad cultural scale, that if we care for the well-being of children we must care for the well-being of their caregivers. (70)

LaChance Adams argues that mothers do not just devote themselves to children because of social norms but because it is easier for them to give up their freedom: "Indeed, maternal devotion is the most culturally glorified escape from freedom for women. It provides a false release from the risks of having one's own projects and facing their potential failure and futility" (178). The devotion that pervades both helicopter parenting meta-helicopter parenting is due certainly to true affection, but such parenting is also a way to escape having to think carefully about one's situation and all of the aspects of one's social world that may demand attention.

Yet if one throws such larger concerns aside and in bad faith focuses solely on a child's success, one finds that success is difficult and complex to obtain. Even if one understands this idea in the most reductive of contemporary fashions—economic success—that too is a path directly threatened at every turn by an interconnected global economy far beyond anyone's control or comprehension. Johanna Oksala points out the manner in which neoliberalism has reduced all of our human endeavours to the calculus of commerce: "social practice and policy—not only economic policy—must be submitted to economic profitability analyses and organized according to the principles of competition" (140). The discussions of economic success and college admittance in the meta-helicopter parenting books work within this paradigm. Indeed, the idea of your children as investments is backed by a study that argues parents were more likely to engage in overparenting if they were paying for college (Lowe et al.). Scholarship recipients had less hyperinvolved parents, suggesting that parents want to protect their financial investment.

In this framework, success is impossible to secure, since it is constantly threatened. To quote Marx and Engels, the neoliberal ideology "has left remaining no other nexus between man and man than naked self-interest, than callous cash payment" (475). How does one achieve financial success as a personal project? How many constant threats to this project await? At any moment, even if the most recent battle is won, future combat awaits. The success of another is even more difficult to secure. Devoting oneself to one's child's success can easily eclipse all other projects in life. One's child will do well, but each good performance, each time he or she seems above average, will likely also produce anxieties about maintaining this precarious success. When the child does poorly, even more effort must be extended to support her. The more one can fit other demands, other projects, and other situations within the socially normalized desire to do what is best for the child, the more one can avoid considering the broader social structure that broadcasts these ideas of success.

A refusal to consider ambivalence pervades parenting ideologies today. If a parent has mixed feelings about parenting within contemporary life, the myth of an easy past promises a straightforward solution: realign to the "natural" style of parenting. Of course, in reality, to be this natural requires knowledge, self-discipline, and careful strategizing. If I find myself feeling ambivalent about my son's school, the dominant ideology indicates that I should work on these feelings just as I would work on a paper I am writing. My child, as an extension of me, is also a project and by careful attention to studies about the right styles of education and upbringing, I can increasingly make him perfect. No one wants to be a helicopter parent, once one learns what that is. Once I start to see his achievement in independence results from our parental discipline, I can congratulate myself and judge those whose children do not display the same kinds of self-efficacy.

The dominant neoliberal idea of the self as a project clouds thinking about structural situations, indicating that we should focus on personal-familial situations that can be individually improved. I can work on my son's soccer skills, the proper grip on his pencil, and his independence. The more I focus on what I can choose to do alone, the less I focus on what I need others' help to achieve. Johanna Oksala writes the following: "The idea of personal choice effectively masks the systemic aspects of power—domination, social hierarchies, economic exploitation—by relegating to subjects the freedom to choose between different options while denying them any real possibility for defining or shaping those options" (125). A neoliberal system would have us believe that success depends on individual effort and talents, meaning responsibility lies entirely with the individual (or the individual's parents). Political solutions are unnecessary. As my students often say—you can do anything you set your mind to! For those who believe in the fairytale of unrestricted choice, self-government and self-management are the preeminent political messages, especially if they appear to promise success.

As LaChance Adams writes, an alternative to the glossing over of ambivalence is to consider conflicting feelings not as problems to be solved but as a sign of the need for thoughtful reflection. In many cases, these considerations will bring to light how we are individually situated within our most pressing contemporary issues, such as environmental degradation, the collapse of the middle class, endless warfare, poverty, and the ruin of public education in poor neighbourhoods. These are structural problems in the social edifice that individual solutions will not resolve. Paradoxically, however, the difficulty of resolving them leads many to cling to neoliberal ideology with more fervour than before. For example, the solution proposed to failing public schools in the U.S. is to give people more choices by allowing parents to use vouchers to opt out of low performing schools. Instead of engaging in collaborative work to improve schools for the long term for everyone, one is told to remove one's children from bad schools and send them to private school or better public schools.

The question—what is the right parenting style?—occurs in this vacuum of neoliberal choice. In the face of academic studies and popular press manuals exhorting us, as parents and educators, to facilitate the best environment for emerging adult success, little space exists for questioning this individual approach, in which each child or emerging adult is seen as a product of proper choices. The academic studies on overparenting lead me, as an educator and a parent, to worry about what is best for these students with low self-efficacy, risky behaviour, and depression. But, of course, I also wonder if such behaviours and moods are not necessarily indicative of something wrong with the students and their lack of taking up their limited choices with independence—this major or that major, this job or that. This is a concern that should be reflected on more seriously. Just as LaChance Adams calls upon us to think about maternal ambivalence, perhaps we should think about emerging adult ambivalence. We live in a world of endless war, divisive politics, racism, radical environmental change, and decreasing opportunities for the working and middle classes. Perhaps depression is not a result of not having enough self-determination, or bad parenting, but a result of the larger situation that cannot be solved by individual choice models.

In conclusion, critical discussions of helicopter parenting are often simply variations on the same theme—parental behaviour management. Such critiques use the myth of an easy, natural past to cover the fact that they are actually parental disciplinary tracks not different in kind but merely in style from helicopter parenting. They exploit the very real existential difficulties of parenting and offer cheap relief. If we are knowledgeable, disciplined, and make the right choices, then our children's success and conflict-free happiness will fall into place. Neoliberalism supports the myth that we have personal control over our lives, ignoring critical sociopolitical issues and obscuring difficulties that no choice could alleviate. It is a thoroughly unambiguous worldview. LaChance Adams draws our attention towards the struggles of mothers, not to blame them, but to point out how failure, ambivalence, and confusion are permanent and necessary parts of ethical life: "Recognizing the prevalence of ethical ambivalence means we cannot so easily dismiss, pathologize, or demonize those who fail" (195).

Feminist accounts of parenting need to discuss both structural and existential issues, as well as their intertwining. Certain problems must be addressed collectively. The social goods that these efforts produce— such as quality public education, environmentally sustainable living, and a truly democratic and inclusive society—are of value to everyone. Even if one's child continues at private schools, the need for a world of educated persons capable of taking up their own freedom remains integral to his future success and happiness. As LaChance Adams notes, "the exercise of one's freedom depends on others," particularly the case of any projects I wish to engage in (159). I need others as audiences, as collaborators, and as continuers of my most vital projects. Thus, they must not just live but thrive. This existentialist view of freedom, as dependent on the freedom of others and therefore integral with ethics, restructures what we see as lives worth living—away from the narrow, and I would think rather unfulfilling, model of individual cost-benefit analysis.

The neoliberal model would have us take on children as personal projects, which may succeed or fail. But this relationship is fundamentally different from an economic investment or a personal wager; it is ethical. This means that the outcome is not ours to achieve. What we can do, in anticipation of our children's futures, is to strive with others to create a world in which everyone can thrive. Children, as both transcendent and immanent beings, are headed towards their own successes and failure that their parents cannot anticipate. As Simone de Beauvoir writes in *Ethics of Ambiguity*, "So it is with any activity; failure and success are two aspects of reality which at the start are not perceptible" (129). For all of these reasons, perhaps all parents are doomed to fail. Nevertheless, it is in the cracks of our attempts to perfectly shape our children that they can flourish in their own ways.

Works Cited

Arnett, Jeffrey. *Emerging Adulthood: The Winding Road from Late Teens through the Twenties.* Oxford University Press, 2004.

Barker, J. E., et al. "Less-Structured Time in Children's Daily Lives Predicts Self-Directed Executive Functioning." *Frontiers in Psychology,* vol. 5, 2014, pp. 1-16.

Bandura, Albert. "Self-efficacy: Toward a Unifying Theory of Behavioral Change." *Psychological Review,* vol. 84, no. 2, 1993, pp. 191-215.

Beauvoir, Simone de. *Ethics of Ambiguity.* Translated by Bernard Frechtman. Citadel Press, 1976.

Bettleheim, Bruno. *The Empty Fortress: Infantile Autism and the Birth of the Self.* Free Press, 1972.

Cline, Foster W., and Jim Fay. *Parenting with Love and Logic: Teaching Children Responsibility.* Pinon Press, 1990.

Ginott, Haim. *Between Parent & Teenager.* Macmillan, 1969.

Glass, George S., and David Tabatsky. *The Overparenting Epidemic: Why Helicopter Parenting Is Bad for Your Kids ... and Dangerous for You, Too!:* Skyhorse Publishing, 2015.

Freud, Sigmund. "Psycho-analytic Notes on an Autobiographical Account of a Case of Paranoia (Dementia paranoides)." *The Standard Edition of the Complete Psychological Works of Sigmund Freud,* vol. 12, edited by James Strachey, Hogarth and the Institute of Psycho-Analysis, 1953, pp. 1-82.

Freud, Sigmund. "Three Essays on the Theory of Sexuality." *The Standard Edition of the Complete Psychological Works of Sigmund Freud,* vol. 7, edited by James Strachey, Hogarth and the Institute of Psycho-Analysis, 1953, pp. 125-245.

LaChance Adams, Sarah. *Mad Mothers, Bad Mothers, & What a "Good" Mother Would Do.* Columbia University Press, 2104.

Lahey, Jessica. *The Gift of Failure: How the Best Parents Learn to Let Go so Their Children Can Succeed.* Harper Collins, 2015.

LeMoyne, Terri, and Tom Buchanan. "Does 'Hovering' matter? Helicopter Parenting and Its Effect on Well-Being." *Sociological Spectrum*, vol. 31, no. 4, 2011, pp. 399-418.

Lowe, Katie, et al. "'If I Pay, I Have a Say!': Parental Payment of College Education and Its Association with Helicopter Parenting." *Emerging Adulthood*, vol. 3, no. 4, 2015, pp. 286-290.

Lukianoff, Greg and Jonathan Haidt. "The Coddling of the American Mind." *The Atlantic*, Sept. 2015, www.theatlantic.com/magazine/archive/2015/09/the-coddling-of-the-american-mind/399356/. Accessed 12 Dec. 2019.

Lythcott-Haims, Julie. *How to Raise an Adult: Break Free of the Overparenting Trap and Prepare Your Kid for Success.* Henry Holt, 2015.

Nelson, Larry J., et al. "Is Hovering Smothering or Loving? An Examination of Parental Warmth as a Moderator of Relations between Parenting and Emerging Adults' Indices of Adjustment." *Emergent Adulthood*, vol. 3, no. 4, 2015, pp. 282-85.

Marx, Karl, and Friedrich Engels. "Manifesto of the Communist Party." *Marx-Engels Reader*, edited by Robert C. Tucker, WW Norton, 1978, pp. 469-500.

Oksala, Johanna. *Feminist Experiences: Foucauldian and Phenomenological Investigations*, Northwestern University Press, 2016.

Padilla-Walker, Laura M., and Larry J. Nelson. "Black Hawk Down? Establishing Helicopter Parenting as a Distinct Construct from Other Forms of Parental Control during Emerging Adulthood." *Journal of Adolescence*, vol. 35, 2012, pp. 1177-90.

Reed, Kayla, et al. "Helicopter Parenting and Emergent Adult Self-Efficacy: Implications for Mental and Physical Health." *Journal of Child and Family Studies*, vol. 25, 2016, pp. 3136-49.

Richardson, Sarah S., et al.. "Society: Don't Blame the Mothers." *Nature*, 2014, www.nature.com/news/society-don-t-blame-the-mothers-1.15693. Accessed 7 Dec. 2019.

van Ingen, Daniel, J., et al. "Helicopter Parenting: The Effect of an Overbearing Caregiving Style on Peer Attachment and Self-Efficacy." *Journal of College Counseling*, vol. 18, 2015, pp. 7-30.

Vision, Kathleen. "Hovering Too Close: The Ramifications of Helicopter Parenting in Higher Education." *Georgia State University Law Review*, vol. 29, no. 2, 2013, pp. 423-52.

Chapter Ten

Sustainable Ambivalence

Kate Parsons

In the summer of 2015, I was presented with the opportunity of a lifetime. A colleague of mine secured a Fulbright-Hays group travel award to Brazil—one of the places I had always dreamed of visiting—and invited me to join her on a five-week, seven-city excursion. The grant, designed for U.S. educators to study the opportunities for and obstacles to environmentally sustainable practices, fit beautifully with my work on environmental ethics. My heart leapt upon receipt of the invitation.

But, almost simultaneously, it ached. Before becoming a mother, I would have signed on without hesitation; travel excites me and motivates me as few other things do. As a kid, I would feign sleep at bedtime, waiting for the moment my door closed so I could browse travel books with a flashlight. My favourite memoirs are stories of women who have trekked solo in places utterly foreign to them. I love the feel of new languages on my tongue, of cracks emerging in my comfort zones, of the peace that comes with learning how to be contentedly disoriented, and then, as Anaïs Nin suggests, of savouring it all again[1]—curling up with a journal and writing down what I've seen, heard, felt. And this—five weeks! Seven cities! The trip included excursions through the Amazon rainforest and an opportunity to attend lectures near the beaches of Rio de Janeiro. My imagination whirled with exoticized images—of piranhas and river dolphins and futebol and samba—and then suddenly vaporized. My kids. In place of Brazilian simulacra, their faces popped into view. I would be away from their kissable cheeks, their muscly little arms hugging me tight before bed, the sparkle in their eyes when new discoveries rocked their world. Five weeks... I could Skype with them, and my partner is an excellent parent who would care for them beautifully. But this still felt like pushing it; five weeks was too long to be away from bedtime stories and boo-boos that needed kissing and training wheels that were just about to come off. My eyes welled up at the thought of them wanting me, needing me, and crying softly without my arms around them.

Of course, nothing monumental was at stake, and this was no tragic decision: to go or to stay was not a dilemma brought on by a war I was fleeing or heading into, and this was not a life-supporting job that I was taking or leaving. No one's livelihood was at stake, and I couldn't even claim (in good conscience, anyway) that this trip was absolutely necessary to my professional development as a professor. Whether to accept or decline was what my students guiltily call a "First World problem." So I resolved just to suck it up, regretfully decline, and not mourn this not-a-problem problem.

For days, though, I couldn't send the email with my regrets. I wasn't quite willing to let it go, and couldn't quite see myself as someone who would let this go. I was captivated by the potential to be one of the solo-trekking women in the memoirs I had loved, and I couldn't reconcile this with good motherhood. Good mothers stay with their children. Good mothers don't abandon their kids for their work, let alone go trekking three thousand miles away without sufficient reason. Good mothers are there for their kids, meaning they don't go. Good mothers, I told myself, would decline, knowing all the while that a good mother did not quite capture what I wanted to be.

Serendipitously, I didn't have to send that email. As if by the hand of a feminist fairy godmother,[2] my colleague offered to let my kids and partner come on the trip, as long as all of their expenses were on our dime and my partner could take care of the kids during the lectures and lessons I would attend. Having spent many years navigating international travel with her now-grown sons, my colleague's offer to bring my family came from her own academic struggles and successes while navigating her professorship with young ones in tow.[3] Other factors helped the dilemma dissolve as well: I had just won a teaching award that came with a large no-strings-attached cash prize,[4] which could cover the family's travel expenses and make up for my partner's (a self-employed contractor with schedule flexibility) loss of income for the month. A colleague in the department was willing take over my duties as department chair for the summer, and my kids would be out of school. With all of these things in place, the timing and circumstances simply could not have been better. So I said yes, barely able to contain my enthusiasm.

As we prepared for the trip, I adopted a kind of tunnel-vision optimism in the face of friends' and family's concerns: yes, the kids were only three and six, and the three-year-old may not even remember the experience. Yes, their routines would go out the window, as we would be moving hotel rooms every three or four days. Yes, there was a risk they may cause annoyance by slowing down the group. Yes, we would end up logging thirteen thousand miles of air travel, which would surely exhaust us all. But this would be a life-changing experience, I told them (and myself). What better way to help our kids broaden their horizons and comprehend the contingencies of their own cultures? When would an opportunity like this ever come again? I ignored those who stared at me blankly and focused my attention on those who nodded in assent. We could do this; we were doing this.

Throughout the five weeks, my partner and I told ourselves repeatedly that we had made the right decision. Ours kids were surrounded by thirteen educators, ages ranging from mid-twenties to early sixties, who quickly became adopted nieces and granddaughters to a range of loving and generous people. The kids' periodic grumpiness was eased more quickly when consolation came from someone other than their parents, and when their legs got tired (a feeling they learned to feign too quickly), there were multiple offers to carry them for a while. My worries that the kids would prove to be a burden on the group lessened as I watched them give academics who were strangers to one another an excuse to express childlike wonder and to provide distraction and cuddles when the adults needed it themselves.

The kids were having the time of their lives, and my partner and I were, too. Yet there were plenty of moments when I still felt ambivalent about their presence—when they simply would not try a new food, when a good intellectual conversation was interrupted by an urgent need for the potty, when it was clear that the potential for a tantrum was too great to risk joining the group for the 9:00 p.m. theatre performance. At times, I wished I had come alone, but I could barely acknowledge this ambivalence to myself. I was so grateful for the opportunity to be there, for everyone's kindness to my kids as well as for the privileges that made the whole thing possible in the first place that I couldn't quite make sense of the fact that I also longed to be free—free from picky eating, slow walking, whiny talking, and early bedtimes. Any ambivalence, even kept to myself, seemed illegitimate.

Until it got a little stronger. As the trip progressed, there were more opportunities for adult experiences that I resented having to miss: hikes that were too long and too difficult for preschool legs, a boat trip under Iguaçu Falls that would have been too cold and intense, and excursions that required longer bus rides than could be managed without a bathroom break. Tired of telling them not to whine when I wanted to as well, I started to whine to myself: I wanted to go on the hikes, I wanted to go exploring, and I wanted to join everyone for after-hours drinks. Maternal ambivalence was moving from a simmer into a slow boil.[5]

One night, when my resentment was running high but there was absolutely nothing I could do about it—the kids had fallen asleep the minute they flopped onto the hotel beds and it was clear we would have to stay grounded for the night—I took a long bath and tried to think it through. And as I relaxed, it dawned on me that the kids may not be the only ones who needed more rest. If I were being perfectly honest, my own agitation and resentment might have been enhanced by the fact that I was burning the candle at both end and that I had had little down time to take care of myself as well. I was so focused on seeing everything, doing everything, and experiencing everything that turning down any opportunity for more seemed like a waste—a failure to get the most out of the trip. When I took a good look in the metaphorical (and hotel bathroom) mirror, I was tired and needed to slow down. And in the midst of my resentment of the kids, it struck me that a little bit of self-care wouldn't be such a bad thing.

In her fascinating book *Mad Mothers, Bad Mothers, & What a "Good" Mother Would Do: The Ethics of Ambivalence*, Sarah LaChance Adams argues that when one views maternal ambivalence as a "phenomenon to be understood" rather than a "problem to be overcome," we open the door to ambivalence's "potentially positive, creative aspects" (8). LaChance Adams does not romanticize maternal ambivalence in the slightest or gloss over its potential to result in abuse or violence; several of the central examples explored in the book are heartrending examples of mothers who end up abusing and/or killing their kids. But she also notes that moments of maternal ambivalence—ones in which we simultaneously love and want to push away our kids—may give us glimmers of insight into the "fundamental structures of our relationships with others" (8). In her complex analysis of the ways in which mothers in contemporary, Western contexts (though not necessarily limited to these) often find themselves torn between their own needs and desires and those of their children, LaChance Adams claims the importance of recognizing "a world ... where self and other share a relation of interdependent co-origination, yet conflict between self and other can still be made sense of" (5). Following leads offered by Simone de Beauvoir and grounding her work in phenomenological theory, LaChance Adams helps provide insights into the complexities of motherhood, wherein women feel tension not only between themselves and their dependent others but also within themselves about their own identities in relation to their dependents.

Both sorts of tension were, I think, grounding my ambivalence about my kids' presence on the trip. Part of my initial angst about whether to go or stay could be attributed to my feeling—as well as the strong cultural narrative supporting it—that I had to choose between their needs and my own. And when there were aspects of the trip in which a choice actually needed to be made between me and my dependents, this source of the ambivalence became quite clear. Yet a portion of my ambivalence was surely also heightened by conceptions of who a good mother is and its conflicts with feminist consciousness and goals. The "good mother" trope dictates that she always chooses the needs of her kids over her own, but feminists have learned to recognize and identify the ways in which constant self-sacrifice rarely does mothers (or anyone, for that matter) much good. Although my not-a-problem problem was not monumental and came about through much privilege and luck, I suspect I could not write the email with my regrets about not attending the trip because some part of me knew the ambivalence was not mine alone and had larger implications for my personal and political identity as a mother.

Although my personal ambivalence certainly lessened when I was presented with the opportunity to bring the family along—when my desire for travel was not so strongly pitted against my desire for time with them—the ambivalence didn't entirely dissolve, even though both desires were being satisfied. LaChance Adams provides insight into this experience in her analysis of an article by Naomi Wolf and a memoir by Jane Lazzare. Both authors offer narratives of themselves as mothers who "wanting time to themselves ... are also directed against that part of themselves that wants to be with their children" (53). In the descriptions of their feelings, each experiences "a rupture within the woman herself, between her own competing desires, between equally valued parts of herself" (53). This rupture is attributable less to either/ or conflicts between the self (mother) and dependent other (child), and more to a conflict or tension between competing identities, ideals, and narratives we hold for ourselves. LaChance Adams notes the following: "Where women expect to have an independent identity [as a writer, artist, professional, etc.] and yet, as mothers, are fundamentally intertwined with their children, there may be no way to avoid feeling torn" (53).

This helped me make sense of the fact that I would often stare, in awe, at my kids' passports, with their pigtails and shyly-posed smiles, and feel a deep sense of appreciation for having them with me. I acquired my first passport at thirty, not three, and I was overwhelmingly grateful for the opportunities my kids would have to realize dreams I had held as a child—to get glimpses of flora and fauna hitherto seen in story books and to experience that disorienting but delightful feeling of communicating with speakers of different languages. Yet I was also plagued by the nagging annoyance that a large part of what I had always cherished about travel was missing: the alone time, the opportunity to observe a new world around me, to try new foods, hear new music, talk with strangers, and then to retreat into my thoughts and write about it. LaChance Adams writes that "opportunities for self-expression frequently mean hours away from children," (54) and on this trip, it was challenging to reconcile loving both, since it was hard to make all of those things happen at once.

The tensions I was experiencing are not often considered to be ethical ones by mainstream philosophical ethicists in the Western tradition. The struggles of mothers, when internal to the family (private) and not implicated in choices about humanity as a whole (public), are largely rejected as pertaining to philosophy and relegated to the realm of psychology. In her book *The Ethics of Care: Personal, Political, and Global*, Virginia Held highlights the mistakes in such rejection, explaining why evolving feminist work in care ethics has been so important and revolutionary. Leading ethical theories in the Western tradition tend "to interpret moral problems as if they were conflicts between egoistic individual interests on the one hand, and universal moral principles on the other" (12). In contrast:

> The ethics of care ... focuses especially on the area between these extremes. Those who conscientiously care for others are not seeing primarily to further their own *individual* interests; their interests are intertwined with the persons they care for. Neither are they acting for the sake of *all others* or *humanity in general*; they seek instead to preserve or promote an actual human relation between themselves and *particular others*. Persons in caring relations are acting for self-and-other together. (12)

Care ethics—an approach that still struggles in the shadows of mainstream ethics textbooks but is slowly and steadily gaining appreciation as it continues to be articulated, explored, and refined by feminist theorists—stems from the recognition that women's socialized modes of understanding themselves and their obligations are typically forged in relationships, both with particular other adults and with dependent others. Care ethics highlights a lack in Western traditional ethics, in that it has tended to construe obligations and responsibilities as formulated in abstraction. Care ethicists have worked hard to highlight the fact that loving relationships need not be contrasted with ethical ones—that the former are not merely natural (read "partial," "biased," and "instinctual") and, thereby, distinct from the ethical. Loving relationships require work and their development and cultivation requires analysis by ethical theorists; scholars in this tradition have appealed to the deep bonds formed between mothers and children to illustrate this claim.

In an effort to build and improve upon care ethics' insights, LaChance Adams centres her work not on the connections but rather on the disconnections and ruptures that often occur in these caring relations for mothers. Although there are many contexts in which it makes sense to claim that mothers are "acting for self-and-other together," there are also plenty of ways in which symbiosis between self and other is challenging for mothers, particularly when their own interests are experienced as coming into conflict with care for their children. LaChance Adams expresses her support for care ethics' challenges to mainstream approaches, yet she also argues that it is critical not to try to dissolve or deny the challenges of tension and conflict between self and others, especially in caring relationships. Affirming, building upon, and aiming to expand care ethics, LaChance Adams offers the critique that it has paid "inadequate attention to the contradictions of mother-child relationships" (6). She worries that "in its emphasis on inter-dependence, care ethics often ignores the need for personal flourishing" (24) and calls for "an ethical theory that accounts for the needs to care, to be cared for, *and* to maintain independence" (6). Although I think recent work by care ethicists such as Virginia Held are more sensitive to this need, and earlier expressions of care ethics (such as those offered by Nel Noddings, for instance) have been lacking in this regard, LaChance Adams takes the literature a step further by digging more deeply into the instances in which there is tension between oneself and cared for others. This tension is often present for justifiable reasons: we need to have distinct boundaries at times and individual, unique interests. And sometimes the tension is heightened and exacerbated by oppressive cultural contexts that compel women to self-abnegate and self-sacrifice—to place the needs of dependent others always before their own.

In my bath-time "aha!" moment, in which I realized I was burning the candle at both ends, I resolved to slow down and take care of myself. But the question that next bubbled up (years of studying philosophy has killed my ability to stop with one question) was whether this was a tension of gender-neutral origin or whether it was exacerbated by the patriarchal context in which I was mothering. Was the point of taking care of myself simply to get better at ignoring or declining what I wanted to do, too? It may be that all I needed was a full night's sleep, if the point was to quell my whining, but would that simply be aiming (whether consciously or not) to deny the existence of the tension I felt in order to make myself a more patient and self-denying (i.e., "good") mother?

In the messages disseminated in contemporary U.S. pop culture, the answer may be a resounding yes. It has become common for women to repeat—sometimes in a mantra-like style—"you have to take care of yourself." At times, this is uttered as advice for handling illness or extreme stress; and once and a while, it's offered as social and political advice to those who consistently put others' needs above their own. Most often, it is the trite advice of the personal care industry—in enticements towards solutions for the supposed needs of our skin, nails, and hair, which, left to their own devices, will presumably run amok and squash our chances at feminine beauty and success. Although men are not immune, and are increasingly targeted by such industries, the imperative for women's (marketed as feminine) self-care both speaks to and entrenches a supposed need of all women (though the marketing aims primarily at, and centers the experiences of, cisgender, heterosexual, white, wealthy, able-bodied women).

Of course, it is arguable that women do need personal care advice, aside from the feminized beauty genre. Women are still performing the second shift at an alarmingly high rate, with disproportionate burdens placed on women of colour and working-class women. We probably do need to spend more time taking care of ourselves. But this is easier said than done, particularly for mothers, when structural injustices provide constant obstacles to the goal. When childcare is prohibitively expensive, when paid family leave is lacking, when school hours do not coincide with work hours, and when health insurance does not cover reproductive care, "take care of yourself" easily becomes a pipedream.

Yet the mantra to "take care of yourself" holds much cultural sway and in a form that keeps our attention on the personal rather than the political. As we try to manage and have it all, we sometimes hear only the shallow remedies offered, not the causes or the structural solutions to it. Indeed, as if instructed by the cliché, my chosen form of escape in the hotel was a bath (even though I had no miracle bath products to help "take me away").[6] It is perhaps no accident that my culturally influenced imagination came up with that particular feminized space and activity for my escape.

Why do we keep buying this message (literally and figuratively)? The brilliance of the personal care industry's mantra to "take care of yourself" is that it seizes on a social narrative that gels with aspects of the women's movement. Consistent with the claim that liberated women must stop constantly sacrificing their happiness and dreams for the sake of their children, partners, and parents, the personal care industry confirms that women are not at all selfish when they shift their attention to themselves. It is purportedly common knowledge that women from all walks of life need some "me time"; the problems is that it seems to matter little whether such time comes through the affordance of a room of one's own or of a bathtub with nourishing bubbles through which one can pamper themselves.

This liberated twist on "me time" has not entirely eschewed the traditional feminine justification. The importance of taking care of yourself is communicated, buttressed, and ultimately justified by the benefits it bestows: when you take some "me time" you'll take better care of others. You'll not only look and smell better, but you'll be more relaxed and patient with children who draw on the walls, with that spouse who forgot the dry cleaning (again!), and with that boss who calls right in the middle of dinner. As Audre Lorde argues, "Caring for myself is not self-indulgence, it is self-preservation and that is an act of political warfare" (131). Yet many of us forget that she was not calling for bath bubbles and spa treatments; she was calling for Black women's survival in the face of patriarchal white racism. Sadly, as the meme with her face makes its way around social media, this context gets lost in translation.

The tug of war that operates in the background, of course, is my needs vs. theirs (dependents' or otherwise), and it continues to be a very real tension. What seems more liberatory than the struggles of our 1950s foremothers, of course, is that the tug of war is now acknowledged (at least implicitly); no longer must the modern woman pretend that she is always happy catering to the needs of others. These days she can (with more cultural acceptance) let the phone ring, the kids squabble, and the boss wait, just for a few minutes. What is less liberatory than it seems, however, is that the justification for "me time" is still others. You may take care of yourself, one is now told, because in doing so you will be more effective at taking care of others. You are taking care of yourself so that you may take care of them.

With this justification, if I were to slow down so that I could be a better mother—more patient and more self-sacrificing—my resentment of my children would likely contain itself at a high simmer, though perhaps remain poised to move into a rolling boil at the slightest thing. For feminists cognizant of the destructiveness of the traditional message that maternal success equals self-abnegation, it may always be hard to care for others without feeling that one is choosing others over oneself.

Yet in this kind of slowing down, in which I was spending time pondering the sources of my ambivalence, I was beginning to recognize, I think, that the justification for self-care cannot always be the other, and I was trying to sort through whether this ambivalence was for good reasons or for culturally pernicious and oppressive ones. It was making some sense that the goal need not be, as LaChance Adams counsels, to rid myself of the ambivalence entirely but to sort through its causes as well as some potential creative solutions. And the solutions may not dissolve the ambivalence entirely but rather shape its manifestations, help me live with its likelihood, and negotiate the terms through which it is presented.

And as I continued to ponder this (it was a very long bath), it struck me that the rhetoric—sacrifice yourself so that you can take care of others—in some ways mirrors the rhetoric that bubbles up in my environmental ethics classes. Bringing myself back to the academic point of traveling to Brazil—to explore environmental ethical issues through an international lens—I reflected upon the fact that my students often express their desire to increase their care for their planet and their environment, but when it comes to trying to put this commitment into practice, they also express resentment over the self-sacrifice that seems to be required. It's hard, they say, not to drive a car when their friends are; it's hard to find meat alternatives and to research the foods and products they consume. It's easier just to use the paper or plastic at the grocery store and to toss refuse in the trash when a recycling bin is not easily accessible. And while part of the complaint is that it takes extra time and work, the resentment seems to come from the fact that they're sacrificing themselves for others—either others who are not doing to the same or others who do not yet exist (posterity)—and that the benefits of such sacrifices may not end up coming back to them in obvious or tangible ways.

The self-care vs. other-care split that I had been navigating was not isolated to my relationship with my kids; it tapped into another kind of ambivalence. It was an ambivalence based in my own love of travel but that recognized the challenge that this love presents to a conception of myself as an environmentalist. As I glanced over at the empty water bottles that were piling up near the sink after only three days in our current city, I felt a sinking feeling, almost a horror, at the environmental damage I was complicit in, simply by travelling to observe and experience great environmental wonders. While it was thrilling to experience the Amazon rainforest and Iguaçu Falls, of listening firsthand both to the heroics and the drudgery of the Greenpeace warriors who work to save the trees, one could argue that the amount of bottled water I was purchasing to avoid stomach issues from tap water, and the ballooning of my carbon footprint from the flights I took every few days, was counterproductive to my identity and goals as an environmentalist. In my sustainability classes, I reviewed routinely the carbon footprint of taking one round-trip domestic flight, yet here I was taking myself and three other people on an international round trip, plus eleven domestic ones.

Returning to LaChance Adams's notion that maternal ambivalence holds in it potential for insight into one's relationships and "potentially positive creative aspects," I considered whether the ambivalence I felt, as a self-identified environmentalist yet a globally wealthy[7] member of the Global North whose life regularly wrought environmental havoc, I returned to the self vs. other construction that exacerbated my resentment as a mother. Just as the patriarchal narrative counselling me to take care of myself so that I could be a better caretaker of others was problematic and ultimately unsatisfying, the advice that my students hear (take care of your planet for the sake of posterity) feels hollow and lacks motivation for them. Likewise, when most of us begin truly contemplating our own complicity in environmental destruction and climate change, the narratives about what "needs to be done" seem constantly to involve self-sacrifice, at least for those who live in the Global North. Being an environmentalist in this context seems to mean giving things up, giving things away, and rarely sounds fun, attractive, or enticing. What environmentalism seems to require of us is mostly self-denial, when the self that we're denying has interests and desires that conflict with sustainable practices.

There are good reasons for this, of course. The U.S., in particular, which makes up only 5 per cent of the world's population, currently consumes more than 30 per cent of our global natural resources. We take and use up and throw away things with reckless and unethical abandon, and from the perspective of the rest of the world, some sacrifices on our part are long overdue. What is troublesome, however, is the fact that even when we recognize and acknowledge this, few of us feel particularly motivated to give up the things we have or to self-sacrifice in other meaningful ways. When it comes to trying to live out or put into place our professed commitments, many of us feel ambivalent at best.

In fact, the only contexts in which environmentalism seems not to involve self-sacrifice—the depressing denial of all that is fun, exciting, easy, and new—is when talk turns to the wild. In wilderness experiences, the opportunity for adventure, challenge, and excitement is sometimes articulated with enthusiasm that mirrors some people's excitement over the latest iPhones and technological innovations. Motivated by the opportunity to see new things that others have rarely experienced (rare species of flora and fauna or unique and fragile ecosystems), environmentalists (particularly from the West) sometimes erect strong dichotomies between culture and nature, wherein culture represents all that is environmentally destructive and nature becomes that which is wholesome and good.

In many of the same ways that care ethicists have worked to demonstrate that it is not always easy, useful, or ethically responsible to draw sharp lines between one's obligations to oneself and obligations to others, environmental ethicists have been working out whether it makes sense to sharply distinguish between culture and nature. Much good writing has been done to betray falsely dichotomous thinking in pitting one against the other, (Kaebnick, Moriarty, and Cronon), but the point that particularly interests me is the absence of relational thinking within the pitting of one against the other as well as the ways in which this absence can exacerbate ambivalence.

Gregory Kaebnick, drawing on the work of William Cronon, points to multiple practical and conceptual problems that arise from adopting a "dualistic vision" of the human and the natural realms. In much the same way that some mothers struggle with wanting the deep connections we get from our loving relationships with our kids and moments later (even simultaneously) wanting separation between ourselves and our dependent others, many environmentalists desire separation from cultural norms that result in so much environmental destruction yet feel ambivalent about giving up modern technological comforts to sustain a deeper connection with nature in wilderness areas. For many Global North, Western, self-proclaimed environmentalists, this can lead to a kind of bifurcated lifestyle, in which one dons professional clothes during the week, drives a car to and from work, lives in a climate controlled house, perhaps eats highly packaged and processed food, and then leaves it all behind on the weekends, pulling on hiking boots to spend some time in the wilderness. Maria Mies critiques Global northerners "for whom the cities are centres of 'Life', of freedom, of culture, [and yet] rush away from these very cities whenever they can" (132) and claims that we are unwittingly destroying the very experiences we seek. While these patterns may be rightly called hypocritical (and I myself have intimated as much in the past), condemning it as such may not solve any of the environmental damage it results in, particularly if we don't have a good sense of what this bifurcated living stems from.

Fleeing the city on weekends and returning during the week is perhaps an attempt to work out an ambivalence whose sources are, in some instances, perniciously constructed and damaging and, in others, inevitable tensions of contemporary living—Western middle-to-upper-class living, to be specific—in relation to our natural environments. Kaebnick, via Cronon, writes the following: "Wildnerness gets us into trouble only if we imagine that this experience of wonder and otherness is limited to remote corners of the planet, or that it somehow depends on pristine landscapes we ourselves do not inhabit" (92). The "trouble" is, on the surface, a problem of our commitments and desires failing tests of consistency, but it may also tap into lack of coherence in our conceptions of who we are and how we think about ourselves in relation to those around us. The ethical implications of this lack of coherence seem worth consideration. In a fascinating passage in his book, again drawing on the work of Cronon, Kaebnick points out the following:

> Attending too much to wilderness can actually free us from attending seriously to the effect we have on the environment: "[T]o the extent that we live in an urban-industrial civilization but at the same time pretend to ourselves that our *real* is in the wilderness, to just that extent we give ourselves permission to evade responsibility for the lives we actually lead" [quoting Cronon]. It can lead us to try to protect rain forests in other countries (perhaps at the expense of poor peoples who live in those countries) rather than attending to environmental issues in our own communities and homes. It can lead us to avoid the kind of active management that may genuinely be needed to protect the environment. (91)

Maria Mies makes a similar point:

> With the advent of cheap, mass-tourism we are increasingly urged by the media to undertake 'adventure' travels and tour. To see "cave people," "cannibals," "wild head-hunters," "stone-age people" in the Philippines, Malaysia, Papua New Guinea, the Amazon and so on. Like the fifteenth and sixteenth century

adventurers and pirates, affluent, late twentieth century men are urged to experience the challenges of early "discoverers" and to commune with Nature—and suddenly you feel like John Wayne! Man feels like a man again in his confrontation with "wild Nature." (132)

Reading both of these authors upon return from the trip, I was struck with the sickening feeling that this may not be an unfair characterization of my fascination with, and angst about, my unfulfilled desire to immerse myself in riskier, less child-friendly experiences I might have embarked upon during my trip in Brazil. Even though I was a seasoned enough traveller and thinker to know that the dream of getting an authentic experience in this "other" culture has imperialist undertones, if I were really honest with myself, I may acknowledge that a part of me was probably aiming to live out a modern-day masculinized, raced, imperialist fantasy with a sordid past. I desired to venture as an explorer into the wild falls and the jungles of the Amazon—a desire fuelled, in part, by the images Mies alludes to. I wanted to be independent and unfettered by ties to my dependent others—freed from responsibilities and innocent in my explorations—but the frequent calls for potty breaks and the periodic need to find food that resembled a grilled-cheese sandwich were seriously cramping my colonially manufactured style.

What may opening the door to ambivalence's "potentially positive, creative aspects" (LaChance Adams 8) mean in a situation like this? Perhaps it held the opportunity to examine both the privileges I held and the unhelpful dichotomies that were preventing me from addressing them in meaningful ways. My maternal and my environmental ambivalences were both stemming from a life of serious privilege in relation to many others. Although every mother is a working mother, not all mothers have equally gruelling schedules or demands in their working conditions. In my current profession, I enjoy a much higher degree of autonomy, flexibility, and earning power than most. And although all environmentalist work is critical, it's important to recognize the difference between those whose commitments to sustainability involve pleas to stop clear-cutting so that we still have some wild spaces to venture into for pleasure, and those whose pleas to stop clear-cutting are motivated by the dire need to protect their immediate livelihood, where they themselves live.[8] My ambivalence about where to direct my caregiving energy was due not merely to my inability to decide where to focus my energy but also due to the fact that some aspects of these responsibilities I experienced as optional.

When it comes to figuring out what I'm responsible for and to whom I am responsible in such cases, it may be particularly unhelpful to draw hard lines between myself and others (or culture and nature) and engage in aspects of previously described dichotomous thinking. When the choice is to care either for me or my dependents or for me or posterity or for culture or nature, I am caught in a bind that cannot be sustained and will likely only lead to resentment. Perhaps, in these cases, the "potentially positive, creative aspects" of acknowledging ambivalences come from efforts to contextualize and historicize their sources so that I can negotiate points of overlap in my ability to engage in care for myself and for others and to identify contexts in which I simply cannot easily do both. Finding the cracks in the otherwise hard lines in the dichotomies of self and other (immediate dependents or future generations) may lead to some creative solutions in caring for both. To illustrate the problems with the related nature vs. culture distinction, Kaebnick asks of his readers the following:

> Consider wind turbines. If we are looking for a simple definition of "natural," wind turbines will be perplexing. A modern wind turbine is an ingenious device; considered strictly in terms of the human ingenuity and effort invested in it, it must be considered well removed from the natural.... But another way to gauge their "naturalness" is in terms of their effect on the environment. Understood in this context, as an environmental intervention that lessens the human impact on the world, a case could be made for considering them a comparatively "natural" form of energy. (17)

The distinction between nature and culture is not obliterated in such historicized, contextualized thinking; it still makes sense to appeal to what is more and less natural when aiming for environmental sustainability. But the notion that sustainable solutions will emerge simply from choosing one side or the other of the nature vs. culture dichotomy is an oversimplification:

> If the concept of 'nature' is not explained as tracking a bright line running down the middle of the cosmos.... It must be understood

historically rather than metaphysically. It must be *naturalized*—made a topic of empirical inquiry. To talk about whether a place is natural is to address the causal story that can be told about how the place came to be the way it is and the role of humans in that sequence. (Kaebnick 96)

Such consideration applies not merely to the sustainability efforts connected to untouched or wilderness areas. In the environmental justice movement—whether on a global scale or a national scale—activists rethink and repurpose traditional appeals to nature as something distinct from culture. Rather than referring to it as something far from where folks in cities live, environmental justice advocates remind us that nature exists where people live. It foregrounds the livelihoods of many people in rural communities, and does not cease to exist in suburban and urban people's backyards, in the water in their pipes, and in the cracks in the sidewalks. They remind us that the dichotomies that "we" live by have often been erected by "us" (privileged ones of us) and that the stories behind them have raced, gendered, and classed power relations embedded in them as well.

Along these lines, the creative potential, I suppose, of sinking into maternal and environmental ambivalence comes when I look at the destructive patterns and mindsets I appeal to and employ while recognizing that some of these can shift with personal effort and some will require larger scale, structural changes, which happen through identifying patriarchal and colonial thinking and practices. I may always continue to experience the ambivalences I have felt as a mother and as an environmentalist, yet I feel hopeful that the resentment and the angst that the ambivalence leads to can be lessened by the "potentially positive, creative aspects" LaChance Adams suggests. Maternal and environmental ambivalence serve as a starting point through which I can both self-reflect and envision collective, social, and political changes. Transforming our culture so that responsibility for childcare is more socially supported and economically subsidized, as well as offering social and financial incentives for activities that take into account our environmental impact on future generations, will likely ease the tensions my ambivalences highlight. And, in turn, the choices between me and my dependents (immediate or generations from now) may not be so sharply experienced as an either/or.

Endnotes

1. "We write to taste life twice, in the moment and in retrospect" (13).

2. Sara Maitland describes feminism as a "fairy godmother" because in the Cinderella story, the magical godmother stopped Cinderella from "sitting at home rather pissed off" and instead transformed the world around her. While I find the appeal to the Cinderella story somewhat problematic, I am also drawn to the notion of feminism as a kind force with transformative power. Maitland is cited in Kolmar and Bartkowski, 2013.

3. For her willingness to make easy for me what surely never was for her, I owe Deborah Trott Pierce my deepest gratitude.

4. My sincere and humble thanks go to the William T. Kemper Foundation and Webster University for this award.

5. Yet it's so hard even to write this. My heart hurts at the risk of my children reading this someday and feeling devastated by the thought that at times I might not have wanted them around.

6. Those my age and older will recall, with an eye roll, the bath ads by Calgon.

7. Although I would not be considered wealthy by most American standards, I refer here to wealth in terms of earning power on a global scale. In contrast with the 900 million people worldwide who earn $1.90 per day—the poverty line set by the World Bank—calling myself globally wealthy does not seem inaccurate.

8. Ramachandra Guha and Juan Martinez-Alier in "The Environmentalism of the Poor" note that environmentalism in the Global South is typically "interlinked with questions of human rights, ethnicity, and distributive justice" whereas in the Global North environmentalists are absorbed "not so much with relations within human society as with relations between humans and other species" (309).

Works Cited

Cronon, William. "The Trouble with Wilderness; Or, Getting Back to the Wrong Nature." *Uncommon Ground: Rethinking the Human Place in Nature*, edited by William Cronon, W.W. Norton: 1995, pp. 69-90.

Guha, Ramachandra and Juan Martinez-Alier. "The Environmentalism of the Poor." *Earthcare: An Environmental Anthology,* edited by David Clowney and Patricia Mosto, Rowman & Littlefield, 2009, pp. 297-313.

Held, Virginia. *The Ethics of Care: Personal, Political, and Global.* Oxford University Press, 2006.

Kaebnick, Gregory. *Humans in Nature: The World As We Find It and the World As We Create It.* Oxford University Press, 2014.

Kolmar, Wendy, and Frances Bartkowski, editors. *Feminist Theory: A Reader.* 4th ed. McGraw Hill, 2013.

LaChance Adams, Sarah. *Mad Mothers, Bad Mothers, & What a "Good" Mother Would Do: The Ethics of Ambivalence.* Columbia University Press, 2014.

Lorde, Audre. *A Burst of Light: Essays.* Firebrand Books, 1988.

Mies, Maria. "White Man's Dilemma: His Search for What He Has Destroyed." *Ecofeminism,* edited by Maria Mies and Vandana Shiva, Zed Books, 1993, pp. 132-63.

Moriarty, Paul Veatch. "Nature Naturalized: A Darwinian Defense of the Nature/Culture Distinction." *Environmental Ethics,* vol. 29, 2007, pp. 227-46.

Nin, Anaïs. *In Favor of the Sensitive Man, and Other Essays.* Harcourt Brace & Company, 1966.

Chapter Eleven

Ambivalence and Identification: Avenues for Reification or Change

Joan Garvan

A significant development in the second part of the twentieth century has been changes to gendered practice. This is, however, a cultural revolution that is being stalled by harking back to so-called traditional roles within families. The vast majority of couples aspire to a form of gender equal or egalitarian family, yet after the birth the child, they tend to gravitate towards traditional gender roles (Broderick; Kaufman; Golberg and Perry-Jenkins; Cowdery and Knudson-Martin; Cowan and Cowan). The plethora of blogs and books with women reflecting on their experience as mothers is indicative of this flux. Women struggle to find new ways of being while maintaining their sense of self. Titles such as *Mother Shock* (Buchanan), *The Divided Heart* (Power), *The Mask of Motherhood* (Maushart), *This Is Not How I Thought It Would Be* (Maschka), *Dispatches from a Not-So-Perfect Life* (Fox), and many more depict an experience of disruption and disjuncture.

In this chapter, based on the data gleaned from interviews, I explore ambivalences held by first-time mothers in light of contemporary understandings of interpersonal dynamics between mothers and their infants. The chapter draws from a qualitative study carried out in 2004 and 2005 in Australia.[1] Issues related to identity after the birth of an infant were evident among the research participants. The mixed feelings expressed by these mothers in the early years after the birth during the transition to parenthood were influenced by changes in their relationships with their male partner. There was an expectation that the mother would attend to the housework as a matter of course while attending to their child. This is the work that has been gendered and privatized within the family and is generally associated with traditional roles. Disruptions to their relationships were also felt bodily—through the women's disassociation from their breasts or in their decreasing sexual connection with their partners.

My research was concerned specifically with the participants' experience of their transition to parenthood, from pregnancy to the second year after birth. The first born for most of these women was between sixteen months and two years. Ten of the sixteen women had a second child at the time of the interview, although my focus was on their experience of the first. The respondents clearly experienced mixed feelings about their new life as a mother. The women prioritized the care of their child over the housework both through the week and on the weekend, which at times became a point of significant tension with their male partner. Furthermore many of these women experienced ambivalence in regard to their sense of self. When they became a mother, their life changed in ways that were different to that of their partner, which evoked a self-reassessment.

My in-depth, semi-structured interviews concerned the avenues in which these women expressed their agency when they were new mothers. My analysis of the interview data is within categories formulated by Cornelius Castoriadis and Jessica Benjamin. According to Castoriadis, all social relations must pass through symbolization, as an interactive process, to become meaningful. Meaning, or social imaginary signification, is embodied in the institutions of a given society. For example, notions of family, mother, or child are shaped by both social policy and everyday practice. Individual identification includes identification with a social group through socially mediated signifiers. Many women experience incongruence in their prescribed roles as new mothers, which is often an unfamiliar and ill-fitting costume. They do not relate fully to the dispositions often associated with being a mother, such as selflessness and endless patience. This leaves many women grappling to salvage their identity. Where do I fit? What is mothering? Is gender equality possible? Is gender equality desirable after the birth of a child? They describe tensions between a desire for equity and a desire to care for their child that arise from privatized care within the heteronormative family form. Ultimately, many of these women attempt to resolve conflicts between their social role and their experience through identification with their mother or with the interests of their child.

Jessica Benjamin elucidates the complex dynamics of mother-child relationships by drawing on the notion of intersubjectivity. This concept understands the mother's identity as formed in concert with recognition and response to the emergent subject of the child. The mother-child relationship entails both interpersonal (mother-infant) and intrapsychic dynamics (internal to the woman-as-mother) and within this intrapsychic dimension identification is at play. Indeed, many of the women I interviewed spoke about their relationships with their own mothers, either as a role model or by way of contrast to their own way of being a mother. Meanwhile, they also identified with the perceived long-term interests of their child. This chapter highlights these struggles as well as the mediating role of identification. I propose that the unsettling nature of ambivalence—the interviewees' dealing with and responding to these mixed feelings—is evidence of social change. The meanings and practices associated with being a mother are in the process of change and are expressed in individual concerns with maternal identity. Castoriadis and Benjamin help to elucidate the processes behind the reproduction of norms as well as avenues for reflection and change.

Conflicts Concerning the Self and Relationship Changes

Research on the transition to parenthood within heteronormative families shows high levels of anxiety and depression (Nystrom and Ohrling; Cowan and Cowan; Golberg and Perry-Jenkins; McHale et al.; Nicholson and Woollett; Rosenberg).[2] Australian research demonstrates that 15 to 30 per cent of new mothers are found to experience depression or raised levels of anxiety (AIHW; Hasler; Beyond Blue). There are high levels of marital dissatisfaction, which arise from changes to relationships with their male partner (Glade et al.; Golberg and Perry-Jenkins; Cowdery and Knudson-Martin; Grote,Clark and Moore; Cowan and Cowan; Corney and Simons; Kluwer; Dempsey). Furthermore, new mothers often experience issues related to identity;

this was a finding in the transition to parenthood research, but it underlies much of the introspection contemporary women engage in after becoming a mother and is evident in the ever expanding genre of motherhood literature. Tension between delight in one's child and disappointment over the need to put aside activities and associations central to one's identity was a common theme in the interviews.

The median age of the women interviewed for the project was thirty-two; and most of the women had extensive life experience, through travelling, working, or social connections. The requirements for the care of their infants radically changed their lifestyle. The expectation and desire to attend to the baby's every need was often described as a disconnection from the self. This often led to a questioning of the self. Who am I? What do I want? Hilary remarked the following:

> I think that is probably the hardest part about it, trying to work out, well, who are you? What is your best—you have to, at some point, work out without all these bits and pieces, you know, without the career, or the job, or the children, and you have to understand at the core, who you are. It is when you are faced with some sort of crisis, like being a mother, and suddenly you are trying to redefine yourself, you do have to then, go back to saying, well, this is me, apart from being a mother.

Hilary's remark goes to the heart of this dilemma for women today. She expresses her concern in terms of a crisis of identity.

Similarly, Carol spoke of experiencing motherhood in terms of loss of the self; "Well it's a wonderful and rewarding experience, but it is very hard to lose the sense of who you are because you just become this machine that is purely there to serve everyone's needs. And, at times, I don't remember who it is just to be a wife, let alone just to be."

The problem of identity arises, in part, as a response to living in contradiction with ideals of gender equity. Lesley reflected on the messages she was giving her children in terms of her conflicting values:

> I would like the boys to see more equality between men and women. I'm in a position of being the mother at home, the stereotype mother at home, while the dad goes out to work. That's ... not a stereotype to me because it's what I've chosen to do, but I wouldn't like my children to see that as this is what

happens. Most of the women I know—that is what happens as well.

Lesley is foregoing her aspiration for equity to accommodate the requirements of care in a gendered context that disadvantages primary caregivers.

Another woman describes several internal tensions in her new role between her religious beliefs and a desire for equity. When I asked "How do you see the relationship between yourself and your husband in terms of family?," "Does your partner have the final word in decisions?," "Do you have the final word?," and "How do you make decisions?"—Peta replied "I would like to say that he has the final word on decisions, but I don't know that he has." She continued: "This is part of my Christian upbringing that he is the head of the house." It was clear, however, through her expression and disposition, that she was uncomfortable with this arrangement. She felt in a bind. She subscribed to a belief that the male should be the head of the household, yet she was uncomfortable with this in everyday practice. She talked about challenging his decisions and that this caused her distress. Peta stayed home with her children because she did not want to send them to childcare; she wanted to be there to provide for their needs herself. However, she did not like the fact that because she was at home, it meant that she became responsible for the cooking, cleaning, and shopping throughout the week, but also on the weekend.

Peta is not alone in her frustration. Consistent with the research indicating a decline in marital satisfaction with the birth of a child, at least six of the interviewees struggled in their relationships with their male partner. The dynamics for three of these couples had changed dramatically since the birth. There were conflicting expectations negotiating housework. Two participants entered long-term counselling to help them process the change and to adapt. A third interviewee said that her husband was a trained counsellor and, therefore, brought to the relationship good communication skills. Another participant had migrated to Australia from Peru. Both she and her husband had grown up in houses where there was home help—a prospect they were unable to afford in Australia. Her husband left the housework and the care of their two young children to her, and she felt tired, bitter, and cheated.

Marina suffered postnatal depression with her second child. She harboured resentment about her husband, as they had not talked about how they would share the new responsibilities and she ended up doing most of it:

> I think you just assume that you'll both know what to do, but probably because I took more control, he just, maybe, didn't know what to do in the end.... You build up resentment, I think, not knowing how to handle things; that's the first reaction. Oh come on do this, do that, and then you're looking after the baby, and then that all snowballs.

The resentment Marina felt led to depression and an inability to cope with the requirements of care.

Beverley had spent many years working as a nanny so when she became a mother she brought extensive knowledge and experience. Yet when she attended her eighteen-month appointment with the maternity and child nurse, her frustrations came to the fore: "I cracked". They asked me "how are you"—it could have been anybody. "I was ready to crack. I was so frustrated by that point and so overwhelmed by emotion and frustration and sort of doubting whether you are doing a good job. It had been such a long road." This outburst was fuelled by financial and relationship concerns. Beverley wanted to be a mother. It was important to her, and she had a strong sense of what this meant in practice, yet she clearly struggled. The notion of "derivative dependency" is relevant here. This concept is used by Eva Kittay to describe the social location of the primary caregiver, whereby familial relations are negotiated within a social framework that economically advantages the independent, autonomous individual.

All of these women had been in the workforce before having children, and were used to an independent income. Most had joint bank accounts with equal access, so theoretically they could withdraw money if they needed it. A couple of the participants organized the family finances or paid the bills, although there was evidence of an unspoken sense of entitlement associated with the male gender and the breadwinner role. Lesley expressed it like this:

> He's supportive of my role as a mother, like, the stay-at-home mum, but when we have arguments. Like, if we have an argument that can be, not even a big issue, but he can, sort of say, well you stay home. I work so you can stay home all day, and I do feel a bit

like I should be making some money, but at the same time, we're both aware that the work that I do at home and the importance of it, if you know what I mean.

Lesley and Dan made the decision together that she would attend to the everyday caring needs of the family, yet she felt ambivalent. Others grappled with this disjuncture and were happy to do some part-time work so that they could also contribute financially to the family or have access to an independent income. Lesley continued:

It's not like you're not working is it, or contributing ... like, you are making a huge contribution, but I think, again, in terms of the culture we live in, because it's not counted as work, what you're doing, even though it is work, it can slide into that thing, well, you're just at home with the kids, like, that's not doing anything.... He does see it as a job, but at the same time, he's the one with the money.... The real importance is on who earns money and that sort of status thing, which is a bit of a—it doesn't add up properly.

The work of Marilyn Waring is relevant here. The daily care of dependents—including infants and children, the infirm, and aged—is work that has been privatized and gendered within the family. This work is not counted in the gross national product, and without adequate paid parental schemes, the primary caregiver is left financially vulnerable.

The women interviewed also described a steep decline in time, opportunity, and/or desire to maintain a sexual relationship with their male partner. The couples had often lived together for some years before having children, and the reality of becoming parents led to a tiring spiral of events. These couples were attempting to meet the great expectations they had for themselves and their children, often with little support. Most said that their relationships had suffered as a result of life with a baby. When I asked about reconnecting sexually with her partner, Barbara stated the following:

I think, well for me personally, it has changed dramatically ... I've personally found that just, not weird, but like you're in mummy mode, and then all of a sudden you're in wife mode again. Especially when you're breastfeeding, it's kind of like, it's a real—and you can't—I think trying to get a male to understand is just impossible.

This divide between the breast as nourishment and sexual pleasure was explored by Paz Galupo and Jean Ayers. They identify issues related to the identity of the woman-as-mother that Barbara was struggling with. Pregnancy, birth, breastfeeding, and childcare are highly physical but are also interlocked with emotional and psychological arenas. Two other interviewees spoke about a continuing difficulty to reconnect physically with their husbands. Earlier in their relationship, Lesley had an abortion, and then later when she became pregnant, she was fearful that she would miscarry: "Every day I was terrified that it was going to happen." After the birth, Lesley said this resulted in her being angry with her partner for a long time, "But I didn't realize, like I said, it was under the level of resentment and so that affected our sex life." Hilary said, "I've had very little interest in a sex life at all—that has been something that has been severely neglected ... I've just been too tired." Other participants had renegotiated a pathway that was generally spoken of in terms of their male partner's needs.

In the first few months after the birth, the mother was often the only source of nourishment for the infant. Feeding became important in the emotional connection between mother and her infant, and a means of soothing and comforting the baby. However, breastfeeding also had the effect of distancing the woman from her body, sometimes to the extent where the breasts were felt to be disconnected; they seemed to be there only for the child's benefit. Celia had this to say: "Suddenly parts of your body are kind of free for all—I gave myself over to her."

Barbara, like many others, had lost much of her sexual desire. She mentioned breastfeeding, with a sense of having lost some control over her body. And the toddler, now nearly two-and-a-half, had just moved out of their bed—"that's a good killer right there," she said. The most common side effect of mothering was a lack of sleep. Barbara said, laughingly, "I find sleep stimulating. I'm afraid I'm just not a Wisteria Lane princess [a reference to the television show *Desperate Housewives*]. For me, it's kind of like, ah you give it to me, ah it's good, but I like my sleep". This physical and sexual outcome from birth and caregiving has been given little attention in the discourses around both motherhood and/or sexuality (Seidman et al), although they are importantly linked to the women's sense of self and processes of reconnection between the parents.

With one exception, pregnancy and birth were part of the life plans for all of the interviewees—the fulfilment of an important life ambition. The birth of an infant can bring couples together, but the interviewees reflected on tensions between discordance and cooperation, which were unearthed within their relationships. They all strove to preserve their connections with their husbands so as to hold the family together, and this required them to subsume personal difficulties. Many grappled with the consequences of the birth, not their commitment to their babies but their new social location. In each of these cases, the women found themselves disenfranchised through the social structuring of care. Their connection with their infant through care located them socially and culturally differently to that of their male partners. The resolution to this gender divide requires institutional change; meanwhile, women are left with conflicting relations between self and other.

Intersubjective dynamics provide for the emergence of something new—"a third space"—a symbolic space between self and other which feeds into symbolic representation and identification. This psychic work that is associated with care represents affect and assists in processing the pain of separation between the mother and her child (Benjamin). Accordingly, the mother, or primary caregiver, attends to and, thus, recognizes this emergent self in the child while she is representative of the other.

A failure to acknowledge, recognize, or legitimize the ability of the mother to determine a future separate from her infant propels many women to project themselves into the future through their child—a merging of self and other through the symbolic. This often appears as a projection of the good of the child into the future, which assumes a disembodied mother and disenfranchises the woman-as-mother, disables action, and promotes the objectification of women. Indeed many of my interviewees spoke of the necessity for unselfish mothering, yet they realized that the responsibilities of motherhood require both attention and self-assertion. In a culture that emphasizes the benefits of the infant at the expense of the mother, motherhood can be experienced as disempowering, and this was a message that came through the interviews.

It is important to recognize that the processes of maternal engagement with infantile psychic development takes place within a social context that contributes to the outcomes for both infant and mother. The experience of women when they become a mother in the contemporary context is characterized by contradiction and ambivalence. Because care is privatized through the family, this disjuncture is individualized and is evident in unfulfilled expectations. Demystifying the maternal relationship, however, through ambivalence can reveal the double-sided nature of interactions between the mother and child.[3]

The Mother's Mother and the Interests of the Child

It is evident in the emergent body of literature on mothering and motherhood that women are reflecting on its meanings and practices. Popular representations of mothers do not reflect the complexities of women's lives, and they find a need to reimagine themselves. There was evidence in the interviews of tensions between individuals negotiating and/or transgressing structural influences while reflecting on their experience of being mothered. They were determining new ways of being a mother within the confines of institutionalized and gendered constraint. But what keeps them there? How do women think of themselves as mothers?

To varying degrees Hilary, Beverley, and Peta were in awe of their mothers and set out to mirror them. However, they often felt unable to reenact the patience and understanding they remembered. Beverley was inspired by what she remembered of her mother's uncomplicated calm. Yet when I asked what being a mother meant to her, Beverley replied with the following: "Well, it means, meaningfulness. There is a lot of meaning that comes into your life; more meaning than ever. It's when all those little accomplishments, the growth. You see your son growing, kisses, and hugs he brings to you, and all of those things, and it brings meaningfulness to your life." It is not uncommon for women to say this of mothering, but I suggest the meaningfulness Beverley referred to is related to questions of identity and identification. These women's commitment to their children was not simply a replication of their mothers' lives or a part of their life course. The world in which Beverley was mothered was in some ways less complicated; the work of care was clearly associated with a gendered role—the housewife and mother. Beverley attributed her experience of frustration and stress to finances, tensions between work and family, and to her relationship with her husband. These factors acted as constraints to what she saw as the most important challenge of her life. The privatized and gendered nature of care individualizes the responsibility whereby women, like Beverley, saw the work associated with the care of her child as critical to his development, and she strove to indulge his experience of these early years. This is a significant generational difference.

Lesley believed her style was not markedly different from her mother's, yet there were clear generational changes in their parenting. Lesley's husband, as with most of the interviewees, was much more involved with both the care of the children and the housework than her father had been. Although her mother had stayed at home while Lesley was growing up, Lesley struggled with this as an option in terms of her sense of self. She worried about what she was teaching her children about gendered roles. There was a common belief with earlier generations that children were to be seen but not heard, whereas, today, there is much more emphasis on child development. Contemporary women often aspire to provide stimulating experiences for their children, engaging with them in play or talk, yet there is a tension between this focus and an expectation that they will at the same time attend to domestic tasks.

Barbara reflected on changes to her sense of self when she became a mother, as the experience had made her constantly question herself. She understood that there were no absolute rights or wrongs about parenting, but she felt obliged to question her decisions. Barbara thought her anxieties stemmed from a difficult relationship with her mother, personal insecurities from her own life experience, and she was overcompensating so as to promote a good relationship with her child. "I dance on a sixpence most of the day, which is just ridiculous because they're going to be fine, but it's just that constant when you don't have anyone necessarily there to bounce off while doing this." Barbara's response stood out from the others in this regard. Many of the interviewees admired their mothers and were emulating the best of their mothers' practice. Barbara did not have a good relationship with her mother, but this was still an important influence on her mothering.

Tamara's mother was in the workforce from when she was very young: "She even went to work with me in the car ... she just had to have me there. She didn't have anyone to look after me." Tamara was in childcare from the age of three. This meant that she spent a lot of time apart from her mother, with her grandmother or at after-school programs. Although Tamara was committed to having her partner be involved with the childcare in an equal way, she was also determined to be there for her children. Her childhood was moulded around the work commitments of her parents. Like Barbara, Tamara's experience of childhood had an important and contrary effect over her style of parenting: she wanted to do it differently from her mother.

In contrast to many other interviewees, Emily appeared not to have prioritized the needs of her child above her own aspirations. The couple planned to have a baby while she was completing her studies because of the flexibility this allowed. It is interesting to consider her decisions in terms of her life experience and, in particular, the role played by her mother. Emily's mother held a professional position while bringing up her daughter—a job with the flexibility to combine work and family. When Emily was ten, her mother worked overseas for three months, leaving her in the care of her father and grandparents, and at the age of thirteen, her mother returned overseas for a further twelve months. This was a jolt to Emily because her mother had been the primary caregiver. Her choices regarding the care of her child were in concert with her life experience, and thus contributed to a secure sense of self.

Hilary, like most of the interviewees, had a toddler and a baby. There were silences throughout the interview, although it was still clear that she appreciated an opportunity to articulate her thoughts on mothering. The first two years of her child's life included innumerable adjustments and challenges, and what sustained Hilary was her unshaken belief in the model of care and nurturing embodied by her mother. However, avenues for articulating new ways of being, separate from experience or tradition, are evident through the tasks she was redefining. Hilary had clearly thought about what her children needed. When I asked whether she felt a sense of purpose in her day-to-day life as a mother, she replied as follows:

> That is something I really struggled with to begin with, for sure, and there are still days when I struggle with that actually because it's just not as simple as a paid job where. Yes, you have certain things that you need to have achieved by the end of the day. So there are days when it feels like I'm not achieving, and I do feel a bit lost.... Well, they [her two children] are the ones that matter and for them, for their perception of their day, that is what is important, that they have felt happy and loved during the day ... that's been something that I've had lots of trouble trying to just understand.

These women grappled with the question of how to contribute to the wider world while caring for their children. A solution for many was to pass on their life learning to their children through modelling and care. Even though Celia had been a passionate and committed teacher, she was now thinking about finding a job in which she would be just "turning pages." This disengagement was evident when I asked, in terms of her sense of self, in what ways had she changed and in what ways had she stayed the same. Celia had this to say:

> I think it's both. In some ways ... [I have changed] because, you know, as I've said I've got someone else to think about, and I don't have to think about myself so much, but in other ways, I think I'm still essentially the same person, the same interests, the same beliefs about things ... but I think I'm a little bit in limbo in terms of what it is to, kind of, be a mother, what kind of mother do I want to be in the future. What kind of role model do I want to be for her? And, so I suppose, I've thought a little bit more about also finding my own interests because I haven't really. I don't have things that I'm particularly passionate about ... I don't just want to focus on her.

Celia reflects on herself in terms of the present and the future wellbeing of her child. She is aware of a need to delineate herself from her child, but she expresses this in terms of the child rather than herself. Paradoxically, she struggles between being a role model (which she believes means she should have her own interests) and how this is in conflict with the energy and attention demanded of mothers.

When reflecting on the meaning of their lives, mothers can often project themselves into the future through their children.[4] Two statements by Carol go to the heart of this tension. The first came up after she had talked about the importance of being a mother. She said that becoming a mother had made her more mature: "It just helped me take that final step into, yes, I'm happy with my life. Yes, I'm where I want to be. Yes, I have the things I want to have and should just settle down and stop learning." But then, the most important lesson Carol wanted to pass on to her children was that "there comes a time where you just have to believe in your passions and pursue them regardless, and that's what I want my children to have, that fearlessness." The naturalized association between women and mothering conveys the message that this maternal role is the pinnacle and provides for contentment and life-long satisfaction, bringing together the love for one's children with a passion for life. Carol's passion is meant to be her children, yet they are separate from her. They are essentially the other, with their own needs, interests, and passions. This conflation of the interests of mothers with their children, in combination with the intensive demands of motherhood, negates the self-interest of the woman—passionate connections not associated with their child.

Conclusion

Over the last few decades, there have been great changes in terms of traditional gender roles, yet the tensions and ambivalences that many of the interviewees expressed are indicative of continuing concerns. Women prioritize the care and development of their child, which conflicts with many of their other values and priorities. A gendered and privatized style of care exists within the family that disadvantages the primary caregiver both financially and in their health and wellbeing. The complex, interpersonal relationship between mothers and their children is overshadowed by the expectations of their social role. These conflicting dynamics are evident in the gap between the expectations and the experience of women as mothers and are played out in their relationships, with their male partners and through their sense of self.

Individuals negotiate the sense of self through identification with socially mediated signifiers; however, the meanings associated with being a mother are in flux. While women are redefining the meanings and practices associated with being a mother, they are also looking back to their experience of being mothered. Identifications with their own mothers and/or the long-term interests of their children have the effect of eclipsing women's sense of themselves as a separate subject of experience.

The tension in the interviews illustrates the radical imaginary in action; the related signification for the woman-as-mother in the social imaginary does not match the way these women see themselves. The disjuncture is a product of change, a faltering relation between women's experience and the symbolic figure of the mother. There is evidence of both continuity and change, and the accompanying ambivalences and contradictions are indicative of movement. It is important, therefore, to understand these processes and the mechanisms by which the individual comes together with the social. Castoriadis's notions of the radical and the social imaginaries as well as the part played by identification are useful. The concept of intersubjectivity, furthermore, provides for a way of locating the subject of the woman-as-mother and can, in turn, facilitate reflexivity and change. If the mother-child relationship is foundational, this is a journey we need to take. If the radical and social imaginaries come together through identification, this period of change calls for renewed and nongendered representations for care and new ways of thinking about what it means to be a mother.

Endnotes

1. All of the women interviewed were in heterosexual relationships. Even though I tried varied avenues, I was unsuccessful in attracting participants from homosexual families. Pseudonyms have been used for the participants.

2. A major European study on work-family boundaries concluded that "gender shapes parenthood and makes motherhood different from fatherhood both in everyday family life and in the workplace" (Nilsen and Brannen, 9)—a finding that is echoed in the finding that "mothers, but not fathers, see themselves as ultimately responsible for child care: (McHale et al. 725). Transition to parenthood is seen as a critical time for achieving gender equal outcomes (Nilsen and Brannen)—a claim substantiated by Australian research by Janeen Baxter et al. in relation to the development of a gender wage gap, which has been labelled "the motherhood wage penalty" (Budig and Hodges; Lewis and Giullair; Waldfogel; Summers; NATSEM; and Drago et al.). The transition to parenthood was also identified by John Dixon and Margaret Wetherell as a key point in the "transformation in the material circumstances of domestic life" (184) and a site for exploration.

3. These dynamics are fleshed out in the work of Wendy Hollway "The Capacity to Care," who highlights the critical role of differentiation between the maternal subject and the child in working through these dynamics. In *The Shadow of the Other*, Benjamin emphasizes the associated tension between what she describes as "comp-

lementarity and mutuality," in contrast to paradox and contradiction. Complementarity describes an instrumental relationship between the "doer" and the "done to," which does not rely on a reflexive position, whereas the second mutuality draws on an understanding that the mother is not only separate but is also a centre of subjective experience. The dynamics are complex and fraught; however, they provide a basis from which to promote differentiation and creativity.

4. The everyday knowledge that is a product of Celia's experience is invaluable to her workplace, theoretically and practically, yet her circumstances distance her from it. A relationship that does not facilitate the expression and development of an alterity between mother and infant can be understood from the perspectives of justice, equity, and citizenship (Lister; Moller Okin). But what about the wellbeing of the mother and infant?

Works Cited

AIHW, *Perinatal Depression Data from the 2010 Australian National Infant Feeding Survey, Information Paper.* Australian Institute for Health and Welfare, 2010.

Baxter, Janeen, et al. "Life Course Transitions and Housework: Marriage, Parenthood and Time on Housework." *Journal of Marriage and Family*, vol. 70, no. 2, 2008, pp. 259-72.

Benjamin, J. *Like Subjects, Love Objects Essays on Recognition and Sexual Difference.* Yale University Press, 1995.

Benjamin, J. *The Bonds of Love Psychoanalysis, Feminism, and the Problem of Domination.* Virgo Press, 1988.

Benjamin, J. *Shadow of the Other Intersubjectivity and Gender in Psychoanalysis.* Routledge, 1998.

Beyond Blue. The National Depression Initiative. *Perinatal Mental Health National Action Plan.* Perinatal Mental Health Consortium, 2008.

Broderick, Elizabeth. *Gender Quality: What Matters to Australian Women and Men in* The Listening Tour Community Report. Human Rights and Equal Opportunity Commission, 2008.

Buchanan, Andrea J. *Mother Shock*. Seal Press, 2003.

Budig, Michelle J., and Melissa J. Hodges. *Modeling the Effect of Children on Women's Wage Distribution: A Quantile Approach*. University of Massachusetts, 2009.

Castoriadis, C. *The Imaginary Institutions of Society*. Polity Press, 1987.

Castoriadis, C. "Radical Imagination and the Social Instituting Imaginary." *Rethinking Imagination*, edited by G. Robinson and J. Rundell, Routledge, 1994, pp. 134-154.

Castoriadis, C. *World in Fragments Writings on Politics, Society, Psychoanalysis, and the Imagination*. Stanford University Press, 1997.

Corney, R., and J Simons. "Transition to Parenthood: The Impact on Relationships and Health." *International Journal of Psychology*, vol. 39, no. 5-6, 2004, pp. 350.

Cowan, C.P., and P.A. Cowan. "New Families: Modern Couples as New Pioneers." *All our Families: A Report of the Berkeley Family Forum*, edited by M. A. Mason et al., Oxford University Press, 1998, pp. 169-192.

Cowdery, R.S., and C. Knudson-Martin. "The Construction of Motherhood: Tasks, Relational Connection, and Gender Equality." *Family Relations*, vol. 54, 2005, pp. 335-45.

Dempsey, Ken. "Who Gets the Best Deal from Marriage: Women or Men?" *Journal of Sociology*, vol. 38, no. 2, 2002, pp. 91-110.

Dixon, John, and Margaret Wetherell. "On Discourse and Dirty Nappies Gender, the Division of Household Labour and the Social Psychology of Distributive Justice." *Theory and Psychology*, vol. 14, no. 2, 2004, pp. 167-89.

Drago, Robert, et al. "Gender and Work Hours Transitions in Australia: Drop Ceilings and Trap-Door Floors." *Working Paper*. Melbourne Institute, 2004. (29 pages) IZA Discussion Paper No. 1210. https://ssrn.com/abstract=569185. Accessed 16 Dec. 2019

Fox, Faulkner. *Dispatches from a Not-So-Perfect Life or How I Learned to Love the House, the Man, the Child*. Harmony Books, 2003.

Glade, Aaron, et al. "A Prime Time for Marital/Relational Intervention: A review of the Transition to Parenthood Literature with Treatment Recommendations." *The American Journal of Family Therapy*, vol. 33, 2005, pp. 319-336.

Golberg, A.E., and M. Perry-Jenkins. "Division of Labor and Working-Class Women's Well-Being across the Transition to Parenthood." *Journal of Family Psychology*, vol. 18, no. 1, 2004, pp. 225-236.

Grote, N.K., et al. "Perceptions of Injustice in Family Work: The role of Psychological Distress." *Journal of Family Psychology*, vol. 18, no. 3, 2004, pp. 480-92.

Hasler, Jane. *No Bloody Wonder – Exposing the Relationship between Postnatal Depression (PND) and the Gender Order*. Dissertation. University of Sydney, 2009.

Hollway, Wendy. *The Capacity to Care Gender and Ethical Subjectivity*. Routledge, 2006.

Kaufman, Gayle. "Do Gender Role Attitudes Matter? Family Formation and Dissolution among Traditional and Egalitarian Men and Women." *Journal of Family Issues*, vol. 21, no. 1, 2000, pp. 128-44.

Kittay, Eva, editor. *The Subject of Care Feminist Perspectives on Dependency*. New York/Oxford: Rowman and Littlefield Publishers, 2002.

Kittay Feder, Eva. *Love's Labor Essays on Women, Equality and Dependency*. Routledge, 1999.

Kluwer, Esther S., et al. "The Division of Labor Across the Transition to Parenthood: A Justice Perspective." *Journal of Marriage and Family*, vol. 64, no. 4, pp. 930-43, 2002.

Lewis, Jane, and Susanna Giullari. "The Adult Worker Model Family, Gender Equality and Care: The Search for New Policy Principles and the Possibilities and Problems of a Capabilities Approach." *Economy and Society*, vol. 34, no. 1, 2005, pp. 76-104.

Lister, Ruth. *Citizenship: Feminist Perspectives*. New York University Press, 2003.

Maschka, K. *This Is Not How I Thought It Would Be Remodeling: Motherhood to Get the Lives We Want Today*. Berkley Publishing Group, 2009.

Maushart, S. *The Mask of Motherhood: How Mothering Changes Everything and Why We Pretend It Doesn't*. Random House, 1997.

McHale, J. P., et al. "The Transition to Coparenthood: Parents' Prebirth Expectations and Early Coparental Adjustment at 3 Months Postpartum." *Development and Psychopathology*, vol. 16, 2004, pp. 711-33.

Moller Okin, Susan. *Justice, Gender and the Family.* Basic Books, 1989.

NATSEM. "She Works Hard for the Money Australian Women and the Gender Divide." *AMP NATSEM Income and Wealth Report.* University of Canberra, 2009.

Nicholson, Paula, and Anne Woollett. "The Social Construction of Motherhood and Fatherhood." *The Psychology of Reproduction Vol. 3: Current Issues in Infancy and Parenthood,* edited by C. Niven and A. Walker, Butterworth Heineman, 1998.

Nilsen, Ann, and Julia Brannen. "Transitions for the EU Framework 5 Study 'Gender, Parenthood and the Changing European Workplace.'" *Interview Study Executive Summary.* Manchester Metropolitan University, Research Institute for Health and Social Change, 2005.

Nystrom, K, and K. Ohrling. "Parenthood Experiences During the Child's First Year: Literature Review." *Journal of Advanced Nursing,* vol. 46, no. 3, 2004, pp. 319-30.

Paz Galupo, M., and Jean F. Ayers. "Negotiating the Maternal and Sexual Breast: Narratives of Breastfeeding Mothers." *Journal of the Association for Research on Mothering,* vol. 4, no. 1, 2002, pp. 20-30.

Power, R. *The Divided Heart Art and Motherhood.* Red Dog, 2008.

Rosenberg, Harriet. "Motherwork, Stress, and Depression: The Costs of Privatized Social Reproduction." *Feminism and Political Economy Women's Work, Women's Struggles,* edited by H. J. Maroney and M. Luxton, Methuen, 1987, pp. 181-96.

Seidman, Steven, et al., eds. *Introducing the New Sexuality Studies Original Essays and Interviews.* Routledge, 2006.

Summers, Anne. *The End of Equality: Work, Babies and Women's Choices in 21st Century Australia.* Random House, 2003.

Waldfogel, Jane. "The Effect of Children on Women's Wages." *American Sociological Review,* vol. 62, 1997, pp. 209-17.

Waring, Marilyn. *Counting for Nothing What Men Value and What Women are Worth.* Allen and Unwin, 1988.

Section III

Mothering in Context

Chapter Twelve

Unpacking Monomaternalism within a Queer Motherhood Framework

Mel Freitag

> Our notions of motherhood [are shaken] and seem to have taken
> the nature out of Mother Nature ... neither nature nor mothers can
> be assumed to be what they were.
> —Schwartz 240

My body is marked as more feminine, so I was the one in the queer relationship that people assumed would carry a child to term. My genderqueer partner decided to carry first for a variety of reasons, including that she is biracial and wanted a biological child who resembled her. Queer motherhoods complicate how parenthood is defined, particularly from the time before conception through to the moment of birth. Even during birth class, the assumption that the biological, moral, and stable mother will innately know more about breastfeeding, as well as be the one taking notes and asking more questions, is situated within a heteronormative parental structure. In our birthing class, I took the notes.

Shelley Park coined the term "monomaternalism" in her recent book, *Mothering Queerly, Queering Motherhood*. Monomaternalism is not only perpetuated by culture but also by biology. In fact, even within the queer world, there are constructions of what it means to be a good queer and a bad queer, and parenthood many times fits a little too safely into a heteronormative framework as "good." Therefore, a nonbiological queer mother resists not only the stereotypical feminine biological mother but also the stereotypical childless lesbian. From the moment a queer-identified couple decides to have a child (Mamo)—and through stories of fertility clinics, donor sperm, naming practices, birthing stories, the birth itself, and into the first year of the beloved's life—their decisions and constructions of motherhood resist not only heterosexual roles (Ben-Ari and Livni) but also femininity and the cult of true womanhood.

This chapter uses a queer motherhood framework (Suter) to situate how I position and name my own nonbiological mother narrative, which resists invasive heteronormative conceptions. Even couples who are infertile and couples who adopt are still supported by a heterosexual master narrative. Queer motherhood, however, transforms parenting practices, such as traditional divisions of labour (Matos), and what it means to be a mother of a child I created (Moraga; Aizley); being with my partner through the moment of conception, pregnancy, and birth changes how nonbiological parenthood is defined. This construction of nonbiological queer parenthood is not parallel with adoptive parents; my child's biological parent is the person I love (Gabb). Perhaps these subversive parenting structures can build better and more egalitarian and vulnerable family constructions. Maternal ambivalence may be a vehicle then for nonbiological mothers to have a voice—that is, because of their position within the institutional hierarchy of motherhood, nonbiological mothers are vulnerable and find themselves forced to choose between two worlds. In this case, I will argue that nonbiological mothers are caught between aligning themselves with fathers, which many do, or producing a new form of queer motherhood that transgresses the mother-father binary and builds a new paradigm of the queer family.

Naming the "Other" Mother: Defined by What I am Not

Much of the literature uses inconsistent terms for the naming of the "other" mother and what the child calls the parent (Abelsohn). Queer mothers have often been described as the "other" mother; "de novo families" (Hayman 274); "mather"—a hybrid form of mother and father (Padavic 176); nonbiological mothers (Reinmann 716); and, of course, with such adjective as "complex," "tenuous," and "shadowy." All of these terms resist the singular institution of motherhood, the "honoured" (DiLapi 110) or "moral" mother, as well as the notion of the authentic or so-called real biological mother. Clearly, the naming of these identities is situated within larger social assumptions about the institution of motherhood (Rich).

Interestingly, none of these authors attempt to relabel the biological mother category, only to rename and situate the "non" category. By not revising the category of the biological and authentic mother, the essentialized and moral mother stays intact. In order to truly dismantle the problematic aspects of the institution of motherhood, it may be necessary to disrupt and transform the gestational mother's identity as much as the nonbiological one. For example, when the nonbiological mother takes on breastfeeding—or more of the household duties like childcare—or fills out the forms for school or the thousand other duties that are assigned to the traditional biological mother, it begins to dismantle the expectations of traditional motherhood. For this reason, I will continue to use the most conventional term, nonbiological mother, until the biological mother category can also be disrupted and renamed.

Intentional Decision Making in Queer Family Planning

A nonbiological queer motherhood narrative begins well before birth. Decision making has to include intentionally creating a sense of family in a society that does not necessarily fully recognize queer life (Oswald). Much of the literature addresses parental rights as a central issue to nonbiological mothers, since the nonbiological mother did not give birth to the child and might not have been able legally marry the birthmother, especially as the legality of same-sex marriage is not universally recognized.[1] Although assuring parental rights in same-sex motherhood can, in many ways, validate and substantiate true motherhood or at least true parenthood, it is not the panacea that will normalize how queer families are viewed.

For queer families, the decision to parent a child has to be legally and medically intentional—that is, they have to act on and negotiate a variety of legal and medical terrains before they can inseminate. In my case, although my partner and I were married before our daughter was born, I still had to go through second-parent adoption in order to ensure full parentage across state borders while navigating the ever-changing landscape of same sex family law. Often, when we are discussing family planning and the number of children we are going to have, my straight friends will jokingly say, "well, you never know!" I reply back, "actually we do." Whenever we are trying for a baby, we have to march over the infertility clinic and do the insemination. This conscious decision making already resists the heteronormative narrative of a "surprise" or "oops" baby, or that one night of unprotected love making could create another human being.

Linder Erlandsson's work in Sweden on nonbiological lesbian mothers was validating. Through her interviews of nonbirth lesbian mothers, she found that most nonbirth lesbian mothers "felt like everyone else, but not quite," (99). Even though I am in a monogamous relationship, I do not fit in the mother-father binary—a feeling that began in the fertility clinic where we saw images of heterosexual couples and realized their interventions were built on the assumption that we were infertile. In fact, we did not have much guidance once the clinic found out we were a healthy, young lesbian couple, who just needed a few inseminations, which was the least invasive and least expensive procedure there.

In addition to the intentional decision-making process, there are also differences in the way parents choose the donor and whether or not they will meet the donor. In a study surveying both nonbiological mothers and fathers who used "open" anonymous donor sperm. "Open" means the researchers asked whether the parents would eventually like to meet the child's donor, but anonymous up until the child turns 18 years old; 73 per cent of nonbiological mothers indicated they would like to meet the donor, whereas 45 per cent of the fathers indicated the same (Pelka 397). Even though the same procedure and many of the same decisions are made when heterosexual couples use anonymous donor sperm, many of the fathers do not wish to meet the donor. In many ways, this is a consequence of deeply rooted patriarchal thinking that says as long as there is one mother plus one father, the biogenetic relatedness is not as central (Pelka 397).

Irene Padavic and Jungian Butterfield point out that "essential motherhood"—the one biological birthmother structure—is at the top of the motherhood hierarchy (177). Below the biological mother would be not only nonbiological mothers but also single mothers, grandmothers, stepmothers, and the like. Because the Western, Eurocentric definition of "family" is structured around the biological myth that a mother is strictly designated by biology, essential motherhood is central to external and internal notions of what it means to be a woman and a parent. Suzanne Pelka argues that LGBTQ people internalize some of the same biologic-relatedness philosophies, including choosing a sperm donor who looks like the nonbiological mother to ensure more biological similarities. Sadly, LGBTQ people are also not immune to internalizing the notion that authentic motherhood is singular (Suter 459, 467).

It is important to define what co-motherhood means in order to better understand queer motherhood. Elizabeth Suter identifies four tenets of what they call co-motherhood, one of the many names for queer motherhood. The four tenets are:

1. Biological ties are not needed to render mother-child relationships real and legitimate.

2. A child can have more than one real mother.

3. A father's presence is not necessary for raising well-adjusted children.

4. Nonbiological motherhood also equals moral motherhood.

During my own transition to queer motherhood, I thought a lot about the first two tenets of Suter's work. Therefore, queer motherhood, or co-motherhood, transgresses these normative biological assumptions, but is often perceived as not as real or genuine. In fact, some question whether this positioning of a mother is even possible.

Division of Labour in Queer Families

Literature on same-sex families usually includes discussion concerning the division of labour and who takes care of daily household activities, childcare, finances, laundry, dishes, and other day-to-day domestic operations. In 2015, the U.S. Families and Work Institute wrote a report titled *Modern Families: Same and Different Sex Families Negotiating at Home.* They report found that there are typically no significant statistical differences in everyday operations of the household between same-sex couples and different-sex couples. However, the report also had some interesting findings related to childcare; same- and different-sex couples divide up childcare differently. Of the families interviewed, 74 per cent of same-sex couples shared childcare responsibility, as compared to only 38 per cent in the different-sex couples. This included most of the day-to-day childcare tasks (Matos 8). Maureen Sullivan also finds that within same-sex female households, household responsibilities are more equally shared (70); division of responsibilities depended upon the skill set each individual parent had as well as personal preferences, not traditional gender roles. This notion circles back again to Abbie Goldberg's (17) "egalitarian ethic" and how that framework manifests in queer female relationships, especially for childcare responsibilities, parenting styles, and family values. Although biology can still affect the naming of a parental identity, as well as increase isolation and stress for the nonbiological parent, it rarely affects how childcare responsibilities are divided. This was the case even when controlled for breastfeeding.

However, not all queer mothers transgress heteronormative practices. Homonormativity, a term that is used to describe tendencies among nonheterosexuals to assimilate to heteronormative standards, is still surprisingly prevalent in some lesbian households. Abbie Goldberg and Maureen Perry-Jenkins show that if the birthmother believes that biology matters more, she is more likely to perform more of the stereotypical female childcare duties (310). Likewise, if the couple is more committed to an egalitarian philosophy, the childcare duties are more shared. Jordan Downing and Abbie Goldberg also echo this "spontaneously earned" ethic and define it as the couple's philosophy that gender and birth status are irrelevant. With these families, non-biological motherhood formed a new "homonormative way of presenting one's relations [that was] independent of the surrounding heteronormativity" (265). A new queer model of motherhood seems to be developing when looking at division of childcare labour in particular. When reading Downing and Golberg's article, I realized that my family fit into the spontaneously earned model, and it was validating to have a name not only for my own nonbiological parental status but also a name for our family structure and parental values. This spontaneously earned way of thinking of birth and gender as irrelevant contrasts with the deeply embedded heteronormative ideals of parenthood, the nuclear family, and monomaternalism. Further, it not only resists it, but provides a new way of defining motherhoods, and how we shape what it means to be a parent.

Transition to Queer Motherhood

I was the first person to "catch" my daughter after birth, and when she opened her eyes, she saw mine before my partner's. Our eyes locked, and I knew we would be forever connected. Adital Ben-Ari and Tali Livini discuss the curious transformation that nonbiological mothers make. Her research of Israeli biological and nonbiological mothers shows more similarities concerning the physical experience of birth: both parents viewed birth as a mutual process during the labour. Another interesting finding was that in becoming mothers, lesbians have not become perceived as joining heteronormative and mainstream society.

Many heterosexual women experience the necessity of having to do it all, even when they come from a more educated or higher socioeconomic background (Wolf). Even though there is a strong my-husband-is-not-a-babysitter movement, which resists the notion that the bulk of childrearing duties are women's responsibilities, women in straight families generally do more of the childrearing day-to-day tasks as compared to queer families (Chan 402). There is an assumption that the male-identified parent chooses to participate in childcare or is even named as the babysitter because it's so rare that he does any household duties. Breastfeeding was one of the more centralized biological behaviours framing the biological mother as more essential for the child's development and to position the biological mother as the so-called real mother. Surprisingly, even when queer parents have an "egalitarian ethic" (Goldberg) during conception and pregnancy, they usually fall into traditional heteronormative roles. The birth or breastfeeding mother becomes the central figure in the child's life, fitting the master heterosexual narrative. I did not realize how pervasive parenting gender roles still are until I became a parent myself.

In queer families, most parents are committed to egalitarian family structures. This was apparent even if breastfeeding may have initially been front and centre, and led to more traditional employment choices, in which the nonbiological mother was more likely to work and the biological mother was more likely to stay at home. Even when the children became toddlers, the division of labour would sometimes still fall within the more heteronormative framework (Goldberg and Perry-Jenkins 17). This also depended on whether or not the nonbiological mother identified as more masculine or wanted to be a biological mother at some point. All of these factors lead to a complex and diverse understanding of queer motherhood. In short, not all queer mothers queer the idea of the mother-father binary. Some uphold it. In reading through much of the literature, I realized I did not fit even within a queer motherhood narrative; society assumes that the more feminine partner would gestate the child. Biology still remains a silent marker of difference, even within queer families.

The transition to motherhood for nonbiological parents is complicated by the fact that it generally lacks both legal and biological substantiation and has few role models, which can lead to feelings of alienation (Wojnar 58). Some nonbiological queer mothers indicate they may not only feel invisible but perform motherhood, consistent with Butler's (1993) ideas about performing gender. Regarding this performance, Shelley Park argues that nonbiological mothers tend to feel like they are passing: "It is incumbent on us ... to know the script for good mothering well and to audition for the role convincingly" (24). Since pregnancy is defined as solely a female experience, and even as a rite of passage for women, it would make sense that nonbiological queer mothers would align more with the father role. This explains why I felt like I was "almost but not quite the real parent" when my daughter was born. Donuta Wojnar discusses the risk of being invisible and even having a "shadowy" status in between the male-female and mother-father binaries. Sullivan discusses the binary concept of the food mother and the fun mother; one mother makes the food, and the other mother is the "fun dad" figure. This binary, however, still reflects the heteronormative structure, in which the mother provides essential life elements and the father is the playful figure. Pelka discusses the paradox of shared motherhood:

> The puzzle for families headed by two mothers is to psy-
> chologically negotiate each woman's learned expectations that
> she would one day be her child's most central relational object
> and primary attachment figure. When motherhood, a status
> generally defined by its singularity, is shared it can be challenging
> to one's internalized sense of one's own full maternal status,
> particularly if one is not the birth/biological mother. (197)

Because the primary attachment to our child was shared, there was no secondary father figure. However, at times, I still felt like a "half" or "step" mother instead of the essential one. It is a paradox because we both possess maternal qualities and, therefore, had to negotiate how to build a collective versus individual notion of what it meant to be a mother and a parent.

Mothers who do not fit heteronormative expectations experience ambivalence about their role in the family. New schemas for family life, such as polymaternalism (more than one mother figure in a family), provide a new paradigm for defining our shared familial experience. Until we truly begin to dismantle the construction of biological motherhood, all of the other types of motherhood will remain on the margins. When mothers tell me that they are the only one in the relationship that ever does anything, or when mothers post questions on Facebook that address only other mothers and not parents, I can transform the conversation simply by sharing my own experience, but that is not enough. Maybe no variation of motherhood is truly stable, definitive, or certain. Maybe all variations of motherhood are ambivalent, contradictory, and changeable. If we are comfortable living in the ambivalence of motherhood, perhaps then the unattainable expectations of the motherhood role will be more evenly distributed and shared among other players. Only when motherhood is radically dismantled can a new politic of parenthood be born.

Endnote

1. Same sex marriage was legalized in the United States in June 2015; in England, it was legalized March 13 2014; and in Australia, the legislation varies by state, but same-sex couples have been protected by de facto union legislation since 1975.

Works Cited

Abelsohn, K., et al. "Celebrating the 'Other' Parent: Mental Health and Wellness of Expecting Lesbian, Bisexual, and Queer Non-Birth Parents." *Journal of Gay & Lesbian Mental Health,* vol. 17, 2003, pp. 387-405.

Aizley, H. *Confessions of the other Mother: Non-Biological Lesbian Moms Tell All.* Beacon Press, 2006.

Ben-Ari, Adital, and Tali Livni. "Motherhood Is Not a Given Thing: Experiences and Constructed Meanings of Biological and

Nonbiological Lesbian Mothers." *Sex Roles*, vol. 54, no. 7-8, 2006, pp. 521-31.

Bos, Henny, and Frank van Balen. "Children in New Reproductive Technology: Social and Genetic Parenthood." *Patient Education and Counseling*, vol. 81, no. 3, 2010, pp. 429-35.

Butler, Judith. *Bodies that Matter: On the Discursive Limits of "Sex."* Routledge, 1993.

Chabot, Jennifer M., and Barbara D. Ames. "It Wasn't 'Let's Bet Pregnant and Go Do It': Decision Making in Lesbian Couples Planning Motherhood via Donor Insemination." *Family Relations*, vol. 53, no. 4, 2004, pp. 348-56.

Chan, Raymond W., et al. "Division of Labor among Lesbian and Heterosexual Parents: Associations with Children's Adjustment." *Journal of Family Psychology*, vol. 12, no. 3, 1998, pp. 402-19.

Ciano-Boyce, Claudia, and Lynn Shelley-Sireci. "Who is Mommy Tonight? Lesbian Parenting Issues." *Journal of Homosexuality*, vol. 43, no. 2, 2002, pp. 1-13.

DiLapi, Elena Marie. "Lesbian Mothers and the Motherhood Hierarchy." *Journal of Homosexuality*, vol. 18, no. 1-2, 1989, pp. 101-21.

Downing, J. B, and A. E. Goldberg. "Lesbian Mothers' Construction of the Division of Paid and Unpaid Labor." *Feminism & Psychology*, vol. 21, no. 1, 2011, pp. 100–120.

Dunne, Gillian A. "Opting into Motherhood: Lesbians Blurring the Boundaries and Transforming the Meaning of Parenthood and Kinship." *Gender and Society*, vol. 14, no. 1, 2000, pp. 11-35.

Erlandsson, K., et al. "Experiences of gay women during their partner's pregnancy and childbirth. *British Journal of Midwifery*, vol. 18, no. 2, 2010, pp. 99-103.

Fineman, Martha. *The Neutered Mother, the Sexual Family, and Other Twentieth Century Tragedies.* Psychology Press, 1995.

Frith, Lucy, et al. "Forming a Family with Sperm Donation: A Survey of 244 Non-Biological Parents." *Reprod Biomed Online*, vol. 24, no. 7, 2012, pp. 709-18.

Gabb, Jacqui. "Imag (in) ing the Queer Lesbian Family." *Journal of the Motherhood Initiative for Research and Community Involvement*, vol. 1, no. 2, 1999, pp. 9-20.

Goldberg, Abbie E., and Maureen Perry-Jenkins. "The Division of Labor and Perceptions of Parental Roles: Lesbian Couples across the Transition to Parenthood." *Journal of Social and Personal Relationships*, vol. 24, no. 2, 2007, pp. 297-318.

Hayman. Brenda. "*De Novo* Lesbian Families: Legitimizing the Other Mother." *Journal of GLBT Family Studies*, vol. 9, 2013, pp. 273-87.

Mamo, Laura. *Queering Reproduction: Achieving Pregnancy in the Age of Technoscience*. Duke University Press, 2009.

Matos, Kenneth. "Modern Families: Same- and Different-Sex Couples Negotiating at Home." *Families and Work Institute,* 2015. www.familiesandwork.org/downloads/modern-families.pdf. Accessed 6 Dec. 2019.

Moraga, Cherrie L. *Waiting in the Wings: Portrait of a Queer Motherhood*. Firebrand Books, 1997.

Padavic, Irene, and Jungian Butterfield. "Mothers, Fathers, and 'Mathers' Negotiating a Lesbian Co-Parental Identity." *Gender & Society*, vol. 25, no. 2, 2011, pp. 176-96.

Park, Shelley M. *Mothering Queerly, Queering Motherhood: Resisting Monomaternalism in Adoptive, Lesbian, Blended, and Polygamous Families*. SUNY Press, 2013.

Pelka, Suzanne. "The Making and Unmaking of Biological Ties in Lesbian-Led Families." *Who's Your Daddy: And Other Writings on Queer Parenting*, edited by Rachel Epstein, Sumach Press, 2009, pp. 83-92.

Oswald, Ramona Faith. "Resilience within the Family Networks of Lesbians and Gay Men:Intentionality and Redefinition." *Journal of Marriage and Family*, vol. 64, no. 2, 2002, pp. 374-83.

Rich, Adrienne. "Of Woman Born: Motherhood as Experience and Institution." New York: Bantam. 1977.

Sullivan, Maureen. *The Family of Woman. Lesbian Mothers, Their Children, and the Undoing of Gender.* University of California Press, 2004.

Suter, Elizabeth, et. al. "Motherhood as a Contested Ideological Terrain: Essentialist and Queer Discourses of Motherhood at Plan in Female-female Co-mothers' talk." *Communication Monoographs*, vol. 82, no. 4, 2015, pp. 458-483.

Thompson, Julie. *Mommy Queerest.* University of Massachusetts Press. 2002

Wojnar, Danuta, and Amy Katzenmeyer. "Experiences of Pre-conception, Pregnancy, and New Motherhood for Lesbian Non-biological Mothers." *Journal of Obstetric, Gynecologic and Neonatal Nursing,* vol. 43, no.1 , 2014, pp. 50-60.

Wolf, Naomi. *Misconceptions: Truth, Lies, and the Unexpected on the Journey to Motherhood.* Knopf Doubleday Publishing Group, 2003.

Chapter Thirteen

Mothering Children with Disabilities: Navigating Choice and Obligation

Sophia Brock

"No one ever asked me what it was like not to have a choice."
—Research participant, Keira, who has a twenty-six-year-old
daughter with an intellectual disability[1]

W
hen we think about maternal ambivalence, perhaps we think predominately of the emotional responses of mothers towards, or provoked by, their children. Mothers can feel love and hate, annoyance and wonder, fury and tenderness, and a number of other seemingly conflicting emotions towards their children. It is possible for a mother to both love her children deeply and wish that she never had children. These feelings and experiences have been posed as a tension, which results in a sense of ambivalence that is perpetuated and reinforced by wider social forces.

Yet it is also possible to think about the ways that maternal ambivalence may not only be a response to the behaviours or conditions of a child. Mothers may indeed experience seemingly opposing feelings towards their children, simultaneously desiring both intimacy and separateness from their child. Yet ambivalence can also erupt as a response to a mother's own reflections about her sense of self. Mothers can experience ambivalence when trying to reconcile and navigate who they are as women and mothers. Some mothers understand themselves as simultaneously defined by their connection to their mother role and by their separateness from their mother role. Some may feel that motherhood and their role as mothers define who they are while also asserting a sense of self and individuality through defining themselves as anything other than a mother. As Suzanne Juhasz articulates, "separation and connection orchestrate the trajectory of motherhood" (403).

This chapter investigates experiences of ambivalence among a number of women who are mothers of children with various disabilities throughout New South Wales, Australia. The participants in this study have children aged between two and thirty-seven, with various levels of intellectual and/or physical disabilities. The reflections of the participants within this research offer a number of important insights into experiences of maternal ambivalence.

Participants express love for their children just the way they are while also wishing that they could take away their child's disability. They reflect on the intensity of simultaneous feelings of joy and sorrow accompanying mothering a child with a disability. Many participants endure a process of grieving the loss of their imagined, nondisabled child. Furthermore, participants contest the ways that "normal" is defined while also situating themselves and their children within these normative frameworks they contest.

This chapter focuses on the ways women who mother children with disabilities experience ambivalence about their sense of self and identity. I connect this ambivalence to the social forces of the ideology of intensive mothering and individualization. Both of these social forces structure and frame participants' experiences in various ways, but together they serve to erupt, exaggerate, and accentuate feelings of maternal ambivalence. Intensive mothering involves assumptions of both obligation and individual choice, and these competing demands exacerbate participants' experiences of ambivalence when reflecting on their identities.

These feelings of ambivalence experienced by the participants were accentuated by inadequate social and institutional support systems for mothers of children with disabilities; social and political attitudes that expect mothers to provide intensive, prolonged, and indefinite care for their children with disabilities; and the ongoing devaluation of mothering and care work.

Individualization

The theory of individualization suggests that in light of modernity, industrialization, globalization, and the rise of technology, the nature of our institutions have changed (Beck). Ulrich Beck argues that premodern societies were based on communal structures in which people formed relationships. He suggests that communal structures moved to collective structures in early modern societies: individuals formed relationships based on shared interests, needs, and wants. Beck contends that we are now in a period of late modernity (or reflexive modernity), in which individual agency takes a primary place over structure, networks are flexible, and individuals lead self-monitoring lives. Individuals are at the centre of their own self-organizing life narratives in this current period of late modernity—they are the authors of their own lives (Beck). This increase in individual choice and flexibility is at the heart of what drives the individualization thesis.

Scholars have debated the effect individualization has had on individual lived experiences and broader social patterns. Anthony Giddens, for example, focuses on the positive potential of individualization to liberate individuals from oppressive institutions and obligations. Beck argues that individualized freedom of choice precipitates the capacity for individuals to author their own lives. Alternatively, Christopher Ray recognizes the ways that individualization has enabled flexibility, but he argues that individuals are now compelled to take personal responsibility for their newfound freedom. This newfound personal responsibility consequently imposes a different type of obligation on individuals (Ray). Alternatively, Zygmunt Bauman argues that the changing nature of our institutions and social obligations, as well as the increase in individual choice, has led to the disintegration of families. The essence of individualization as a social force is that individuals are autonomous agents who exercise choice over their lives and relationships. This sense of autonomy is in direct contrast to the equally pervasive social force of intensive mothering.

Intensive Mothering

There is a plethora of research examining the experience of mothering and its theorization as a social construction (Chodorow; Hays; Goodwin and Huppatz,; O'Reilly; Ruddick; Douglas and Michaels). Based on this research, the concept of intensive mothering has emerged. Intensive mothering is a powerful and pervasive concept that establishes who a good mother is and how she should behave. The good mother is self-sacrificing, ignores her own needs and interests, child centered, not economically self-sufficient, and monogamous; her mothering is exclusive, emotionally involved, and time-consuming (Arendell; Goodwin and Huppatz). Intensive mothering establishes this image of the good mother, through which mothering experiences are mediated, influenced, and judged. The ideology of intensive and good motherhood is frequently and powerfully represented in the media and is perpetuated in popular culture; it ultimately sets unattainable standards of perfection for mothering.

This motherhood ideology is entwined with an image of the "idealized white, middle-class, heterosexual couple" (Arendell, 1194). It is implicitly linked to theories of gender stratification but is also adaptive in its constraints about who can be a good working mother, a good adoptive mother, and so forth (Goodwin and Huppatz 2). Liena Gurevich suggests the that the "good mother" construction is a "modern, expert-defined, and culturally white middle class creation" (521). This image has been drawn from intensive mothering rhetoric and has become has an established normative construct—"a mechanism through which women do what they 'should'" (Goodwin and Huppatz, 4). Anything outside of this construct is seen as deviant, deplorable, or even morally corrupt.

Within discourses of individualization, individuals are defined by agency, autonomy, and the capacity to choose how they lead their lives. This capacity for choice allows them to make decisions governing the course of their lives and exercise freedom of choice in their relationships and personal lives. This has implications for individuals' perceptions of self and identity. Giddens writes about the "reflexive project of the self" within the context of individualization, where an individual's sense of self is something continually reflected upon. Yet understanding the self as a reflexive project within individualization is in direct contrast to the demands imposed on mothers by intensive mothering. Whereas individualization sets up assumptions about choice, intensive mothering discourses set up assumptions about obligation. As Alison Stone argues, "the inherited fabric of Western ideas that define the self [are in] contrast to maternity, and the persistence of these ideas within the contemporary parenting industry" (294).

Intensive mothering has remained the normative standard by which mothering practices and arrangements are evaluated. Mothers who do not conform to this script become surrounded by discourses of deviancy (Arendell, 1195). Thus, while becoming and being a mother can confer a sense of maternal power, it can also be an immense burden of responsibility, as mothers become subject to judgements framed by strong and enduring societal expectations (Arendell 1195-96; Hays 5). Mothers live within assumptions of obligations that are linked with intensive mothering as well as assumptions of agency and choice that are linked with individualization.

The problematic foundation of intensive mothering is that mothers should be self-sacrificing primary caregivers, whose lives are bound by obligations to their children. The problematic foundation of individualization is that all individuals in contemporary social life are, or must become, rational, individualized actors who exercise agency and freedom of choice (Garvan). Herein lies the tension that precipitates experiences of ambivalence within the participants in this study. The tension is between individualization and intensive mothering as well as between assumptions of exercising choice and assumptions of being bound by obligation. Participants are constrained in their capacity to be autonomous subjects who exercise agency and choice, and this constraint is linked to intensive mothering discourses. Due to such constraints and the tension between individualization and intensive mothering, many participants experience ambivalence when reflecting on their sense of who they are and how they see themselves as individuals.

This tension between individualization and intensive mothering, and the resulting maternal ambivalence, echoes Sharon Hays's concerns about neoliberalism and good mothering expectations. Hays argues that the ideology of intensive mothering stems from an ambivalence about a social and economic system that is based on individual suits of self-interest. Hays's identification of such ambivalence reflects the tension I am underlying between individualization and intensive mothering. Hays suggests that we have attempted to deal with the underlying uneasiness about self-interest through imposing unrealistic standards, expectations, and commitments on mothering. This makes motherhood a somewhat contradictory force within a society, which is supposedly fuelled by self-interest. For Hays, motherhood is the way in which cultural ambivalence is played out. Somewhat ironically, the way cultural ambivalence has played out provokes and fuels experiences of maternal ambivalence.

Selfhood

One way that this ambivalence operates is through the participants' reflections of their sense of self and identity as women and as mothers. This chapter and research is based on a social constructionist and feminist phenomenological methodology, which understands the self as constructed and relational: "the self is always to be found in a web of relationships and constituted by such interconnections. This philosophical stance, which always sees the individual in context and as untenable if conceptualized as solitary and self generating, found its way into sociology" (Jallinoja and Widmer 17).

Although participants are embedded within a web of relationships—impacting who they are and how they see themselves as individuals—they also inhabit a multiplicity of subject positions when reflecting on their identities. Juhasz defines maternal subjectivity as a collection of representations experienced by a woman who is a mother. Participants draw on a number of different representations when describing who they are as individuals. For example, some participants make specific distinctions between who they are as paid workers, compared with who they are as mothers. Some participants draw on language positioning themselves as caregivers and other times as mothers.

Participants use on a multiplicity of subjectivities when describing who they are in an attempt to reconcile the ambivalence and tension they experience, which is linked back to the opposition established between choice and obligation, represented and perpetuated by individualization and intensive mothering, respectively. As Stone argues, "Mothers feel that they have fallen into a formless realm that excludes meaning and agency: the agency to organize one's own life and to organize one's own experience into meaningful patterns" (294). In essence, individualization pervades Western discourses, institutions, and culture, and stands in contrast to intensive mothering (Stone 294). Stone's account of the difficulties mothers can face in exercising a sense of agency centre on the problematic assumption that underpins individualization—that individuals in contemporary social life are or, must become rational and individualized actors who exercise agency and freedom of choice. She connects this assumption with the underlying and deep-rooted expectation that for individuals to become autonomous agents, they must break away from their mother. Stone, therefore, argues that "the ultimate explanation for the difficulties of becoming a mother ... is very deep-seated: in Western civilization there has been a widespread tendency to understand the maternal body and the self in opposition to one another" (326).

Because of this definition of individualization, agency is posed in opposition with maternity. Participants experience ambivalence in negotiating their role as a mother because they live within competing frameworks of individualization and intensive mothering. Due to the way in which agency is posed in opposition to mothering, it can be difficult for women who are mothers to see themselves as subjects: "because our cultural tradition casts unified, individual selfhood in opposition to the realm of maternal bodily relations, then, being a subject and a mother or as a mother is rendered problematic" (Stone 397). Therefore, to be a subject, one must not only live through experience but also be the one authoring that experience in order to infuse it with meaning.

Participants, therefore, feel they must assert or experience their subjectivity through drawing on other subject positions besides that of mother because the maternal subject position is not seen as compatible with assumptions of individualized agency. It is in the participants' discussions about their sense of self and how they reconcile their reflections with their identities as mothers that this maternal ambivalence plays out. I will use an example of one participant's experience to highlight how ambivalence over a sense of self connects with the conflicting social forces of individualization and intensive mothering.

Case Study

Katherine lives in a northern suburb of Sydney with an above average socioeconomic profile; she is a married, part-time music teacher, with three children. Her youngest son, John, is six years old and has agenesis of the corpus callosum, resulting in speech, movement, and feeding difficulties, and Katherine describes him as presenting "like a child with cerebral palsy." John went through an intensive period of testing after he was born, which Katherine describes as a "living hell." About this early period, Katherine says the following:

> I remember applying for respite but not being considered because he was a newborn, and I think they thought a newborn needs its mother. But I couldn't even read. I actually could not even read. I couldn't make sense of a paragraph. I was that exhausted. I could not read. And it was part of the trauma. I honestly couldn't, for quite some time.

Katherine experienced, and continues to experience, isolation from her friends and members of her family. She feels as though medical professionals routinely ignore her concerns, yet she has been required to develop medical expertise in order to provide care for her son. Despite her level of education and experience gained while navigating the disability sector, she has found formal support mechanisms and services difficult to access and negotiate. Katherine confronts a number of challenges in mothering her child with a disability not necessarily connected to the needs of her child alone but to the social and institutional frameworks within which she lives.

Katherine's subject position as a teacher is integral to her sense of self and to her life: "I love my teaching. I absolutely love it." During the time that her son was an infant, she could not engage in paid teaching work. However, as his condition has improved—partly due to the intensive, grueling, and endless work that Katherine put into his care—she has started working as a teacher again three days a week:

> I mean I work three days.... I tried to work four days last year but just couldn't. I mean last year I got the shingles; I just got so sick. I honestly physically could not manage. And then this year, I got another job—because I'm part time—so I had a job in three schools and I want all of them. I want all of those jobs. But I've had to let one go, even though it's an ideal, flexible, great job for me to have. I just can't cope with any more than three days.

She positions herself as a mother and a teacher, and maintains that her role as a teacher is imperative for her to continue to care for her son in the way that she does. She says the following about her teaching: "[It] nearly kills me, but it's my creative outlet. Because I'm a creative person I've found it. I have found that I need that. I need something creative to be who I am, and I lost all of that with John." She, therefore, connects the loss of this aspect of her identity with the care work required by her son. Yet Katherine does not see her position as a teacher as necessarily distinct from her role as a mother. In fact, she connects her capacity, skills, and subject position as a teacher to her subject position as a mother: "Well because I'm a teacher, I know where he's at, and I make it my business to look at what's happening and I spend ages researching education programs... It comes quite naturally for me because I'm a teacher but it's a lot of work."

Although Katherine earlier describes the way in which the role of being a mother of a child with a disability has precipitated the loss of her creative self and her capacity to engage in paid teaching work, she still says, "But I really ... love teaching him." Katherine links her subject position as a teacher with her subject position as a mother. Therefore, although Katherine's role as a mother has precipitated a sense of loss, she can still demonstrate the way in which her role as a mother can reaffirm and bolster the enjoyment and regaining of the loss of self and creativity.

Yet despite this, Katherine still emphasizes the importance of her work as a school music teacher as separate from her subject position as a mother: "That's all I was [a mother] for a period of time; now that I'm working again, there's a 'me' out there." The intensity of care that her son requires, and the lack of proper support in providing this care, means that Katherine necessarily shapes the rest of her life around her son's needs. She describes herself as a changed person because of her role in mothering a child with a disability. Her description of her own sense of self captures the multiplicity of subjectivities that the participants have experienced and the ways in which these multiple subject positions provoke ambivalence as to how participants understand and interpret who they are.

While Katherine inhabits a multiplicity of subjectivities through her subject positions of being a teacher who is creative and a mother who is a care provider that draws on the skills of a teacher, these subject positions are inherently related. Katherine does experience her role as a teacher as something distinct from her role as a mother. Yet when she reflects on who she is, she sees a change in herself, which has come from being a mother to a child with a disability. Katherine's ambivalence and struggle to reconcile these differing positions comes from the opposition between maternity and agency that Stone identifies, which reflects the competing frameworks of intensive mothering and individualization. Katherine's struggle also reflects the strong connection she feels to her mothering role and the way it has changed her:

> I just see the big picture all the time. One of my friends said to me, and I think this is true, that it exaggerates your emotions—so you feel the true depth of sadness or if you have a really happy moment you can really see it. Like I get the most immense joy out of a little milestone that he may make, but I'm generally walking on eggshells. I'm very fragile. I can burst into tears, and I don't see it coming. I'm a changed person. I can be at work having a conversation with someone, and they'll say something and it's [a] stab in my heart.... It could be anything. I could see a beautiful healthy child and ca-chow [cutting noise].

Mothering a child with a disability has changed Katherine's perspective on who she is, how she sees others, and how she lives her life. She earlier emphasized the importance of her role as a teacher in providing her with a sense of self separate to her subject position as a mother. Yet in the quote above, she provides an example of a key moment of change, where her subject position as teacher and subject position as mother intersect. By describing how someone at work could easily say something that triggers a stab in her heart, Katherine identifies the context of paid work—a place where she most fully inhabits a sense of self in distinction from her position as a mother—and demonstrates how her subject position as a mother inescapably collides with this supposedly distinct context. Being a mother of a child with a disability has changed Katherine, as she now understands how her self as a teacher and her self as a mother are both distinct yet intertwined:

> I think I'm strong. I think I'm so strong. I'm fragile all the time. But to do what I've done.... I cannot believe what I have endured [whispering]. It's unbelievable.... I've worked so hard. I've gone through hell [whispering]. I've watched him suffer like you wouldn't believe. So I think I'm so much stronger. I don't look resilient, but seriously [tearful] ... I don't think anyone knows—even my husband.

Katherine's reflection on her self is full of ambivalence. She is strong yet fragile. She is a survivor, but she feels broken. What she has endured has brought suffering as well as fostered resilience. Katherine's reflection highlights the type of ambivalence, tension, and complexity that can exist for participants when they reflect on who they are. Such tensions and complexities are the consequence of the competing frameworks of intensive mothering and individualization as well as the resulting assumptions about obligation and choice. For some participants, a sense of coherence is an illusion, which can lead to a sense of ambivalence. Katherine's fragility masks her strength, and her strength masks her fragility. It is within these multilayered understandings of the self that these mothers can challenge maternity being placed in opposition to agency and choice. Katherine understands the ambivalent impact that becoming a mother to a child with a disability has had on her life; she is aware of the constraints this has provoked as well as the ways in which such constraints have highlighted her strength and resilience.

Conclusion

As Katherine's case shows, mothers of children with disabilities can experience maternal ambivalence. This ambivalence does not necessarily only relate to feelings towards their child, but it can be a response to reflexive interpretations of their sense of self and identity. Mothers of children with disabilities can feel ambivalent when reflecting on who they are and how their role as mothers is entwined with their sense of identity (or not).

This ambivalence over their maternal identity is experienced within the context of two competing social forces: intensive mothering and individualization. Intensive mothering discourses create unattainable expectations of what good mothering is and assumes a high level of self-sacrifice on the part of mothers, whereas individualization assumes that individuals today are rational, autonomous agents who exercise choice and agency.

Participants who are mothers of children with disabilities live within the context of these two social forces, and their experiences are framed by the contrasting assumptions of choice and obligation. One of the ways that the tension plays out between these two assumptions is through participants' ambivalence over their identity. The participants, such as in the case of Katherine, try and reconcile such ambivalence through occupying multiple subject positions—that of mother, worker, or anything other than a mother. Occupying these multiple subject positions allows participants to reflect on their identities as women, where mothering is central to who they are but also not completely representative of who they are. The need to create such distinctions through the occupation of multiple subject positions can be interpreted as challenging the ways in which maternity is juxtaposed with agency.

Ultimately, the feelings of ambivalence experienced by mothers of children with disabilities need to be connected and understood within the framework of broader social forces and institutional structures. Experiences of maternal ambivalence for women who mother children with disabilities are also heightened by the following: inadequate social and institutional support mechanisms; social and political attitudes that assume these mothers will provide intensive, prolonged, and indefinite care for their child; the ongoing devaluation of care work and mothering; and social ambivalence about disability itself. The social forces of individualization and intensive mothering are embedded within contemporary Western culture and society, which contributes to and reflects feelings of maternal ambivalence.

Endnote

1. The names of all participants and their children within this research are pseudonyms.

Works Cited

Arendell, Terry. "Conceiving and Investigating Motherhood: The Decade's Scholarship." *J Marriage and Family Journal of Marriage and Family*, vol. 62, no. 4, 2000, pp. 1192-207.

Bauman, Zygmunt. *Liquid Love: On the Frailty of Human Bonds*. Polity Press, 2003.

Beck-Gernsheim, Elisabeth. "On the Way To A Post-Familial Family: From A Community Of Need To Elective Affinities." *Theory, Culture & Society*, vol. 15, no. 3, 1998, pp. 53-70.

Beck, Ulrich. *Risk Society*. Sage Publications, 1992.

Chodorow, Nancy. *The Reproduction of Mothering: Psychoanalysis and the Sociology of Gender.* University of California, 1978.

Douglas, Susan J., and Meredith Michaels. *The Mommy Myth: The Idealization of Motherhood and How It Has Undermined Women.* Free Press, 2004.

Giddens, Anthony. *The Transformation of Intimacy.* Stanford University Press, 1992.

Goodwin, Susan, and Kate Huppatz. *The Good Mother: Contemporary Motherhoods in Australia.* University Of Sydney Press, 2010.

Gurevich, Liena. "Patriarchy? Paternalism? Motherhood Discourses in Trials of Crimes Against Children." *Sociological Perspectives,* vol. 51, no. 3, 2008, pp. 515-39.

Hays, Sharon. *The Cultural Contradictions of Motherhood.* Yale University Press, 1996.

Jallinoja, Riitta, and Eric Widmer. *Families and Kinship in Contemporary Europe: Rules and Practices of Relatedness.* Palgrave Macmillan, 2011.

Juhasz, Suzanne. "Mother-Writing and the Narrative of Maternal Subjectivity." *Studies in Gender and Sexuality,* vol. 4, no. 4, 2003, pp. 395-425.

O'Reilly, Andrea, editor. *Maternal Theory: Essential Readings.* Demeter, 2007.

Ray, Christopher. "Individualization and the Third Age." *Centre for Rural Economy. Discussion Paper Series No. 3.* University of Newcastle Upon Tyne, 2005.

Ruddick, Sara. *Maternal Thinking: Toward a Politics of Peace.* Beacon Press, 1989.

Stone, Alison. "Psychoanalysis and Maternal Subjectivity." *Mothering and Psychoanalysis: Clinical, Sociological and Feminist Perspectives,* edited by Petra Bueskens, Demeter, 2012, pp. 325-42.

Chapter Fourteen

Unnatural Women: Reflections on Discourses on Child Murder and Selective Mortal Neglect[1]

Susan Hogan

T his chapter reflects on historical ambivalence towards mothers, especially a reluctance to prosecute, or harshly punish, women who murdered their newborn babies. I suggest that in nineteenth- and early-twentieth-century England, there was increasing social tolerance towards child murder, which ran counter to the polemical and evangelical religious arguments against the crime.[2] In this chapter, I consider the legal perception of cases of intentional child murder and the debates that took place in court, referring to trial records. This ambivalence about convicting women for murder was manifested in an ad hoc manner with a variety of defence strategies in operation, as will be illustrated. As one may expect, the cases themselves varied tremendously—from a woman in utter despair attempting to kill herself and her baby simultaneously by drowning, to cases in which the murder could be considered to be quite calculated. Although cases in which sickly and possibly unviable infants are "let go" through a process of selective mortal neglect are technically murder, they are quite different from putting a newborn to a violent end. I argue that a variety of social practices and attitudes towards childhood illness obscured a high tolerance of child murder and that the neglect of newborns elicited tacit understanding, if not social acceptance.

Lewd Murderers? The Legal Situation in England

Modern sensibilities are very different from those in the nineteenth and early twentieth century with respect to how mothers who murdered were regarded and depicted in public domains. This chapter will elucidate these profound differences. Using the English Old Bailey Court Proceedings, anthropological as well as historical literature, I reexamine and reframe notions of infanticide and argue that a variety of social practices and attitudes towards childhood illness obscured a high tolerance of child murder.

One of the central ambivalences to be touched upon is that of social institutions towards illegitimate children; the higher than average death rates of such children point to social practices and attitudes that placed less value upon their lives than those of so-called legitimate children. Although there was some social tolerance of child murder, religious arguments proposed fierce retribution for it. In his book *New-Born Child Murder: Women, Illegitimacy and the Courts in Eighteenth-Century England,* Mark Jackson notes that the "path of female ruin from lust through to death" was a leitmotif used in deliberations of newborn child murder throughout the eighteenth century (Jackson 111). For example, Mathew Henry, a Presbyterian minister, chose this text for a cheery prison sermon in England in 1701: "Then when Lust hath conceived, it bringeth forth Sin: and Sin, when it is finished, bringeth forth Death" (James 1.15 qtd. in Jackson 111). Many women awaiting the death penalty for the murder of their bastard offspring might have been subjected to this kind of lecture.

The legal situation was quite different in the periods under discussion in several crucial respects. A harsh law of 1624 pronounced that a woman who tried to conceal a dead baby's body, born out of wedlock, was guilty of murder and liable to the death penalty. The onus was on the mother to prove that the baby had died of natural causes or had been stillborn. However, from 1803, women were considered innocent until proven guilty. Moreover, to secure a murder charge, it was necessary for the prosecution to establish "that the infant was fully born and existing independently of the mother's body at the moment that the crime took place" (Marland 170). It was often difficult for the prosecution to prove that the baby was "fully born" at the point that an act of violence took place—such as strangulation, for example, which could have occurred before the baby's body had fully emerged from the mother's body—and women were given the benefit the of doubt. In many such cases, obvious signs of intent to murder were simply overlooked. The not-fully-born defence was invoked and accepted, I suggest, because of societal ambivalence about seeing women, often in desperate circumstances, being prosecuted for murder of a newborn child. Some of these children were in demographic circumstances that gave them over a 50 per cent chance of dying anyway, as will be further discussed. For this reason, women tended to be prosecuted for the lesser offence of "concealment of birth," a practice associated with wrongdoing, since childbirth was customarily a public event. Concealment carried a sentence of up to two years imprisonment and became a separate offence in 1828. No woman was hanged for the murder of a baby after 1849 (Marland 170). The Infanticide Act of 1938 created the offence of infanticide to be used as an alternative to murder in those cases in which the child was under twelve months of age and "at the time of the act or omission the balance of her mind was disturbed by reason of her not having fully recovered from the effect of giving birth to the child or by reason of the effect of lactation consequent upon the birth of the child" (Infanticide Act 1938, sl [1]).

So here are, as we shall see in the forthcoming extracts of court transcripts, two popular nineteenth-century defense arguments becoming enshrined in legislation. The Infanticide Act allowed for lesser sentences to be handed down (e.g., probation instead of a prison sentence or a conditional discharge). From this Act on, the majority of the cases led to probation rather than to custodial sentences, or were not prosecuted at all (Mackay 209-10). The Butler Report noted the advantage of the infanticide plea over that of "diminished responsibility" was that it permitted the prosecution to seek a sentence of infanticide rather than murder in the first instance (para.19.26). Second, the Butler Report also noted "that by so doing the prosecution conceded with mental disturbance which the woman would not have to prove" (Mackay 209). In other words, the infanticide plea once accepted meant that women did not have to provide further evidence of mental disturbance, as its acceptance was implicit. Indeed murder, as noted in the introduction, is perhaps too emotive a term for some of what I wish to describe, which will include a discussion of the "letting go" of sickly and unviable infants.

Of Milk and Madness

The two main forms of insanity identified were called puerperal mania and puerperal melancholia, and as we shall see, instability associated with lactation was also a dominant trope. Then, as now, there were occasional sensational accounts of murders of babies and older children by women who appeared to have become insane. Women who were usually placid were described as showing frenzied and altered states of behaviour. Robert Gooch, who wrote on the subject of puerperal insanity, suggested in 1829, that the process of gestation and birth were potentially destabilising:

> During that long process, or rather succession of processes, in which the sexual organs of the human female are employed in forming, lodging, expelling, and lastly feeding the offspring, there is no time at which the mind may not become disordered; but there are two periods at which this is chiefly liable to occur, the one soon after delivery when the body is sustaining the effects of labour, the other several months afterwards, when the body is sustaining the effects of nursing. (54)

Women suffering from postpartum delirium (child-bed fever) might harm their infants in a moment of frenzy (Hogan, "The Tyranny of the Maternal Body"). There was the possibility that the symptoms of delirium caused by puerperal fever could be mistaken for mental illness, in which case the mother could be imprisoned as insane. Women who harmed their babies in a state of mania could be incarcerated indefinitely "during His Majesty's pleasure" or "be detained till His majesty's pleasure be known" (Hogan "The Tyranny of the Maternal Body"). They suffered a complete loss of liberty and could languish indeterminately. Yet women could be released if it was deemed they had recovered, so a claim of temporary insanity could be advantageous. Consequently, claims of temporary insanity via postpartum mania became a popular defense. To give an example, Elizabeth Hodges, indicted for the wilful murder of her infant daughter in 1838, was found not guilty because she was "insane at the time of committing the offence." The court records note that "it is not unfrequented [sic] for women during parturition, and shortly after, to be affected with a mania peculiar to that state—it is called puerperal mania—deficiency of milk, and the milk flowing upwards, would very probably cause such consequences."[3]

To a modern reader, the notion of the milk flowing the wrong way is odd if not frankly comical, but the idea of temporary insanity—puerperal mania—allowed a women to escape the death penalty if she killed her infant in a delirious condition. Furthermore, she could potentially avoid custody entirely. Medical and gynecological literature frequently drew links between breastfeeding and disorders of the mind or brain. Lactation that was protracted or which stopped suddenly was thought to be problematic and was often listed by asylum doctors as causing insanity. Precise explanations for this varied but could include the breast being in such a state of irritation that it extended its influence to the brain (Digby 201).

In fact, the links to the production of milk are not as absurd as they first appear. Milk stasis, a buildup of milk within the breast, can be serious. Mastitis is a condition that causes a woman's breast tissue to become painful and swollen and can include feverish states in which she may well not be fully mentally competent due to bacteriological infection. Nevertheless, my suggestion is that in many such cases, the insanity defense represents a desire not to convict women of murder; the mania is presumed rather than necessarily seen. Ambivalence, or indeed outright distaste for seeing such mothers prosecuted, led to such presumptions, as will be illustrated.

This attitude can be seen in the example of Emily Batt who drowned her baby near London Bridge in 1883 and tried but failed to drown herself at the same time. Testimony at the court case suggested that a "woman who has had a child may suffer from puerperal mania for some months and lack of food would very probably produce mental aberration." Although she was found guilty of manslaughter, the jury recommended mercy and she was given a one-year jail term.[4] Here we have a very clear example of a jury supposing that the women in question might have had a starvation-induced mental condition, which coupled with puerperal mania caused the aberrant behaviour. In addition, since the woman was in a situation in which raising a child was difficult or improbable, the jury might have been more sympathetic.

In a similar case, Maxwell Rae was indicted for and charged with the wilful murder of her newborn child in 1888, but she was found not guilty as "when the prisoner committed the offence she was suffering from puerperal mania, and was not accountable for her actions." Furthermore, a surgeon testified that the injuries sustained by the infant might not have been inflicted until after the death of the child.[5] She was given the benefit of the doubt as to when the injuries were inflicted, whether upon a corpse or a living child. This is another fairly straightforward account in which a murderess was found not responsible for her actions.

Puerperal mania was not always a successful defense. Minnie Wells who killed her daughter in 1894 is another example in which the mania defense was attempted but unsuccessful. There was considerable debate in the court records about whether puerperal mania could "come on suddenly," how much the women would recall, and what her conduct had been prior to the offense.[6] The respectability of women could have a bearing on how harshly they were viewed. Even when unsuccessful, the debate about the possibility of sudden onset of puerperal mania certainly shows an attempt to use this defense. In a similar case, Julia Lee was found guilty of the murder of her baby daughter in 1894. Puerperal mania was briefly considered as a cause, but then depression exacerbated by alcohol was thought more likely. She was found guilty of manslaughter and sentenced to eighteen months hard labour.[7] The puerperal mania defense did not work for Louise Beaumont either, whose newborn infant was found alive but mortally injured in 1903. The court conjectured that a fall might have caused the injury, with the weight of the mother falling upon the infant having caused the harm. She was found guilty of manslaughter and given five years' penal servitude.[8]

In 1904, Louise Lunn, a domestic servant, having given birth in her room, murdered her newborn daughter by tying a handkerchief around her throat, hid the body up the chimney, and feigned dropsy for the need to rest. She admitted to the murder when challenged by a doctor, who had been called by her employers to tend to her and to fetch the dead baby, which had been wrapped in a brown paper parcel tied up with string. One of sixteen children herself, she was noted to have been very kind towards her siblings. Although she was found guilty of manslaughter, Lunn was discharged.[9] This case illustrates a compassionate attitude and an unwillingness to prosecute, even after a full confession.

Another case that illustrates a compassionate attitude and tendency towards leniency, even after a full confession, is that of Clara HIlderbrand, an alleged rape victim, who was charged with the willful murder of her newborn child in 1905. There was evidence that the infant had received a blow or blows from the blunt end of a meat chopper and that she then disposed of the body in the water closet. She had clearly admitted the crime by saying, "I am exceedingly sorry. I did not mean to murder the child, but I was so worried I did not know what I was doing." The court could not decide if she had been suffering from a transitory mania or not, and gave her the benefit of the doubt, with a lenient sentence of twelve months imprisonment for manslaughter.[10]

Another case from about the same period records depression due to suppressed milk, recorded in the court records as "puerperal melancholia." Puerperal mania was noted as "a form of mental illness not un-frequently following childbirth" and suggests that those committing infanticide could be perfectly lucid. In this case, Florence Britt was found guilty of murder, though not responsible, for her action at the time. Nonetheless, she was detained at Her Majesty's pleasure. The court testimony stated as follows:

> Persons suffering from that disease are fully aware of what they are doing—sometimes there is no motive for committing the offence—very often the woman is seen to be affectionate a short time before the act—the suppression of milk is a frequent cause—I understand this child was not suckled by its mother—there is always depression in such a case as this.[11]

This discussion is interesting in its dogmatic assertion that depression is inevitable in such cases where the mother cannot breastfeed her child.

Liminal Lives

Murder and manslaughter account for a small proportion of nineteenth- and early-twentieth-century infant deaths in Britain; infants in their first week of life suffered high mortality rates (Rose 8). Many working women also suffered multiple miscarriages, and certain occupational groups had higher rates of infant mortality than others. For example, in Preston in 1844, death rates for newborns to five-year-olds were listed as 17.6 per cent for the gentry, 38.2 per cent for tradesmen, and an astounding 55.4 per cent for the offspring of "operatives" (factory workers) (Rose 141). Infant mortality was, therefore, an omnipresent phenomenon, affecting some groups more than others.

A comparison to the anthropological work of Nancy Scheper Hughes is enlightening to consider here. She argues that "high expectancy of child death is a powerful shaper of maternal thinking and practice" (Scheper-Hughes 344) and that it has resulted in women delaying their emotional attachment to infants. They are sometimes thought of as temporary "visitors" until a certain age. Scheper-Hughes further argues that the repeated experience of infant death results in an existential doubt and an attitude that "allows the mother to reject as a child not worth keeping, a child without a knack for life" (Scheper-Hughes 359). Notwithstanding the grim reality of the precariousness of life in shantytowns and slums, maternal expectations did play a definite role in the premature death of infants in the Alto de Cruzeiro in Brazil (Scheper-Hughes 356). Many sickly infants were thought to be "as good as dead." As one of Scheper-Hughes' interviewees put it:

> They come into the world with an aversion to life. They are overly sensitive and soon fed up [abusado] with milk, with mingau— food doesn't interest them; it doesn't hold their attention. You see, they are neither here nor there. (Scheper-Hughes 368)

Little is done to keep infants alive in this transitional or liminal state; they are seen as neither here nor there. Some of these babies are born looking quite normal but soon demonstrate that they have too little resistance or fight. They die of "mingua," a slow and gradual neglect. Scheper-Hughes notes that most of these infants were simply "tiny famine victims" whose hunger was often complicated by diarrhoea and dehydration; they were perceived to be just wasting away, shrivelling up (368).

I certainly do not want to make too strong a comparison between Scheper-Hughes's work in the Brazilian Alto de Cruzeiro and nineteenth-century and early twentieth-century maternal attitudes in Britain; however, as she puts it, there are "some resonances and resemblances with mothering practices at other times" (Scheper-Hughes 344). Some of the English mothers practicing selective mortal neglect may have had ambivalent (meaning mixed or contradictory) feelings towards their offspring. A woman living in poverty in Britain in the early twentieth century watching her sickly infant die might have felt sadness, relief, and guilt. However, this chapter argues that thinking about the mothers' actions in relation to social processes, rather than with specific regard to individual psychology, has value in understanding the phenomenon. In both cases, a collective social schema developed to explain their actions.

In the nineteenth century, common infectious diseases (diphtheria, scarlet fever, smallpox, whooping cough, and measles) killed a relatively small proportion of infants (Rose 7). What killed Victorian babies? More commonly, they died of "wasting diseases," which included the effects of congenial defects, injury at birth, want of breast milk, atrophy, debility, marasmus (a form of severe malnutrition in children), and prematurity. "Diarrhoeal diseases" (including gastritis and enteritis) were the next biggest killers. These were followed by respiratory disorders, such as bronchitis and pneumonia. Convulsions, a blanket term to cover an array of maladies, came next:

> Most infant deaths were due to natural deficiencies: maternal exhaustion and malnutrition producing sickly offspring; and unhygienic conditions; wrong feeding, and a damp foetid atmosphere producing respiratory infections; whilst maternal venereal infection, and contamination of the bloodstream with alcohol or poisonous abortifacients would have been responsible for many of the "congenital defects" as vaguely classified in the official returns. (Rose 7-8)

Given the vagueness of many of these maladies, neglect could go unnoticed:

> For a mother so inclined, it would not have been difficult to will death upon her infant by neglecting it and inducing one or other of the symptoms described. Such causes were so common anyway that the child's death *was unlikely to attract any suspicion*, and we can never know how many child-murderers were concealed under these generalised symtomological terms. (Rose 8, my emphasis)

Lionel Rose argues that it was not just compassion towards women that was at play; there was a variety of social practices involved. The children of wet nurses (lactating women who were paid to breastfeed the children of wealthy women) might perish while their milk nurtured a wealthy women's offspring. At the other end of the social spectrum, funeral insurance could become enticing for the most impoverished in times of dire necessity, and who could rightly condemn those struggling to feed their existing children in not wanting the burden of another infant? Charities for the rehabilitation of fallen women emphasised getting women back to respectable work following childbirth, and their infants would often perish after a too-short period of breastfeeding (frequently one month). Childcare practices, such as sedating infants with laudanum or other medicines containing opium, were commonplace, and "accidental poisoning" was a typical coroner's verdict. "Overlaying," which was the accidental suffocation of babies in bed, and "accidental suffocation" were also common verdicts (Rose p.60). Given these widespread causes of infant death, there was a general reluctance to prosecute an individual mother—a myriad of opportunities to lose an unwanted baby existed.

Margaret Arnot makes the point that newborn babies and older infants were regarded differently because of their external relationships. Newborn child murder could sometimes be used as a form of late abortion in Victorian England. For this reason, it is important to distinguish between the death of a newborn, whose existence is hidden and unknown, and that of older infants who had developed relationships with others (149-150). The liminal status of the newborn is particularly evident in this period (Hogan, "The Beestings"). Consequently, the loss of a newborn infant received greater social tolerance. Of the entire English legal system, Rose notes the following:

> Their [coroners'] "why-bother?" attitude towards inquests and post-mortems in the case of infants was induced by the workings of the judicial system. Even if an autopsy *was* held, and a verdict of "murder" *was* returned, leading to the mother's trial at the assizes, the chances to a suitable conviction (assuming the police bothered to prosecute in the first place) was very remote. (61)

Rose's discussion of "baby-farming" scandals in the 1860s underlines the point that infanticide was tolerated and that there was a general reluctance to prosecute women. Following a suspiciously high infant mortality rate, noticed by the registrar following a sequence of applications for death certificates for babies boarded at her establishment, Mrs. Chard's baby farm came under scrutiny, whereby the coroner's inquest noted that profound neglect was evident: the infants were "scarcely recognisable as human beings" (42). Nevertheless, the jury's verdict regarding the latest death was based on the immediate symptoms of death—"debility"—rather than on the obvious and wilful neglect that had caused it (Rose 42). Another baby farm, run by a Mrs. Jaggers, contained infants clearly suffering from the symptoms of starvation. Yet the jury's finding in the case of a fatality was that the baby's death was from "glandular fever." However, Jaggers was censured for failing to call a doctor earlier (Rose 43). Both babies mentioned above were illegitimate, and death rates of illegitimate babies were higher than legitimate ones. These examples show that if there was a reluctance to prosecute even those who could be regarded as wicked baby farmers who slaughtered babies in a flagrant manner, there was even less prospect of individual mothers quietly practicing selective mortal neglect coming under attack. The women who came to court tended to be those who had acted in a flagrant manner or who had confessed, so their actions were hard to ignore. The rare conviction of a criminal baby farmer in 1870 drew cold irony at the prospect of a hanging: "We shall witness in our midst the edifying spectacle of a woman strangled as a concession to one of those outbursts of public virtue" (Rose 101).

Hillary Marland summarises popular sentiment in the 1850s and 1860s as "public revulsion" regarding the death penalty for women: "The severity of the penalty for infanticide, death by hanging, compared with the mildness of the punishment for concealment was picked out as a particular failing of the law" (Marland 170). The fact that the fathers were not prosecuted was also a point of concern, as women could be coerced or raped by men who then were not brought before the law. This added to the general ambivalence about prosecution and reluctance to find women guilty of murder.

Conclusion

Marland sums up the dominant ideas associated with child murder:

> Infanticide represented the antithesis of female nature, a total rejection of maternal ties, duties and feelings. Puerperal insanity could explain this, with the mother becoming, as the result of her mental disorder, confused, despondent or driven to murderous fury ... the idea that women were likely to fall prey to puerperal insanity became increasingly acceptable.... Judges and juries appear to have been convinced by this explanation of the mother's madness and crime, while other witnesses eagerly took it up and added to it.... The phenomenon of erratic and even

harmful behaviour on the part of mothers following childbirth had been recognised long before the nineteen century by midwives, doctors, courts and inquest juries. Following the trial of giving birth, involving intense physical effort, pain and disruption of the delicate reproductive organs, and in many cases increased strain on family resources, mothers were seen as liable to become deranged, neglectful or violent. They came to represent a risk to themselves and other family members, particularly the new-born child. (172-73)

Certainly, the plea of puerperal insanity was used widely, as the examples above illustrate. Those who were prosecuted had often very obviously inflicted violence upon their baby or had admitted guilt. However, as seen in the courtroom dialogues cited above, even obvious signs of violence were not necessarily sufficient to secure a conviction, as there could be ambiguity regarding whether an infant was already dead when a violent act was undertaken, or whether the act was undertaken in a temporary fit of mania. A self-confessed murderess could be freed because of sympathy for her predicament. Others were found not guilty because they were not accountable for their actions, regardless of whether the temporary insanity in question had been witnessed by others. It was commonly thought that madness could be assumed to be part of postnatal fragility. I claim that this presumption arose out of an unwillingness to prosecute such women—not necessarily a resolute belief in such madness.

Selective mortal neglect was also practiced at an institutional level, and I have noted the high mortality rates of illegitimate babies in charities for the rehabilitation of fallen women as an example above. This is an illustration of societal ambivalence towards illegitimate offspring. This is a complex and sensitive topic with the liminal status of the newborn baby contributing to a willingness to view the newborn's status differently from that of older developed children. Such "institutional infanticide" continued into the twentieth century, with some institutions experiencing up to a 50 per cent death rate of such infants (McGreevy). Some estimates suggest that illegitimate children born in Ireland in the 1920s had a mortality rate five times higher than the norm.

In nineteenth- and early twentieth century England, child death was, to a degree, seen as inescapable, although there was some obvious ambivalence about this, as evidenced in calls for reform of the baby-farming sector and slum housing that contributed to infant mortality. Others suggested that infant mortality was eugenically beneficial, with the weakest being weeded out of the breeding pool in a misappropriation of Darwin's ideas (sometimes dubbed social Darwinism). Although the dangerous and deranged mother might have become a dominant trope and used in courtroom defenses, this chapter has suggested that we should reframe the notion—since infanticide was doubtless masked within an array of common maladies—as a decision to let go of unwanted and unviable infants, who were seen as suffering from wasting diseases. If there were suspicions regarding such cases of selective mortal neglect, they were seldom reported, and if they were reported, they were not prosecuted, which suggests a certain amount of tacit social tolerance of widespread infanticide practices. This finding contradicts what has become the dominant trope of the deranged mad woman as a predominant killer of infants—a trope which endured and was useful as a means of saving women from harsh penalties. Individual infanticide was ignored in those cases where it could be ignored, and many babies were allowed to quietly slip away.

Endnotes

1. Heartfelt thanks to Phillip Douglas for his comments on this essay. I continue to value his insights. Thanks too to my co-editors for their feedback. I'd also like to remember my late mother-in-law Dame Professor Mary Douglas, who I believe would approve of my approach.

2. The term "child: in the periods discussed can indicate a newborn baby, rather than an older child.

3. Old Bailey Proceedings Online (www.oldbaileyonline.org, version 7.0, 15 Oct. 2014), January 1838, trial of ELIZABETH HODGES (t18380129-499).

4. Old Bailey Proceedings Online (www.oldbaileyonline.org, version 7.0, 19 Oct. 2014), October 1883, trial of EMILY BATT (t18831015-969).

5. Old Bailey Proceedings Online (www.oldbaileyonline.org, version 7.0, 19 Oct. 2014), January 1888, trial of MAXWELL RAE (19) (t18880130-282).

6. Old Bailey Proceedings Online (www.oldbaileyonline.org, version 7.0, 19 Oct. 2014), October 1894, trial of MINNIE WELLS (23) (t18941022-849).

7. Old Bailey Proceedings Online (www.oldbaileyonline.org, version 7.0, 19 Oct. 2014), December 1894, trial of JULIA LEE (23) (t18941210-110).

8. Old Bailey Proceedings Online (www.oldbaileyonline.org, version 7.0, 19 Oct. 2014), January 1903, trial of LOUISA BEAUMONT (24) (t19030112-163).

9. Old Bailey Proceedings Online (www.oldbaileyonline.org, version 7.0, 19 Oct. 2014), March 1904, trial of LOUISA LUNN (20) (t19040321-332).

10. Old Bailey Proceedings Online (www.oldbaileyonline.org, version 7.0, 15 Oct. 2014), March 1905, trial of CLARA HLLDEBRAND (23) (t19050306-276).

11. Old Bailey Proceedings Online (www.oldbaileyonline.org, version 7.0, 19 Oct. 2014), September 1903, trial of FLORENCE BRITT (22) (t19030908-766).

Works Cited

Arnot, Margaret, L. "The Murder of Thomas Sandles: Meanings of a Mid-Century Infanticide". *Infanticide. Historical Perspectives on Child Murder & Concealment 1550-2000*, edited by Mark Jackson Aldershot, 2002, pp. 149-67.

Digby, A. "Women's Biological Straightjacket." *Sexuality & Subordination: Interdisciplinary Studies of Gender in the Nineteenth Century*, edited by Susan Rendall, Routledge, 1989, pp. 192-221.

Gooch, Richard. *On Some of the Most Important Diseases Peculiar to Women*. The New Sydenham Society, 1829.

Hogan, Susan. "The Tyranny of the Maternal Body: Maternity and Madness." *Women's History Magazine*, no. 54, 2006, pp. 21-30.

Hogan, Susan. "The Beestings: Rethinking Breast-Feeding Practices, Maternity Rituals, & Maternal Attachment in Britain & Ireland." *Journal of International Women's Studies (JIWS)*, vol. 10, no. 2, 2008, pp. 141-60.

Jackson, Mark. *New-born Child Murder: Women, Illegitimacy and the Courts in Eighteenth-Century England*. Manchester: Manchester University Press. 1996.

Mackay, Ronald, D. *Mental Condition Defences in the Criminal Law*. Clarendon Press. 1995.

Marland, Hillary. "Getting Away with Murder? Puerperal Insanity, Infanticide and the Defence Plea." *Infanticide. Historical Perspectives on Child Murder & Concealment 1550-2000*, edited by Mark Jackson, Ashgate. 2002, pp. 168-93.

McGreevy, Ronan. "Tuam Deaths Need Further Investigation, Says Academic Expert. Prof Liam Delaney Says Deaths Cannot Be Explained by Social Conditions." *The Irish Times*, 6 June 2014, www.irishtimes.com/news/ireland/irish-news/tuam-deaths-need-further-investigation-says-academic-expert-1.1822219. Accessed 9 Dec. 2019.

Old Bailey [Court] Proceedings Online (www.oldbaileyonline.org). As per notes.

Rose, Lionel. *Massacre of the Innocents: Infanticide in Britain, 1800-1939*. Routledge & Kegan Paul Books, 1986.

Scheper-Hughes, Nancy. *Death Without Weeping. The Violence of Everyday Life in Brazil*. University of California Press. 1993.

Chapter Fifteen

"Mother, Is This Our Home?" Mothering in the Context of Lord's Resistance Army Captivity: Understanding the Perspectives of Mothers and Children in Northern Uganda

Myriam Denov

As a result of a brutal civil war, the Acholi people of northern Uganda have been affected by multiple and intergenerational forms of violence and loss. Spanning over two decades (1986 to 2007), the armed conflict between the Ugandan government and the rebel Lord's Resistance Army (LRA) left families torn apart, villages and communities demolished, education disrupted, traditional family and cultural practices degraded, and life's daily activities significantly altered. The war ultimately left tens of thousands dead and forced 1.7 million people into internally displaced persons' camps (Annan et al.; Ledyard et al; Patel et al.). The Acholi people experienced inexorable violations of their individual and collective rights, gradually eroding the social, political, economic, and cultural fabric of society.

In its battle against the Ugandan government, the LRA—led by Joseph Kony—systematically abducted between sixty thousand and eighty thousand children into its ranks (Shanahan and Veale). Girls were targeted for forced marriage and pregnancy (Denov and Lakor; Denov et al.). Although much global and media attention has often categorized women and girls abducted by the LRA as "sex-slaves," their roles and experiences within the ranks of the LRA were multiple and complex (Akello). Thousands of young women and girls served as soldiers, porters, cooks, medics, mothers, and forced wives. Girls were often held in captivity longer on average than boys, and research suggests that roughly a quarter of the women and girls became forced wives to LRA members; at least half of these girls and women gave birth to children in captivity as well as in a context of violence and rape (Annan et al.). According to one estimate, 2,500 children were born to mothers in captivity by 2001, representing one-quarter of all children held by the LRA (Apio).

During the armed conflict, given the precarious circumstances under which females in the LRA lived, pregnancy and the eventual delivery of a child represented situations of great risk for the health and wellbeing of both the mother and the child, making motherhood and mothering during armed conflict and captivity of key importance (Denov and Ricard-Guay). This chapter draws upon a study of the realities and perspectives women who were abducted into the LRA as girls as well as a sample of children born in LRA captivity. The chapter focuses on the complexities of mothering during war and captivity from the perspectives of both mothers and their children. The chapter first addresses the realities of mothers and their experiences of abduction, sexual violence, forced marriage, and mothering in the brutal context of captivity. The chapter then explores the realities of children born of war, their perspectives and connections to their mothers, and the complexity surrounding the mother-child relationship. The chapter concludes with a discussion of the service provision needs of both women participants abducted into the LRA as well as the children born in LRA captivity.

Methodology

Funded by the Pierre Elliott Trudeau Foundation and the Social Science and Humanities Research Council of Canada, the study received ethical approval from two research ethics boards: the first from the Uganda National Council for Science and Technology/Office of the President of Uganda and the second from the Research Ethics Board of McGill University, Canada.

Data collection was carried out between June and October 2015 in the Gulu, Pader, and Agago districts of northern Uganda by a team (led by the author) of Canadian and northern Ugandan researchers. Interviews were conducted with two groups of participants. The first group comprised of twenty-seven women who were abducted into the LRA and as a result of rape gave birth to a child during their captivity. The second group was sixty children born in captivity. All participants were recruited through local northern Ugandan researchers who had ongoing contact with women and children formerly in the LRA as a result of their ongoing work and advocacy for women and children born in LRA captivity. The women participants—who were between the ages of twenty-two and thirty-three at the time of interview—were living in Gulu (eight), Pader (eleven), and Agago (eight) districts of northern Uganda. These mothers were between the ages of nine and fourteen at the time of their abduction, and had been held captive in the LRA between three and nineteen years. The average time these women participants spent in captivity was ten years. Women participants gave birth to between one and six children in captivity. During the same period, interviews were conducted with sixty children born in LRA captivity. Child and youth participants were between the ages of twelve and nineteen at the time of the data collection and were living in Gulu (twenty), Pader (twenty), and Agago (twenty). Participants had often spent their formative years in captivity, ranging from a few months after being born to seven years. All interviews for the study were conducted in Acholi,[1] audiorecorded with permission, and then translated and transcribed into English.

The following sections report on the realities of both groups of participants in relation to their experiences during LRA captivity. The experiences of the women participants are presented first.

Life in LRA Captivity: Abduction, Violence, and Female Resistance

Women participants explained how they were abducted as young girls and adolescents by the LRA in violent ways and at night often while they were sleeping in their homes or at their school dormitories. This woman participant recalled her abduction:

> I was abducted when I was studying in Gulu High School, and I was in senior two. The rebels came to Gulu High School and surrounded one girls' dormitory and one boys' dormitory very

early in the morning when no one had yet got out of bed.... Many students who failed to walk [quickly] or who tried to escape were killed on the way.... Life was not easy because some of our friends who tried to escape ... were killed by animals ... we could see their remains [as we passed by]. The [commanders] would tell us that we should see how those who try to escape suffer and get killed. So we decided to stay with them.

The wartime realities narrated by the twenty-seven mother participants were marked by years of severe and chronic violence, coercion, and deprivation. Abducted and forced into roles as combatants, porters, cooks, wives, and mothers, their lives in LRA captivity were marred by physical, sexual, and psychological violence as well as profound abuse. Their basic survival was a struggle under harsh physical conditions as well as during food and water shortages, in which many perished. They also travelled long distances on foot while injured, sick, or pregnant. This participant described the brutality and horror of captivity:

When we first arrived under Kilak Mountain, I found life very hard. Because every time when we are moving, we needed to carry heavy loads while walking for a long distance without resting, sleeping, and even eating.... If you [walk] slowly, they beat you. So, I found life was so difficult in the bush.... Being a young girl who had never experienced sex, we were forced to have sex by those big men, doing things very fast with tiredness.... Again when we entered in Sudan, we found cholera was very high; there was no food and you had to go and pick tree leaves. We ate very many leaves of different wild plants, and life was very difficult. Whoever fell sick would be taken far away from other people so that they go and die there. They don't even bring you water; they don't care for you, and you stay there for maybe a week and you die there.

When asked what they remembered most about life in captivity, the mothers recalled the brutal forms of physical, sexual, and psychological violence that they regularly witnessed, experienced, and sometimes participated in, which has continued to haunt them in their postwar lives. These participants recounted the following:

I had someone among us who knew our family and out of sympathy he gave me some sandals to wear. But we reached a water source, and I removed my sandals to rush and drink some water. I returned for my sandals, [but] someone had taken them. So I walked barefoot up to Sudan. I developed wounds on my feet that were so bad, and they were preventing me from moving fast; I was practically limping. Some rebels suggested that I be killed, as I could not move quickly and I was slowing them down.... I was close to being killed. These rebels used words which are metaphoric. For example, when they ask you whether you are tired, to them it would mean you are tired of living and, therefore, you would be killed if you said you were tired. I could see that one of the rebels was interested in killing me because I was slowing the rest down.

There is something that I did from the bush, and I will not forget it. When we were abducted and still not used to the bush, one of the abductees tried to escape. The person was followed and arrested, and we were forced to kill that person without a gun and not even with any tool. We were told to bite that person with our teeth until the person died. We killed that person by biting with our teeth. I feel so guilty and feel so bad about it. Whenever people in the community stigmatize and insult me, I keep remembering what we did in the bush.

Interviews with the mothers also revealed that despite the coercive control and violence they lived under, many took courageous actions to resist this control and found ways to protect themselves. Some participants detailed their attempts to escape (even as girls as young as ten), their efforts to fend off sexual assaults by men much older and larger than themselves, and events that gave rise to remarkable strength and resolve to carry on and in some cases to miraculously escape:

Life was so difficult for me, and I was really weak and kept remaining on the edge [of the group] with my children. One day, we were attacked, and the LRA and UPDF [government forces] started exchanging fire. I was left behind alone. The last group found me, and the officer in command asked me with pity: "Don't you have a home?" He said this as he was moving so that nobody could hear him say that. To me, it hadn't occurred to me to try to escape before because I always saw myself as a loser, since I was abducted at ten years old.... I thought I was meant to die in the bush [said with deep pain in her voice]. But after the words of this commander, I started thinking: "Oh yes, I was just abducted, and I have a home." So I imagined how I had been wasting myself since the age of ten. From then on, I started planning to escape, and indeed I did escape.

The Realities of Sexual Violence and Forced Marriage

Young women and girls in LRA captivity faced multiple hardships in the bush; they endured sexual violence, forced marriage, and forced pregnancy. Although the participants' feelings towards their bush husbands were nuanced and complex, they described the beginnings of their forced marriages and the dynamics of this relationship as coercive, forceful, and violent, in which the girls and women were viewed as the exclusive property of men:

> [In the bush], there is no love and no relationships. They just select you and take you to be their women whether you like it or not. We never had any voice to make choices—whether he is old or young. You fear they will kill you so you have no option.

> On Christmas, we were called to a wide field. We were told to line up, and they also told a group of men to line up and our line should face the men in line. Then they told those men to come and choose a lady ... to pick a lady to be his. Then they picked us, and we started crying because it was not our wish to have those men as our husbands. They told us that if we continue to cry, then they would kill us. We kept quiet. Then other ladies who were abducted before us started teaching us how we should adapt to those situations. And that was how we started living with them forcefully. For me, I refused to go and sleep with that man given to me. He went and reported me to the commander that I refused to sleep and have sex with him. Then they decided that I should be killed the next day. My friend leaked the information to me that if I failed to sleep with that man today, the next day I would be killed. She said: "Have you seen those sticks spread in

the sun? ... Those sticks are for caning you until you die." On that day, I forced myself to sleep with that man given to me as my husband.

When I was abducted, they took me straight to that man, and they just forced me to stay with that man ... no dating, no agreement. They would just order you to go and take a bath and get to a house where the man is. The man would rape you or forcefully have sex with you when you are not even ready for the sex.

Despite describing the relationships with their bush husbands as highly coercive, over the course of many years in captivity and because of the complexity of their circumstances, some participants began to perceive their bush husband as a provider and a protector against other LRA members as well as government forces during times of combat. The women also recalled that despite the mistreatment by their bush husbands, these men, nonetheless, loved and provided for their children. Moreover, women realized that, ultimately, they were much more vulnerable to mistreatment if their husband was killed. These participants explained such complexities:

Things were hard when your bush husband was killed. Other soldiers and women gave you a hard time.

The man [husband] died in the bush, and life became hard. We struggled to acquire food, soap, and other basic needs....When he was alive, he would help us acquire those basic needs.

He [bush husband] would come and protect me from the UPDF [government forces].... He cared for me, and I saw that he used to love me.

Similarly, participants recalled certain high-ranking commanders who would look out for them and come to their defense when others threatened their lives. Some participants provided examples of incidents in which they were shown mercy or compassion when they were too young to handle walking long distances, were sick, or were injured:

The commander of the group that abducted me was a bit sympathetic with me. Whenever he would look back and he didn't see me, he would turn and go back to find me. He would then encourage me to move faster. I had luggage which he took from me because he saw I was too tired and also weak. I was close to being killed.... This one commander questioned [other commanders] why those abducted were being killed whenever they were too weak to walk. He asked: "Why have you abducted them if you have resorted to killing them?"

Forced Pregnancy and Giving Birth in Captivity

Forced pregnancy was a key LRA military strategy. Commanders were expected to impregnate their wives and father children to be raised as Kony's next generation of fighters (Denov and Lakor). In addition to the girls' young age, the violence accompanying their forced impregnation, and the loss of power and agency over their bodies further intensified the difficult circumstances under which their children were conceived and in which they became mothers. Among the twenty-seven mothers interviewed, the average age a girl had first pregnancy was age thirteen, giving birth to her first child at age fourteen. Participants gave birth to between one and six children that were conceived or born in captivity.

Feelings towards Pregnancy

During their first pregnancy, participants reported that due to a lack of knowledge of their young bodies, they did know they were pregnant, or they were in denial when other women commented on the signs of pregnancy they observed. Some participants recalled feelings of fear, anger, or resentment during pregnancy. Reflecting on the negative implications of birthing a child in the bush, some were fearful that their bodies were not physically mature enough to withstand childbirth. Others were resentful because they were young, and they believed that their futures would be ruined because of the baby or because the pregnancy was not conceived out of love. Some wished to die or to abort the baby. These participants explained their varied responses and reflections as follows:

I was unhappy about the pregnancy because I saw that my parents were not there now. I'm pregnant and would be going back with a child whose father is not there. My education was spoiled. How will I keep the child?

I felt bad [about getting pregnant] because if I give birth in the bush how, will I escape with the child? How will I keep the child in the bush? This meant that I would die in the bush.

With the first child, I didn't even know that I was pregnant. People would say, "Ooooh your stomach is getting bigger" and "In the past your stomach was not that big; what is happening to you?' I didn't take it seriously…. I didn't even realize any signs [of pregnancy], but people were consistently saying that my stomach is getting big. I started getting scared that maybe I am pregnant…. How will I give birth when am still this young? … I was still very young, and I was thinking that I may even die during delivery…. Giving birth was not easy for me, and it was God who helped me survive.

It is important to note, however, that in some cases, pregnancy was viewed by participants as protective. During pregnancy, girls and women were often exempt from carrying heavy loads and physical labour; they were not targeted for direct forms of violence. Therefore, pregnancy sometimes offered a reprieve from violence and abuse.

The Birth and Delivery of a Child

Other women usually assisted with childbirth, acting as midwives and nurses to the mother during the birthing process. Women with a lower rank within the LRA remembered being mistreated by these women immediately following the birth. Food and water would sometimes be withheld, or the new mother was forced to walk long distances despite having just given birth. Several of the women suffered serious medical complications during and after childbirth, or reported a difficult delivery:

When I was pregnant, I kept thinking "How am I going to manage with this pregnancy?" I kept wishing that if I had some kind of medicine that would help me abort, I would have used it to get rid of the child in my stomach. But because I could not get any medicine, I endured my pregnancy until I gave birth. Even during my labour, when it was time for me to deliver, I had a lot of difficulty giving birth. If I had been in the hospital, they would have opted for a Caesarean. The person delivering [the baby] kept beating me. Thanks to God, I managed to deliver. Even after giving birth, I was still mistreated. They poured hot water on me.... I developed bruises on my stomach.

Mothering in Captivity: Ambivalence and Vacillation

For some mothers, the birth of their child was seen as a gift from God or a reason to persevere and overcome their difficult circumstances, whereas for others, a child was unwanted and hated. In the bush, the arrival of a child represented a profound burden. Girls knew that having a child to care for would significantly reduce their chances of a successful escape from the LRA and would potentially even threaten their survival. Having a child could be dangerous—an encumbrance slowing girls down during ambushes and fighting when they were required to run with children on their backs or at their sides. Mothers were also harshly punished, including being severely beaten if their babies cried, which could draw attention to their position in the bush. Under such circumstances, mothers had varying responses to motherhood and towards their children: children were met with hatred and love, and were perceived as sources of both resentment and joy. These complexities were described in the following way:

> I didn't like her [the baby] at all. In fact, I hated her with all my heart. I wished this child would be born dead so that it could give me time to be free ... to escape [the LRA].

> I first wished that the child would die so that I could look for a way to go back home.

> [The] situation [was not] easy, but when I look at my two children I feel happy and try to forget the past. It's like the two [children] are symbols of what happened in captivity. When I look at them, I get overjoyed and say to myself "God has done something good in my life."

Traditionally, in Acholi culture, a baby may be given a name that reflects the situation of the mother or other circumstances surrounding the pregnancy or birth. Given the extreme hardship surrounding the circumstances of their birth, many children born in captivity held names that were reflective of that hardship. Children interviewed for the study held Acholi names with following meanings: "The world outside my womb is not safe"; "I am cursed"; "Born during the time of war"; "I survived narrowly"; "Born during famine"; "Everything is a struggle I cannot escape"; "Chaos causer"; "Regret"; "Unwanted, everyone hates me"; and "I am rejected." These naming practices served as a reminder of the suffering mothers went through during pregnancy and birth.

Their ambivalent and contradictory feelings concerning the child became clear in the participants' narratives. Birthing and mothering a child in captivity meant that chances at escape, flight from violent government ambushes, and basic survival became more onerous. Under such difficult conditions, mothers struggled with conflicting instincts to save themselves and/or to protect their children. This tension was reflected in the women's narratives—told as discrete moments in time where a choice was made between abandoning the child and running for their lives, or self-sacrificing to ensure the child's survival. These mothers explained this tension in the following way:

> They began firing at us. We were about five in number; they continued shooting at us without stopping. At one point, I ran, leaving my first born child behind. My son kept crying while shouting out my name saying: "Mother, why are you leaving me? Mother, do you want me to die while you remain alive?" I then stopped running and went back for him. I lifted him, and I continued running with my head lowered. When we crossed a certain river, I then carried him on my shoulders.

> My child grew so thin that I thought he would die, but it was God who helped me, and I took care of him. During those days where there was fierce fighting, I would drag my son on his chest. We would begin running from morning until evening. My son's throat developed sores, and he was passing blood. When the fighting would begin, I would sometimes run for a long distance, leaving him behind. But after a second thought, I would go back

for him. I would tell him that "I can decide to leave you behind because we will all die." I struggled hard to ensure that he survived. Sometimes the fighting would separate us, but after the fighting, I would look for him and find him.

Children Born in Captivity: Children's Perspectives and Connection to Their Mother

Children were born in the bush into the harrowing conditions of war and deprivation, and spent their early and formative years under threat of government ambush, violence, injury, and illness. Children born in captivity were witnesses and victims to severe forms of violence, including people being beaten, burned to death, and killed. Many children experienced or witnessed the violent death of a parent or sibling. The child participants interviewed also expressed how they endured starvation, slept under the rain, and walked long distances without rest. The child participants shared how they continued to be haunted by nightmares or traumatic memories of their time in the bush:

The hardest thing I cannot forget is when I saw how my father was shot ... dead, and we ran and left him there.

My mother had already been shot while carrying me on her shoulders.... My mother was shot and fell down, while I also fell lying next to her. One of the people who was running alongside her carried me away and continued running with me.

Life in the bush was unbearable. There was always fighting between rebels and government soldiers. Sometimes you can only take water and go to sleep on an empty stomach.

The children's connection with their biological mother, though often fraught with complex relational dynamics, emerged consistently as the most important and powerful relationship they had. Most children reported a profound and close bond with their mothers. Many of the child participants described bonding with their mother through adversity and felt that their mother was their sole source of love, protection, and financial as well as emotional support:

As Acholi folks say: "Your mother is your richness." So when you are near your mother, she would not wish to see you suffering.

She loves us who were born in captivity more that those one she gave birth from home.

I feel it is my mother [who is the most important person] because she is the one who gave birth to me, and she persevered all the hardship in the bush with me. She knows how it was hard. I feel that if I share my problems with her, she could help me faster because she knows what happened to my father. She also knows ... that there is no one that I can go to apart from her.

The children interviewed frequently used language referring to the "struggle" and "suffering" their mothers endured for them. They described the sacrifices their mothers had made for them, and that because of the war and their birth, their mother lost out on the chance to be educated. Children had an acute awareness of how their mothers had tried to protect them and kept them alive during captivity. Children remembered or were told detailed stories of what their mothers went through with them in the bush, and child participants described incidents of their mothers defending her children at great cost and risk to their own wellbeing:

I asked her when we were still in the bush: "Mother, is this our home?" She replied, "This is not our home." [Interviewer: What made you to ask her that question?] It is because I saw my mother being beaten several times. Whenever she was to receive any beatings, she would first remove me from her back. She would be beaten, and later she would carry me back on her back. That's when I asked her, "Mother, don't we have a home? Who are these people?"

My mother decided to escape and came home with the two of us [children]. She carried an AK 47. She never shot dead anybody during the escape. When we reached a field, my mother saw the LRA moving, and she hid in the bush. She entered a cassava field, and we ate some cassava. We continued with the journey. We got picked up by a Red Cross vehicle.... The vehicle was carrying dead bodies. They saw my mother and she ran back to the bush, but they found her. [My mother] held my hand the whole time. She never left me.

Children born in captivity had a strong sense of responsibility for working hard and taking care of their mothers in the future:

With the suffering we have endured together, when I am grown and have a job, I will buy for her something nice to make her happy.

A salient theme emerging from both the interviews with the children and their mothers was the theme of protection. In captivity and during escape, many mothers employed methods to protect themselves and their children that required self-sacrifice, incredible courage, stamina, and resourcefulness. At times, the mother's need to protect herself was at odds with the needs of the child, and this tension was difficult to negotiate. However, during the fog of war, when choices were highly constrained and options severely limited, most mothers used various methods to try to protect their children.

Addressing the Needs of Mothers and Children Born in Captivity

This study has demonstrated the ways in which girls who were abducted into the LRA and gave birth to children born of rape experienced a broad range of negative, positive, and ambivalent feelings throughout the process of pregnancy, birth, and mothering. During the war, girls and young women living in LRA captivity were forced into motherhood through rape, violence, and coercion—not choice. The ways in which participants made sense of their experience of mothering and their feelings towards their children and their maternal role were complex and varied considerably, ranging from fierce love and protectiveness to ambivalence or hatred. At other moments, they struggled with conflicting instincts to protect themselves or their children.

Ultimately, responses to motherhood shifted across time and were influenced by a myriad of external and internal dynamics and circumstances. Mothering was, therefore, a dynamic and interactional process between mother and child, as illustrated by the feelings love and protectiveness the children have towards their mothers and vice versa. These feelings were born through the challenges they overcame together, as women participants commonly spoke of "struggling alone" with their children. In turn, the children, despite their young age, understood and held profound insight into their mothers' struggles and the sacrifices that they had made for them during captivity. They expressed a deep love and gratitude to their mothers and wanted protect them and provide for them in the future. Although the children often experienced rejection and sometimes abuse by their mothers, many child participants understood the source of this rejection and the complexity inherent to their relationship. That awareness, though, did not make the children's lives easier.

Women formerly abducted into the LRA and their children are in urgent need of local, national, and international supports and services not only to facilitate their postwar reintegration into society but also to foster meaningful relationships with one another and the wider community. Such support is critical, as the women and children continue to experience profound forms of rejection, violence, and loss in the postwar period (Denov and Lakor; Denov et al.). As part of this research project, the interviews with mothers explored their service provision needs and participants' recommendations for both policy and practice. Although participants suggested multiple areas for improved service provision, livelihood programs and psycho-social support were two areas that women participants deemed vital to their and their children's long-term wellbeing in the postwar period.

The most important area identified by women participants was the need for livelihood programs targeting their socioeconomic marginalization through income-generating activities that foster self-sufficiency. Women participants recommended livelihood programs—such as livestock rearing and agricultural projects, vocational training, and other income-generating activities for both mothers and their children born in captivity—that would enable them to feed their children, afford to send them to go to school, rent land, and access medicine and healthcare.

Because of the dearth of follow-up support services available to mothers, and the widespread denial surrounding their children's plight, participants underscored the need for follow-up support for themselves, their children, and their family members in the form of home visits, psychosocial counselling, and psycho-educational workshops that address the concerns, needs, and challenges facing parents and caregivers. Women participants felt that raising awareness and doing follow-up and home visits in the community would send the message that these issues and the rights and welfare of children born in captivity and their mothers are important. The issues identified by mothers included coping with war-related trauma and relational issues, such as family violence, parenting skills, communication, and managing disclosure with their children in terms of their origins, their fathers, and family heritage. In the remote rural regions of northern Uganda, where supports of any kind are scarce, participants stressed the need to mobilize and train the local population, such as religious and local political leaders as well as other formerly abducted persons who are already well-established in the community.

By addressing the immediate and long-term service provision needs identified by participants, the realities of mothering in challenging contexts and the ambivalence of mothers of children born of war can be acknowledged and directly addressed. The scholarship on children's rights and protection has often highlighted the reality that supporting and protecting mothers is one of the most vital ways to protect children (Veale et al.). In the context of northern Uganda, supporting mothers will help improve the individual and collective lives of this group of women who have endured multiple forms of violence and trauma; such support can help to positively affect the lives of their children who have suffered immeasurably in a war that was not of their doing.

Endnotes

1. This research was a partnership between researchers at McGill University and Watye Ki Gen. Watye Ki Gen is made up of a collective of women who were abducted by the LRA and held in captivity. In the postconflict period, the organization is working to strengthen the rights, needs, and collective voice of former abductee women and their children, particularly within mechanisms of transitional justice.

2. Interviews conducted by non-Acholi speakers included Acholi-English translation.

Works Cited

Akello, G. "Experiences of Forced Mothers in Northern Uganda: the Legacy of War. *Intervention Amstelveen*, vol. 11, no. 2, 2013, pp. 149-56.

Allen, Tim. *Trial Justice: The International Criminal Court and the Lord's Resistance Army.* Zed, 2006.

Annan, Jeannie, et al. *The State of Female Youth in Northern Uganda: Findings from the Survey of War Affected Youth* (SWAY). Feinstein International Center: Tufts University, 2008.

Annan, J., et al. "Counseling for Peace in the Midst of War: Counsellors from Northern Uganda Share Their Views." *International Journal for the Advancement of Counseling*, vol. 24, no. 4, 2003, pp. 235-45.

Apio, E. "Uganda's Forgotten Children of War." *Born of War: Protecting Children of Sexual Violence Survivors in Conflict Zones*, edited by C. Carpenter, Kumarian Press, pp. 94-109.

Carlson, Khristopher, and Dyan Mazurana. *Forced Marriage within the Lord's Resistance Army, Uganda.* Feinstein International Center, 2008.

Denov, Myriam, and Alexandra Ricard-Guay. "Girl Soldiers: towards a Gendered Understanding of Wartime Recruitment, Participation, and Demobilisation." *Gender & Development*, vol. 21, no. 3, 2013, pp. 473-88.

Denov, Myriam, and Atim Angela Lakor, A.A. "When War is Better than Peace: The Post-Conflict Realities of Children Born of Wartime Rape in Northern Uganda". *Child Abuse and Neglect*, vol. 65, 2017, pp. 255-65.

Denov, M., et al. "Mothering in the Aftermath of Force Marriage and Wartime Rape: The Complexities of Motherhood in Post-War Northern Uganda. *Journal of the Motherhood Initiative*, vol. 9, no. 1, 2018, pp. 156-74.

Ledyard, E., et al. "Invisible Conflicts/the Dwon Madiki Partnership." In C. E. Stout (Ed.), *The New Humanitarians: Inspiration, Innovations, and Blueprints for Visionaries, Vol 2: Changing Education and Relief*, edited by C. E. Stout, Praeger Publishers/Greenwood Publishing Group, 2009, pp. 129-61.

McKay, Susan, and Dyan Mazurana. *Where Are the Girls?: Girls in Fighting Forces in Northern Uganda, Sierra Leone and Mozambique: Their Lives During and After War.* Rights & Democracy, 2004.

Patel, S., et al. "Comparison of HIV-Related Vulnerabilities between Former Child Soldiers and Children Never Abducted by the LRA in Northern Uganda." *Conflict and Health,* vol. 7, no. 1, 2013, pp. 1-15.

Schomerus, Mareike, and Emily Walmsley. *The Lord's Resistance Army in Sudan: A History and Overview.* Small Arms Survey, 2007.

Shanahan, Fiona, and Angela Veale. "How Mothers Mediate the Social Integration of Their Children Conceived of Forced Marriage Within the Lord's Resistance Army." *Child Abuse & Neglect,* vol. 51, 2016, pp. 72-86.

Veale, Angela, et al. "Participation as Principle and Tool in Social Reintegration: Young Mothers Formerly Associated with Armed Groups in Sierra Leone, Liberia, and Northern Uganda." *Journal of Aggression, Maltreatment & Trauma,* vol. 22, no. 8, 2013, pp. 829-48.

Worthen, M, et al. "'I Stand Like a Woman': Empowerment and Human Rights in the Context of Community-Based Reintegration of Girl Mothers Formerly Associated with Fighting Forces and Armed Groups." *Journal of Human Rights Practice,* vol. 2, no. 1, 2010, pp. 49-70.

Notes on Contributors

Sarah LaChance Adams is associate professor of philosophy at University of Wisconsin Superior. She is author of *Mad Mothers, Bad Mothers, and What a "Good" Mother Would Do: The Ethics of Ambivalence*. She is co-editor of *Coming to Life: Philosophies of Pregnancy, Childbirth, and Mothering* and *New Philosophies of Sex and Love: Thinking through Desire*. She lives with her family in Duluth, Minnesota.

Sophia Brock was awarded her PhD in sociology from the University of Sydney in 2017. Her research investigated the experiences of women who mother children with disabilities. Sophia's thesis argues that participants' experiences of motherhood, relationships, and the self are framed by competing and highly problematic sets of assumptions, stemming from the concepts of individualization and hegemonic maternality.

Tanya Cassidy is a Fulbright-HRB (Irish Health Research Board) Health Impact scholar, an EU Horizon 2020 Marie Skłodowska Curie Award (MSCA) fellow, a Cochrane Fellow, and a visiting fellow at the University of Central Lancashire (UCLan). While she continues to work with researchers at Maynooth University, she has recently become an assistant professor in the School of Nursing and Health Sciences at Dublin City University (DCU). She lives with her family in Maynooth, Ireland.

Myriam Denov is a full professor in social work at McGill University and holds the Canada Research Chair in Youth, Gender and Armed Conflict (Tier 1). A specialist in participatory research, she has worked with war-affected children and families in Asia, Africa, and the Americas. Denov holds a PhD from the University of Cambridge, where she was a Commonwealth scholar.

Mel Freitag is the diversity officer in the School of Nursing at University of Wisconsin-Madison. She serves underrepresented populations through mentorship, recruitment, programs, and professional development. Freitag strives to transform the curriculum through her work with health equity and social justice. Her scholarship explores how students' voices shape what it means to be a welcoming, supportive, and safe as well as brave school for all.

Joan Garvan was awarded a doctorate in sociology and gender studies in 2010 at the Australian National University. She has worked as an online moderator at the ANU and lectured in sociology. Since completing her studies, Joan launched an Internet site and offered online professional development courses: www.maternalhealthandwellbeing.com.

Susan Hogan is professor of cultural studies at the University of Derby and a professorial fellow of the Institute of Mental Health of the University of Nottingham. She has written extensively on women's transition to motherhood and experience of psychiatry. Her most recent funded research is The Birth Project (AHRC grant ref. AH/K003364/1).

Claire Steele LeBeau is an assistant professor of psychology at Seattle University. She teaches both undergraduate and graduate courses in existential-phenomenological psychology, ethics, developmental psychology, and writing for psychology. Her research interests include Levinasian ethics, embodied collaborative research methods using Gendlin's focusing technique, and the developmental transitions of new parenthood.

Sagashus T. Levingston earned a PhD in literature from the University of Wisconsin-Madison. Her dissertation focused on mothers "bad moms who do extraordinary things." She is an entrepreneur and a mother of six.

Patricia MacLaughlin is the owner of Sligo Woodland School, which embodies the forest school model. She has lectured in the social sciences at the Sligo Institute of Technology, and her current research interest is outdoor play in the early years.

Bertha Alvarez Manninen is associate professor of philosophy at Arizona State University. Her main areas of teaching and research interests are applied ethics, philosophy of religion, social and political philosophy, and philosophy and film. In her spare time, she likes to be with her two little girls, Michelle and Julia, her husband Tuomas, and her menagerie of cats and dogs.

Kate Parsons is professor of philosophy, director of the Women, Gender, and Sexuality Studies Program, and fellow with the Institute for Human Rights and Humanitarian Studies at Webster University. Her current research grapples with ethical questions related to climate change, international travel, and motherhood.

Amanda Roth is an assistant professor of philosophy and women's and gender studies at SUNY Geneseo. Her recent publications focus on reproductive ethics, pregnancy loss, and lgbtq+ family-making, and draw on her own experiences with these matters. She lives in western New York with her six-year-old daughter and cats.

Gwen Scarbrough is a lecturer in social sciences at the Sligo Institute of Technology. She has worked as a midwife in the U.S., providing care for women from a variety of backgrounds. Currently, her research is focused on maternal and infant care and mothering practices.

Sara Cohen Shabot is an associate professor (senior lecturer), and chair of the Women's and Gender Studies Program at the University of Haifa. Her present research addresses childbirth and the maternal embodied subject through feminist philosophy. Her recent publications deal with obstetric violence as gender violence (*Human Studies* 2016) and with the role of shame in obstetric violence (*Hypatia* 2018).

Aleksandra Staneva has a PhD in maternal mental health. Through employing feminist, critical realist, and postqualitative approaches, she explores experiences of depression and anxiety related to mothering. Her research involves grassroots perinatal interventions. Aleksandra creates art, counsels perinatal women, and lives with her son and partner in beautiful Brisbane, Australia.

Talia Welsh, PhD, is the interim director of women's and gender studies, and a U.C. Foundation professor of philosophy at the University of Tennessee at Chattanooga. Her research has included a translation of Merleau-Ponty's lectures at the Sorbonne, a book on Merleau-

Ponty's child psychology, as well as numerous articles and book chapters on phenomenology, feminist theory, and the ethics of the good health imperative.

Joan Woolfrey is professor of philosophy at West Chester University of Pennsylvania and an affiliated faculty member for women's and gender studies and Holocaust and genocide studies. Her publications include work on the concept of hope, group virtue, and feminist awareness as virtue, ectogenesis and human cloning, and ethical behaviour within a virtual world environment.